STOCK SYSTEM AND STRATEGY

An Engineer's Approach

Prakhar Agarwal

Made with ♥ on the Notion Press Platform
www.notionpress.com

Disclaimer:

This book is for educational and informational purposes only and does not constitute financial, investment, legal, or tax advice. I am not a SEBI-registered investment advisor. All trading and investment strategies mentioned are for illustrative purposes, and please be aware that the author and their associates may hold positions in the stocks discussed. Investing involves significant risk, including the potential loss of principal. Past performance is not indicative of future results. Market data is subject to change, and the author assumes no liability for losses resulting from reliance on information presented here. Please conduct your own research and consult with a qualified financial professional before making investment decisions. Reproduction of this content without consent is strictly prohibited.

Table of Contents

Dedicated to my parents and friends, whose constant support helped me bring this book to life.

To those who believe in taking their destiny into their own hands and changing the course of their future through hard work. The techniques in this book are built to elevate you. They will teach you to take absolute control of your finances and fundamentally change the destiny of your wealth.

Preface: An Engineer's Approach to the Market

From an early age, I have possessed a deep curiosity to understand how this world works. This drive led me to explore a wide variety of subjects, absorbing knowledge from self-help books covering business, finance, personal motivation, and even computer programming.

When I decided to pursue engineering, my natural curiosity pulled me toward the stock market and personal finance. My journey into investing actually began early; a simple SIP I started back in the 11th class, well before I turned 18, gave me a valuable, long-term overview of how investing works. However, at that time, I still lacked hands-on experience with individual stocks.

That hands-on experience began with the savings from my very first job after a full year of work. I read extensively, gathering practical insights and techniques, and began combining them with my own direct observations of market behavior. Over the years, I started documenting the specific methods that consistently helped me identify which stocks and sectors to buy.

With encouragement and inspiration from my friends, I penned those methods down, which ultimately evolved into this book.

I never approached stocks from the traditional perspective of academic finance books or rigid theoretical lectures. Instead, this book is built purely on practical learning and real-world market experience gathered over the years. It represents an engineer's way of thinking applied directly to the market: logical, structured, and focused on what works. My hope is that these pages will help you develop your own clear investment framework and empower you to take complete control of your personal finances.

Introduction

Why invest in equities?

There are primarily four types of assets in investing:

1) Commodities

Gold, silver, and agricultural goods are assets in which most people invest or trade. They offer returns which are, in the long term, comparable or equivalent to inflation.

Commodity prices are mostly dependent on **supply-demand** economics. If the supply of rice is more this year, prices will plummet. Conversely, if demand is more than the supply of rice, the price of rice will rise asymmetrically and may even reach all-time highs before crashing.

Gold and silver usually rise more when the world is going through panics—war, food, economics or health—as a safe haven against currency. **Central banks and governments hold these reserves** to diversify their reserves and reduce reliance on fiat currencies, especially during times of currency depreciation or inflation.

Commodities hedge against currency fluctuations and market volatility. Because the value of gold and silver is not tied to any specific currency or economy, they tend to maintain or increase their worth during periods when currencies are depreciating, or markets are experiencing turmoil. In addition, these precious metals generally have a negative correlation with equities—meaning that when stock markets decline, gold and silver prices often rise or remain stable. This negative correlation makes them effective diversifiers in an investment portfolio, helping to reduce overall risk and protect wealth during financial downturns.

2) Bonds, Debt Instruments, & Fixed Income Assets

Government securities, corporate debentures, fixed deposits (FDs), and debt mutual funds provide stable but often inflation-lagging returns.

These investments focus on **stable, predictable returns**, usually via interest payments. Bank FDs are popular in India but rarely beat inflation. Liquid mutual funds, on the other hand, offer FD-like returns with instant access to cash. Public Provident Funds (PPF) offer a 15-year lock-in with about 7.5% returns and fall under the Exempt-Exempt (no tax on interest, redemption and profit) tax category.

You can earn good in bonds when there are yield **inversion** scenarios—where short-term debt yields more than long-term—can signal strong opportunities. During interest rate cuts by central banks, long-term bonds can offer attractive yields of up to 9–12%, with sovereign guarantees adding a layer of security.

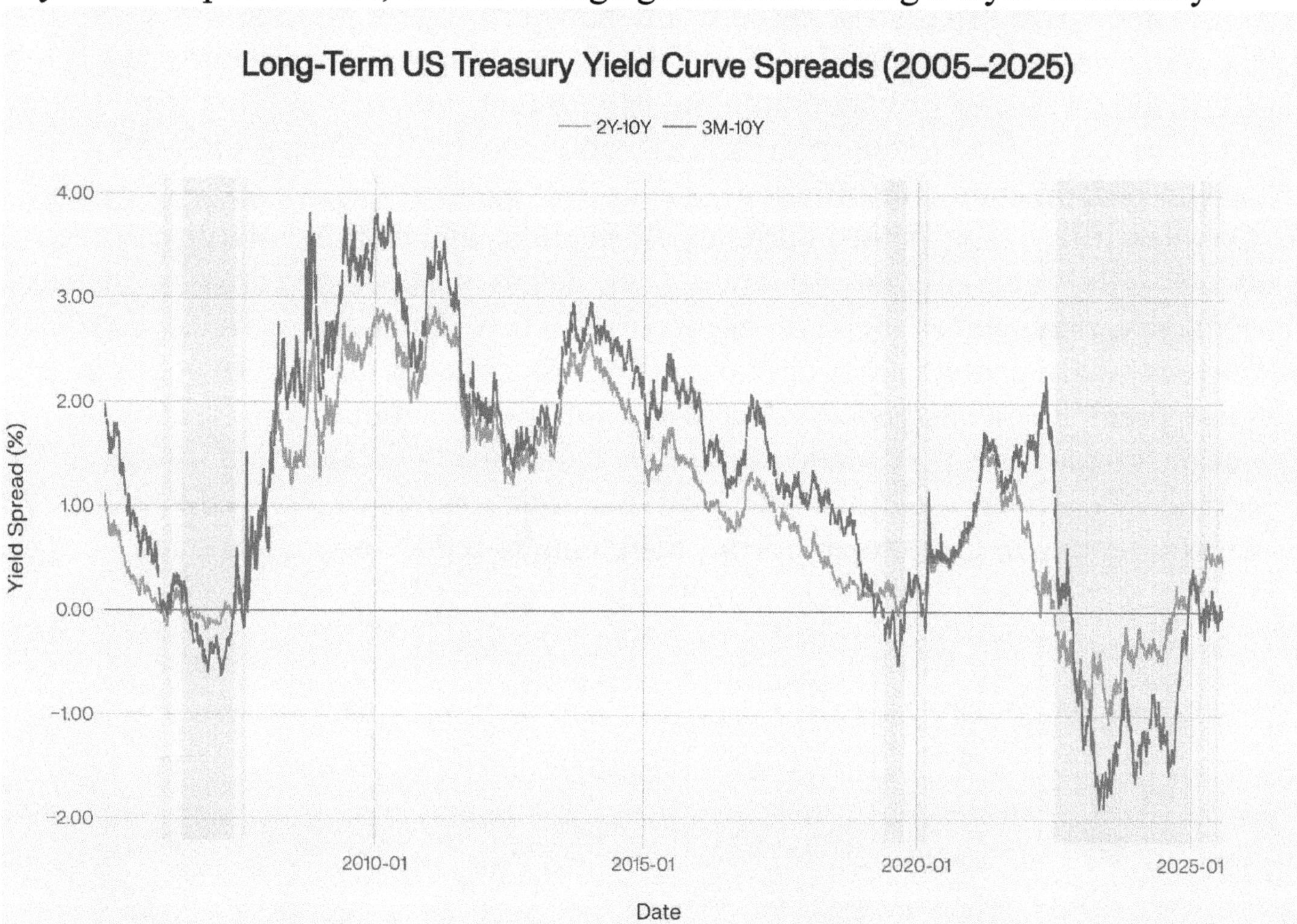

Long-Term US Treasury Yield Curve Spreads showing 2Y-10Y and 3M-10Y from 2005 to 2025

The shaded regions show when spread falls below zero, marking inversion periods. When the yield curve flips upside down—meaning short-term rates are higher than long-term rates on the chart—you get more interest by parking money in short-term bonds or liquid funds. Once the curve turns right-side up again—long-term rates climb above short-term rates—you lock in better returns by buying long-dated gilts.

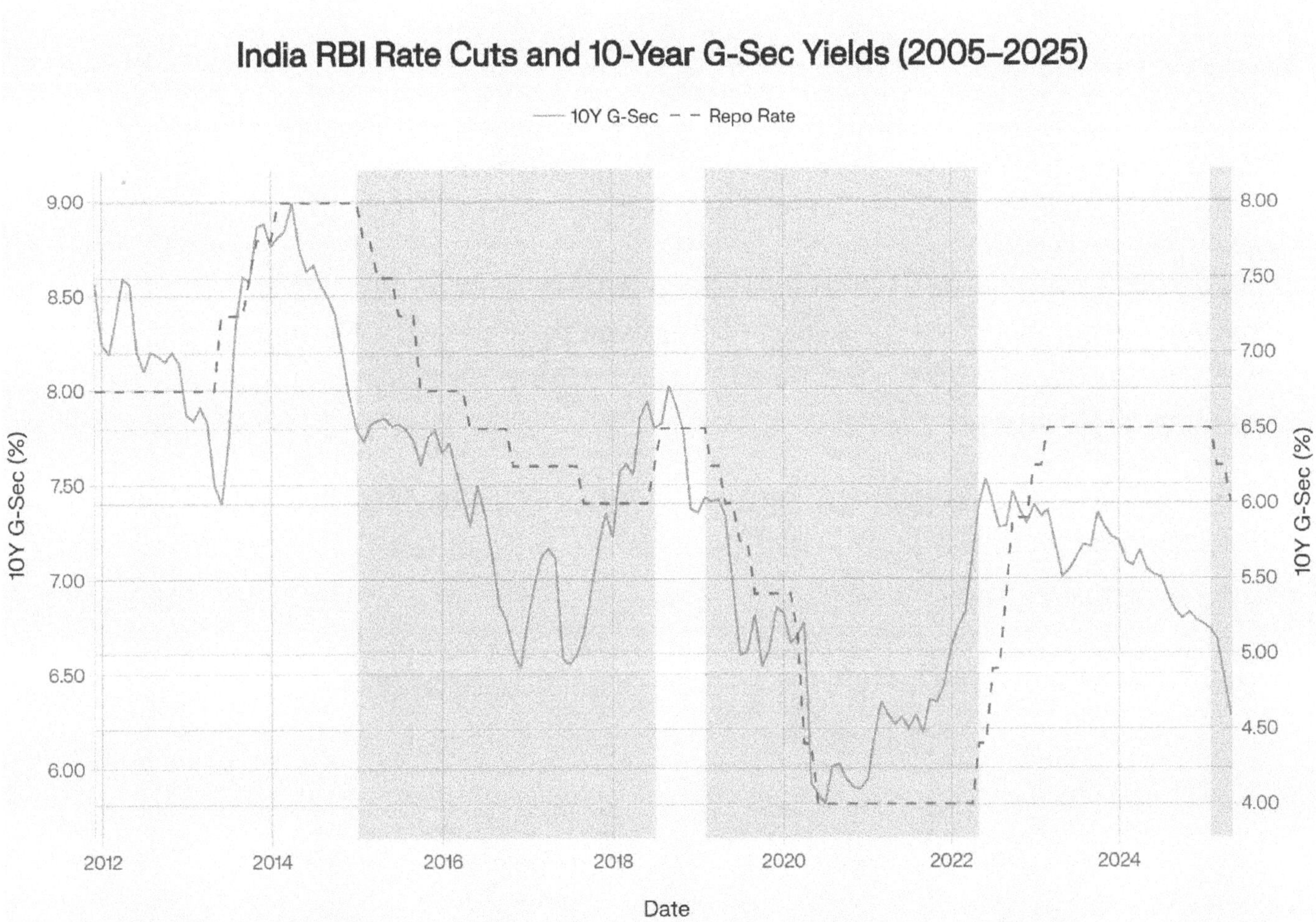

India RBI Rate Cuts vs 10-Year G-Sec Yields (2005–2025)

- Blue line (left axis): 10-year government bond yields.
- Green dashed line (right axis): RBI repo rate.
- Shaded areas on the chart mark each month RBI has cut rates, making it easy to spot when it's a favorable time to invest in longer-dated bonds (gilt funds). When rates are rising like the period after 2022 short-term bonds (ultra short funds, liquid funds) provide better returns.

3) Real estate

Real estate earns about inflation rates in the long term if bought in well-known, discovered areas.
Most of the gains often come from **leverage** (buying with borrowed money), we pay only a part of money borrowed in installments monthly and gains are on the whole amount of property that's why profit numbers look huge.

Real estate's main benefit is that property rarely declines in value—it either grows or remains stable for years. Whenever property prices decrease it is a good way to earn money, also buying in emerging cities or underdeveloped areas can yield big returns.

Paperwork in India is time-consuming and not fully digitized. High transaction costs and long holding periods are typical. Best for those seeking large, long-term investments.

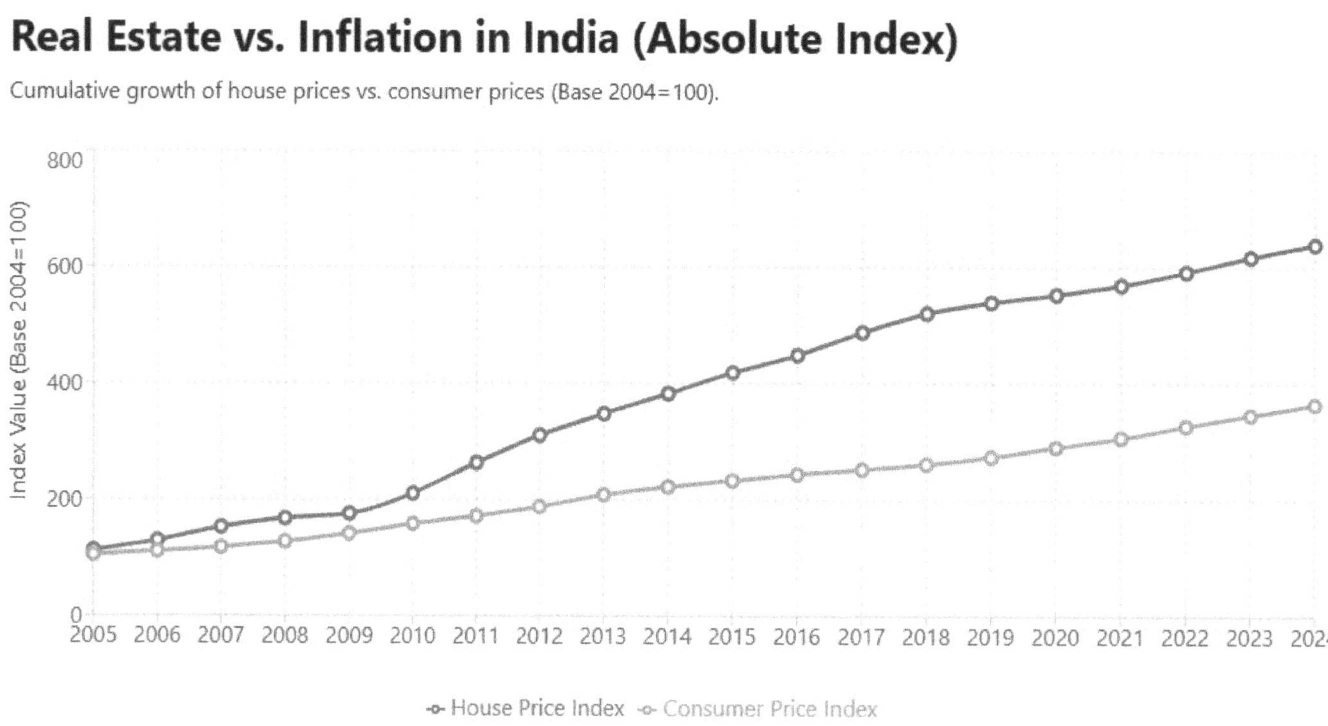

Real estate vs Inflation

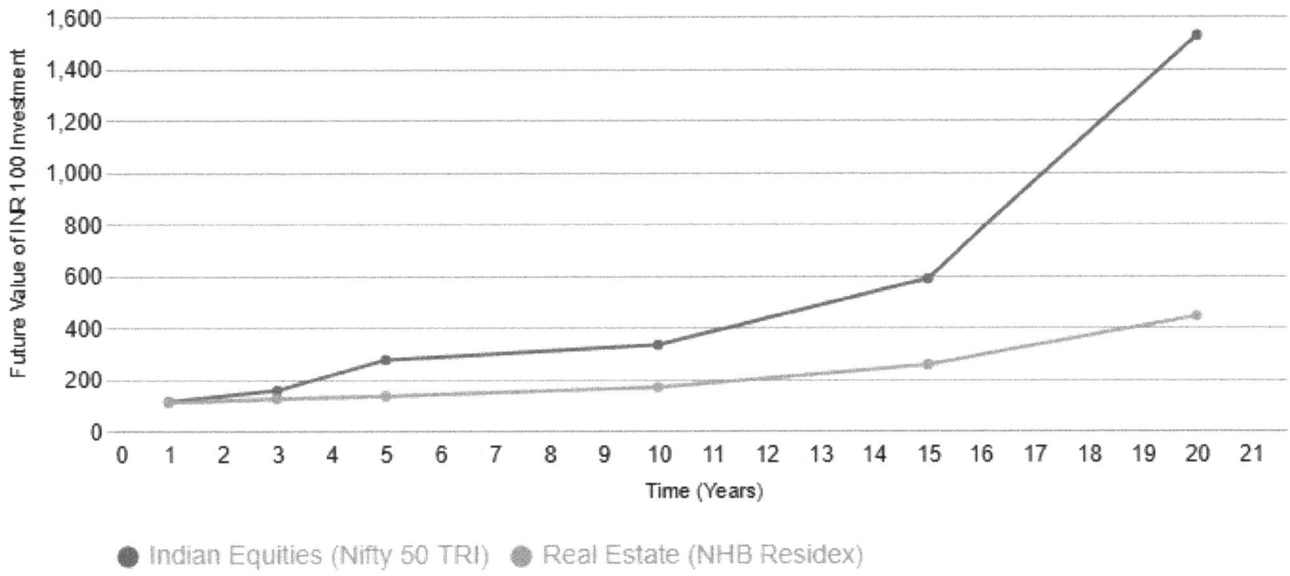

Real estate vs Equity

The NHB Residex is India's official home price index. The National Housing Bank (NHB) developed it to track and provide a transparent measure of changes in residential property prices across various cities in the country.

It serves as a key benchmark for the performance of the Indian real estate market. The key takeaway from the chart is the significant difference in long-term wealth creation. As you can see from the lines, over a 20-year period, the investment in equities grew at a much faster rate, resulting in a substantially higher final value compared to the investment in real estate.

4) Equities

Equity investing means buying shares of companies—either directly or via mutual funds, ETFs.

Stocks can also be obtained from unlisted stock platforms, IPOs, FPOs, ESOPs, right issues and other ways, but we'll be discussing only direct investing through demat/brokers or via mutual funds or ETFs.

Gains from equity depend on your entry and exit price, how long you hold, and the performance of the company because of liquidity nature of stocks we see a lot of unexpected gains and losses from time to time but in long run it beats inflation, if index based is used it also provides additional returns over inflation because it is the **only productive asset class** which means that if the company you own increases earnings stock performs better.

Carefully, observing the chart of commodities in the 10-15 years' time frame, silver has been Range bound (trading below previous all-time highs and above previous lows). Crude oil is also range bound after normalizing for some extreme price spikes. **Most of the commodities are cyclical** and provide inflation-linked returns whereas equity provides returns in the long term generally as (G + I + S) [Δ] not just inflation based.

Most of the fixed income returns are fluctuating with interest rates decided by the state if we take a long-term view on them, then we can see chart of Indian Government Bonds 10 Year Yield and US 10-year yield chart the previous top is higher than current top or chart is in lower high pattern that means from each economic cycle less interest or yield is obtained through fixed income assets, in long term view the **yield of bonds, fixed deposits will be closer to zero** while equity will generate returns based on (G + I + S) [Δ]. Taxation on slab rates also makes them unattractive for long term capital gains.

Δ (G + I + S) stands for GDP growth + Inflation + Speculation. If a country is growing at a rate of 6% and inflation is 4% and assuming speculation gain of 2%, the return of the index should be around (6+4+2) % = 12% over the long run.

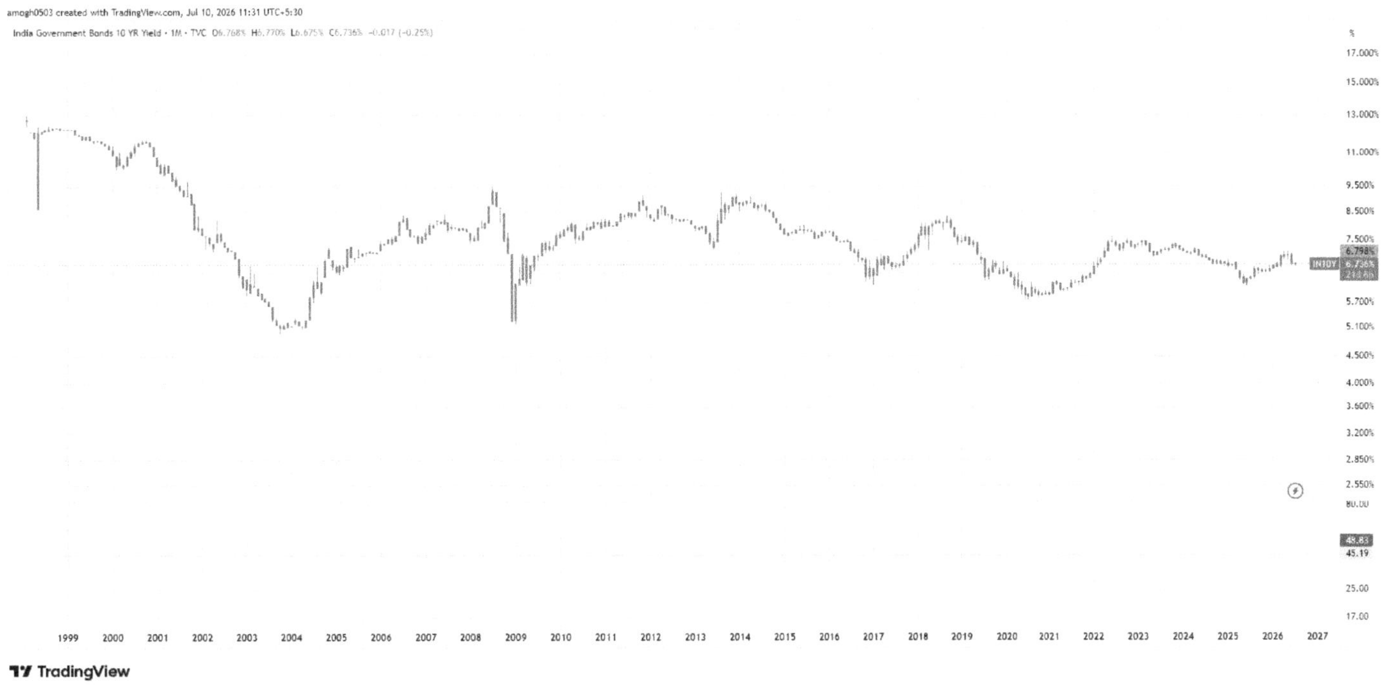

Indian Government Bonds 10 Year Yield

US Government Bonds 10 Year yield

Real estate can sometimes produce returns equivalent or more than equities but the number of people making money out of it is very less and most of the opportunities are in undiscovered areas or new emerging cities rather than well-established cities. Real estate rarely goes down in value, and you can put a huge corpus in investment through housing loans. The decision to favor real estate over equities depends largely on an investor's unique risk profile and liquidity requirements. Investment made in equity using index or mutual fund or ETFs over a long time through a systematic plan without breaking discipline is one of the best ways to generate stable returns. Moreover, you can choose **sector of future,** big business houses, EV makers, AI builders, cloud, great dividend yield, great management, monopoly companies from all the world to invest in, the freedom of choosing investment in equity is its greatest asset and this freedom can also lead to lots of wrong bets too that's why a systematic approach is needed. Small ticket size of ₹100 investing, taxation benefits of ₹1.25 lakhs per year is tax free, makes equity a way for everyone to make money beating all other asset classes.

Nifty 50 Index

From January 1999 to August 2025, a lump-sum investment in the Nifty 50 would have compounded at a 10.02% CAGR$^{\Delta}$, while an equal-amount monthly SIP achieved an 11.70% CAGR$^{\Delta}$. A ₹1,000 monthly SIP started in 1999 would have grown to ₹25,31,592 by 2025, while a lump sum of ₹50,000 invested in 1999 would have become ₹10,76,154 by 2025. CAGR, or Compound Annual Growth Rate, is the average annual growth rate of an investment over a specific period longer than one year.

Chapter 1

Nature of Market

As we begin our journey into equity investing, let me introduce Mr. Market — a fictional character from Benjamin Graham's *The Intelligent Investor*. Mr. Market visits shareholders daily, offering to buy or sell shares at fluctuating prices.

Mr. Market's mood swings wildly between **overly optimistic**, overvaluing stocks, and **overly pessimistic**, undervaluing stocks. These moods reflect volatility driven by **emotions** rather than **fundamentals**.

Key Lesson: Don't take market prices at face value. View them as opportunities, choosing to buy or sell only when prices align with **intrinsic value estimates**.

One of the valuation metrics from Graham's book for returns of the stock market depends on three factors in the long run.

(G + I + S) = Long Term Returns of Stock Market

- **G** — Growth in corporate earnings per share
- **I** — Inflationary growth
- **S** — Speculative growth

If GDP is 7%, inflation is 5%, dividend is 1% and estimating speculation gains to be 2% then Long-Term Returns of Stock Market will be around (7+5+1+2)% = 15% in the long run if the country maintains this growth, inflation numbers in long run.

Market Trends

1) Bull Market

A bull market is a period in which asset prices are generally rising with few downs, often minor correction pricewise or timewise.
Technically, a bull market is a period when prices of a country's major index like Nifty or Sensex rise by 20% or more than previous all-time high.

All bull runs are supported by liquidity, excess liquidity in system whether it is due to booming income of middle-class or interest rate cut by the state (state-mandated interest rate cuts) or government aid (US government aid, package of fiscal stimulus and ultra-loose monetary policy in 2020 due to covid19) and increased interest of public in market also leads to bull markets.

The Federal Reserve releases M1 money supply data on a monthly basis, which is commonly used to assess liquidity in financial systems. Similarly, the Reserve Bank of India (RBI) also publishes M1 money supply figures monthly—these include liquid deposits such as currency with the public and demand deposits with banks.

M1 refers to the most liquid forms of money in the economy: currency with the public (cash and coins) plus demand deposits (savings accounts, current accounts) with the banking system. M2 includes M1 plus other less liquid assets like savings deposits with post office savings banks and short-term time deposits. M1 is mainly used to measure immediate liquidity available for transactions, while M2 provides a broader view of overall money available in the economy—including funds that can be quickly converted to cash but are not used for everyday payments.

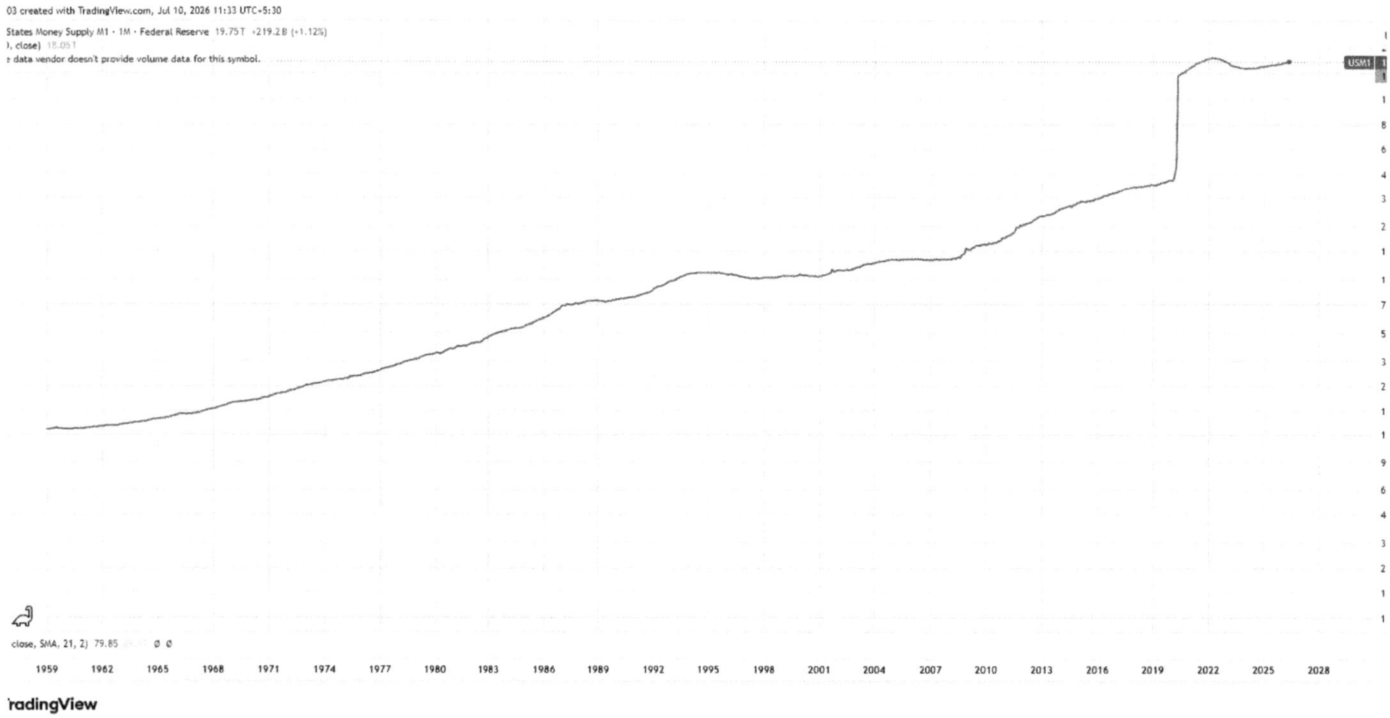

United States Money Supply M1

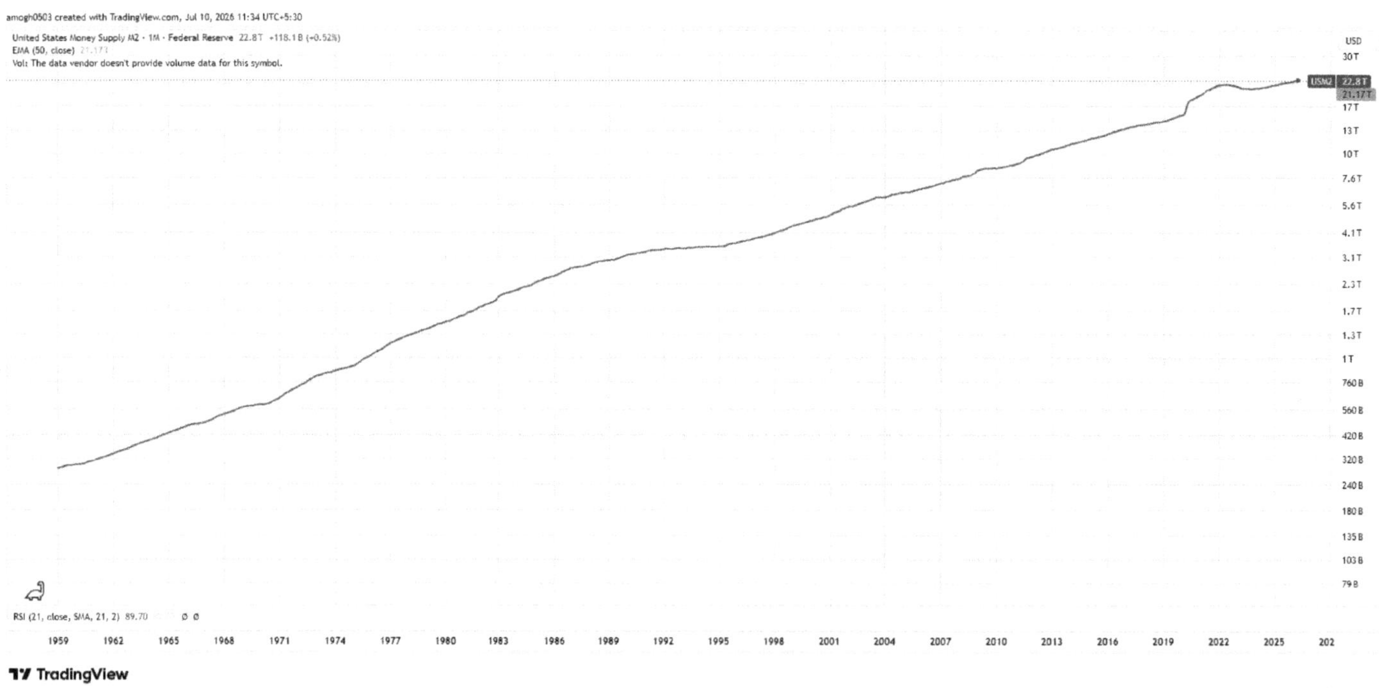

United States Money Supply M2

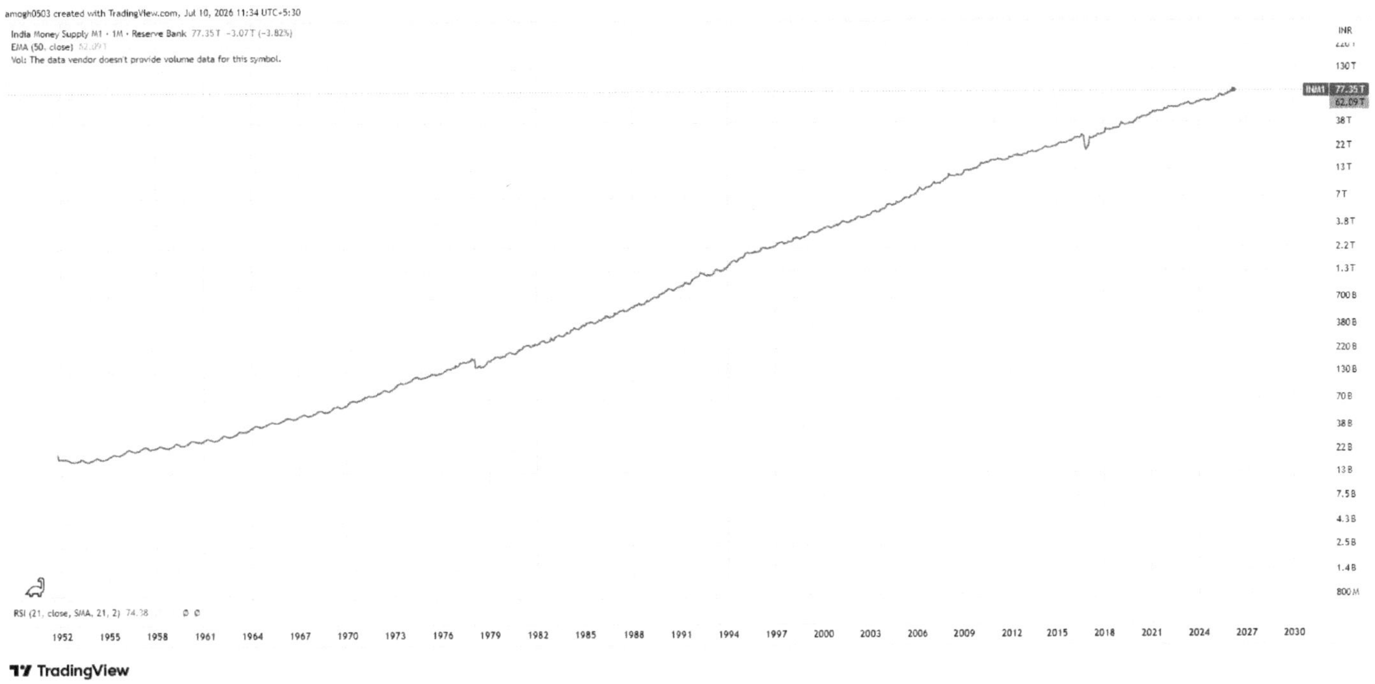

India Money Supply M1

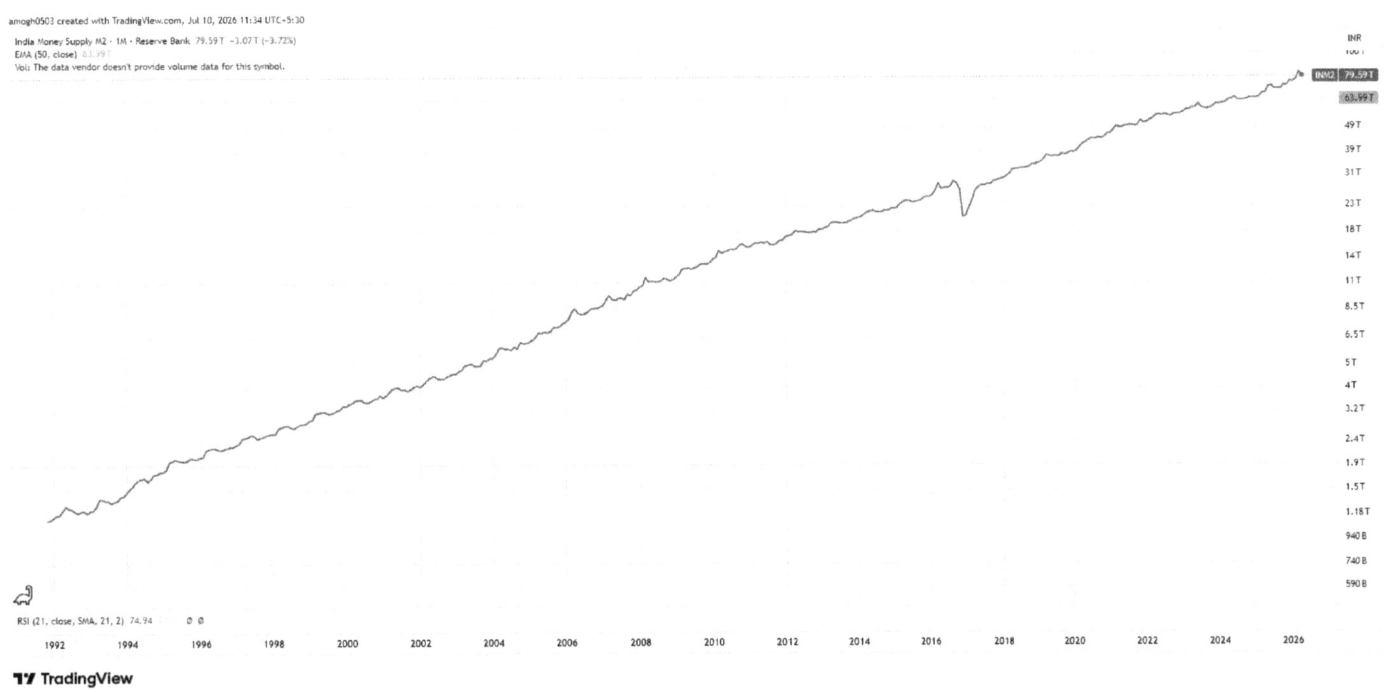

India Money Supply M2

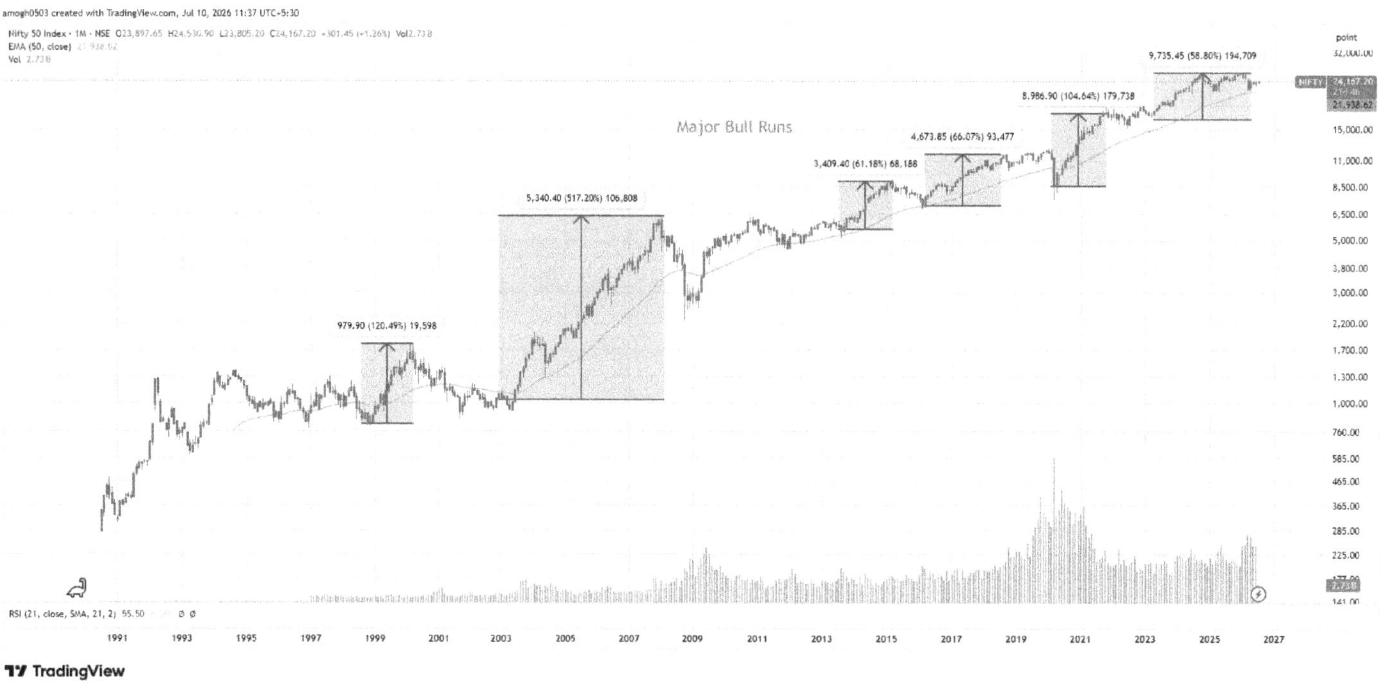

Nifty Bull Market

Nifty EPS Chart - Pink Line Shows Earning Per Share for Nifty, Green Line Shows Nifty Prices

Nifty 50 Major Bull Runs

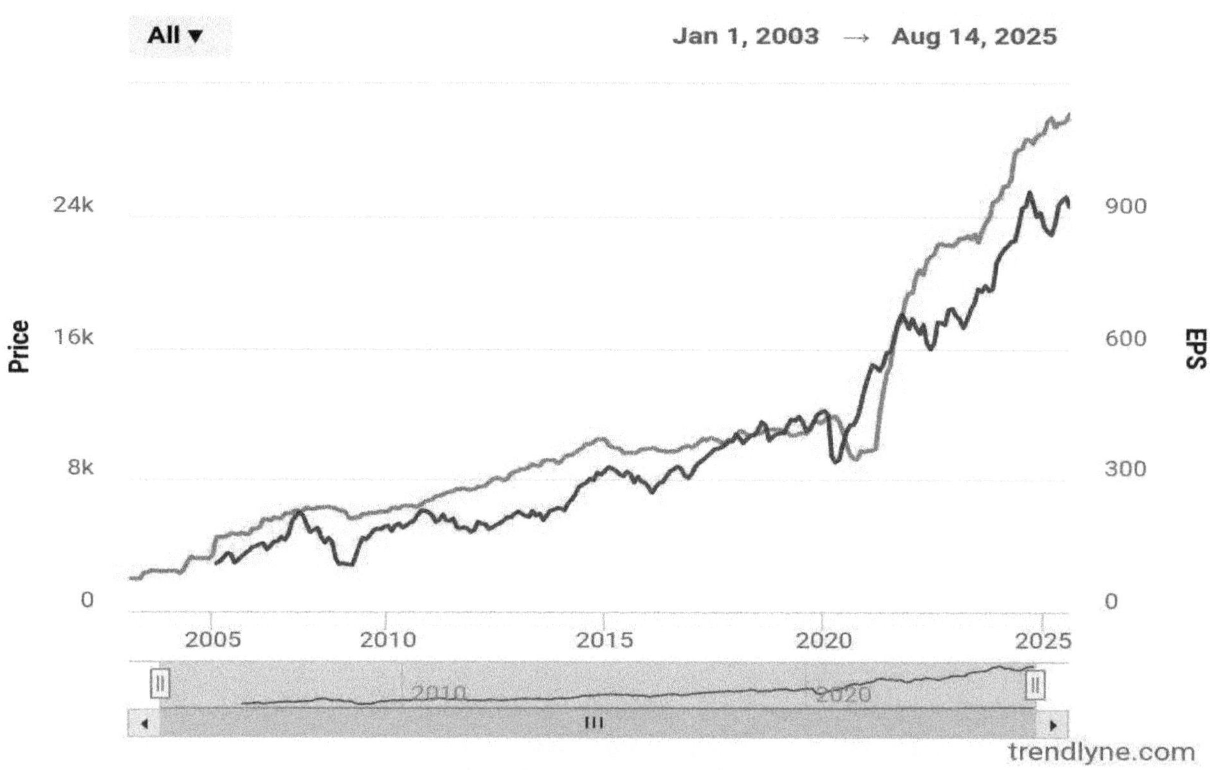

Bull Run	Time Period	Key Characteristics
First Bull Run	1998 - 2000	A speculative rally and boom in technology, media, and telecom (TMT) stocks, which was part of the global dot-com bubble.
Second Bull Run	2003 - 2008	A multi-year, powerful rally driven by strong domestic economic growth, a global commodities boom, and significant foreign capital inflows.
Third Bull Run	2013 - 2015	A sharp rally driven by a change in political leadership and investor optimism about a new era of economic reforms and stability.
Fourth Bull Run	2016 - 2018	A steady, consistent rally fuelled by improving corporate earnings and a period of stable economic policy.
Fifth Bull Run	2020 - 2021	An aggressive "V-shaped" rally and recovery from the COVID-19 crash, driven by massive liquidity injected by central banks and a swift return of investor confidence.
Sixth Bull Run	2023 - Present	The current bull run, characterized by a breakout from a long consolidation phase, with strong support from domestic retail investors and robust corporate earnings.

2) **Bear Market**

A bear market is a period in which asset prices are generally falling with few downs, often minor correction pricewise or timewise. Technically, a bear market is a period when the prices of a country's major index, such as the Nifty or Sensex, fall by 20% or more from their previous high.

Bear markets can be triggered by economic downturns, recessions or other black swan events (events unpredictable beforehand). In these conditions, investors prioritize capital preservation, although long-term opportunities may arise in companies with robust fundamentals and dividend yields. Focus should be on preserving capital rather than seeking growth.

In the long term it is a good time to buy stocks, you can find multi baggers with unbelievable fundamentals like 10-15% dividend yields P/E of 2-10 are common across multiple sectors, it is a good time to own great businesses that are cheaper than ever.

During bear markets, the financial landscape is characterized by steep price corrections (usually a short span of time; sometimes they can even take a long time to recover from fall), weakening corporate earnings and GDP figures.

The public starts losing interest to buy stocks, no new entrant trying to make quick money in the bear market, even companies start showing higher profits see price correction; because there is no incentive on showing better earnings, companies can hoard cash for safety. Be careful, stocks that were leaders of the rally that rose 5-10X in that period may fall to the same prices 50-80%. Safe haven during these times are gold and silver which rises as money shifts to safer assets.

Eventually, the government intervenes and tries to push the index up, by putting money in the system through interest rate cut monetary policy or fiscal policy (giving incentives to consumers or manufacturers).

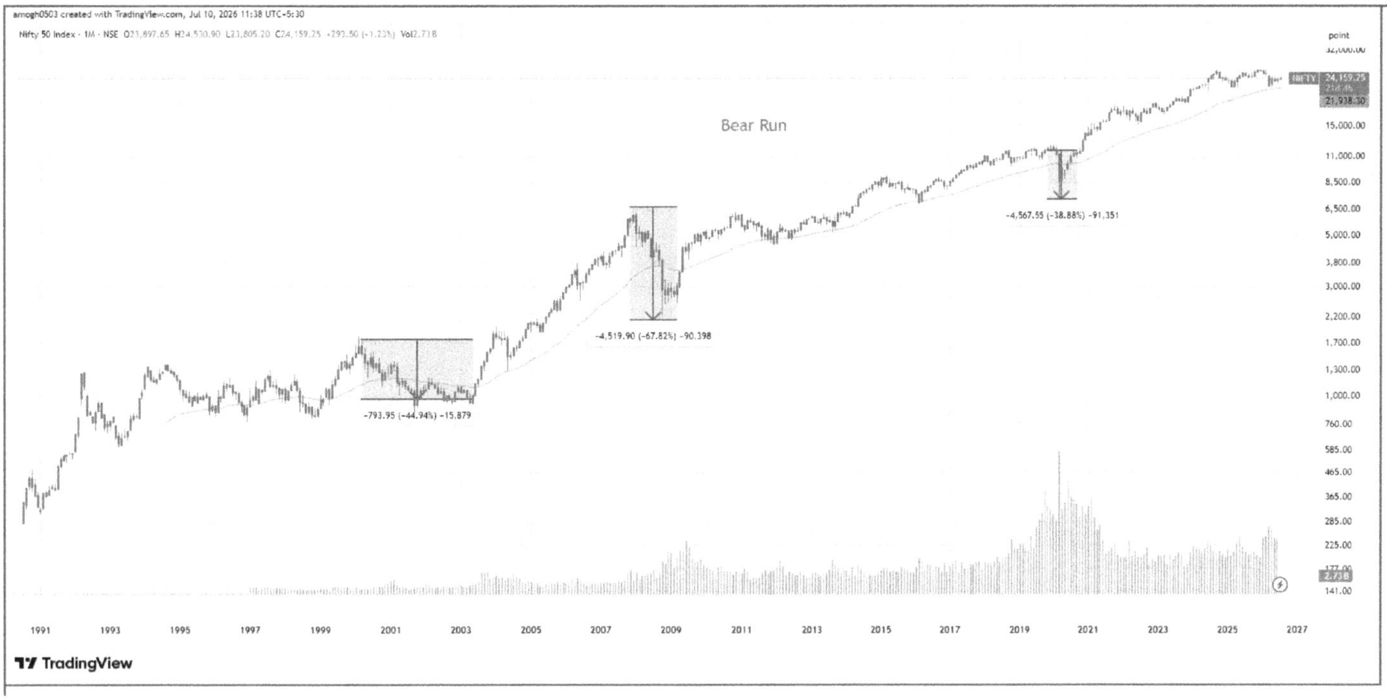

Nifty Bear Market

Here is a table summarizing the major bear markets of the Nifty 50.

Bear Market	Time Period	Key Characteristics
Dot-com Bubble Burst	2000 - 2003	A prolonged and painful bear market triggered by the collapse of the global technology boom, leading to a multi-year consolidation phase.
Global Financial Crisis	2008 - 2009	A deep and severe bear market caused by a global credit crunch and liquidity crisis, resulting in a massive and sustained sell-off.
COVID-19 Crash	Early 2020	A historically fast and sharp bear market triggered by the global pandemic lockdown, which was followed by an equally swift recovery.

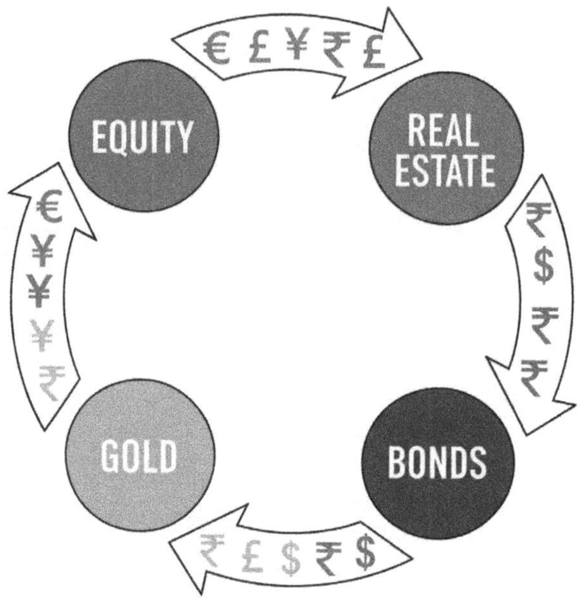

The Money Quadrant

Money is never lost in the system; it is simply being rotated among different quadrants of assets. This rotation assures investors that after each bear market phase, money will eventually return to equity.

During periods of economic uncertainty, investor sentiment drives money out of risky assets and into safer havens, a natural and necessary part of the cycle.

Take the **2000 Dot-com crash** as the first example. As the global tech bubble burst, investors panicked and pulled their money out of speculative stocks. This capital didn't vanish; it simply flowed into other assets, causing the Nifty to fall sharply. Yet, as the over-optimism faded, and sounder companies began to perform, that same capital eventually found its way back into equity, bringing the market back to life.

Similarly, the **2008 Global Financial Crisis** sent a shockwave through the global economy, causing the Nifty to plummet by over 50%. This was a classic flight-to-safety event, where vast amounts of money were reallocated from stocks to perceived crisis hedges like **bonds** and **gold**. As central banks intervened and confidence slowly returned, that capital once again began to flow back into equity, setting the stage for a powerful bull's run.

Most recently, the **2020 COVID-19 crash** demonstrated this cycle in a condensed timeline. The market saw one of its fastest and steepest falls ever as panic-selling took hold. While a huge volume of money left the equity market, it did not leave the financial system. Following swift economic policies and a massive return of liquidity, that capital came rushing back, fueling an equally fast recovery that pushed the Nifty to new highs.

These historical examples show that money is never truly lost from the system. Instead, it is continuously rotating between different asset classes, assuring investors that after each bear market, capital will find its way back to equity.

3) **Sideways Market**

A sideways market or range bound market occurs when prices don't show a clear trend in either direction up or down.
These markets often arise during periods of uncertainty when investors lack confidence to push prices strongly upwards or downwards. After 2020, sideways were created by FIIs selling heavily Nifty based ETFs whereas DIIs and retail bought stocks in every fall creating a range for Nifty to trade upon for 1–2-year period.

After a strong rise in prices of stocks, the market goes in sideways for fundamentals such as sales, earning per share of stocks to catch up and reflect the result of speculations made by seeing growth of stocks previously.

Geopolitical events like Russia-Ukraine war starting created a sideways market, interest rate changes or pausing rates for a long time can lead to a sideways market.

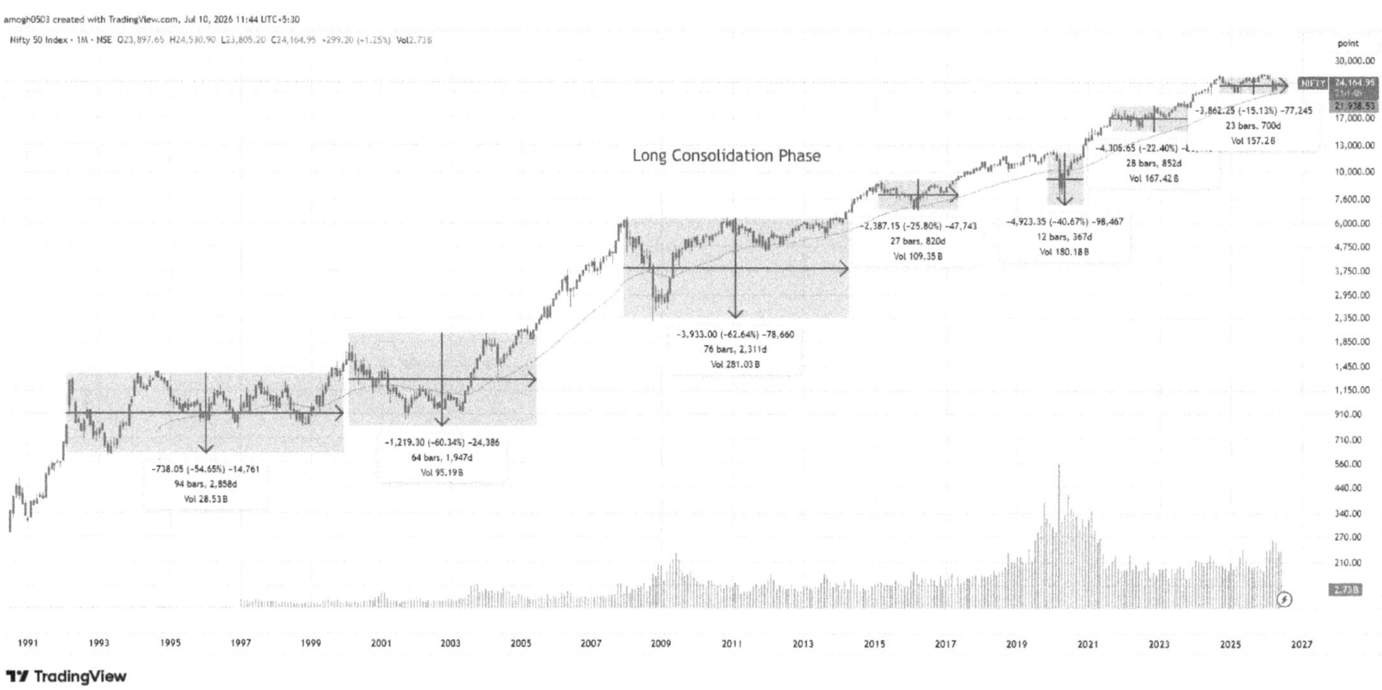

Nifty Sideways Market

Consolidation Phase	Time Period	Key Characteristics
First Phase	2000 - 2003	A long period of sideways trading with low volume, reflecting investor uncertainty after the dot-com bubble crash.
Second Phase	2008 - 2013	A multi-year recovery phase after the global financial crisis, where the market moved within a defined range to build a new foundation.
Third Phase	2015 - 2016	A shorter, two-year period where the market took a breather and traded in a tight range to absorb previous gains before the next major move.
Fourth Phase	2018 - 2020	A period of sideways trading with higher volume, which ended abruptly with the sharp market correction caused by the COVID-19 pandemic.
Fifth Phase	2021 - 2023	A wide-ranging consolidation phase following the rapid pandemic recovery, where the market digested gains before breaking out to new all-time highs.

Chapter 2

Nature of Investors

After knowing the nature of the market, it's important to know about the psychology of investors which creates a different nature of investors that put money in the market. Investors can be classified by their risk tolerance and investment strategy into two broad categories: aggressive investors and defensive investors.

1) **Aggressive Investors**- are investors primarily invested in equities and trying to make maximum profits with every turn of market whether it's a bull, bear or sideways market. Their objective is to get maximum returns often by taking more risks by allocating substantial portions of their portfolio into small cap stocks, emerging markets, or leveraged products (F&O).

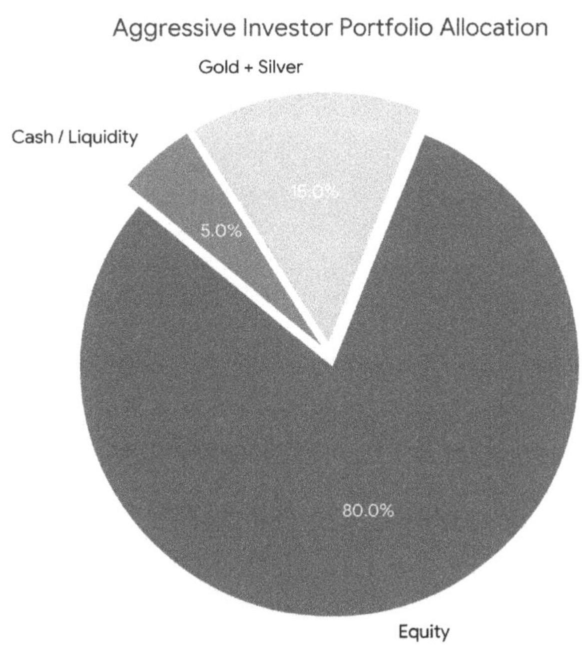

These investors should apply technical analysis on undervalued stocks, growth companies, and use a systematic approach for investing.

Investor should find out about their nature and view of market, do they want to constantly want to manage portfolio of stocks they are holding doing frequent changes in allocation with every tick on screen in hopes of doing better than everyone else and betting on higher gains or want invest in a relaxed manner with minimum changes to allocation believing that markets do well in long run and make money by sitting tight on a portfolio occasionally checking on companies quality and earning potential.

2) **Defensive Investors-** are investors whose primary objective is to avoid serious errors and ensure a consistent moderate return on their investments.

For defensive investors, protecting their principal is key and returns beating inflation; other asset classes along with their focus for accumulation of wealth over the long term.
Defensive investors should maintain a diversified portfolio with bonds, blue chip stocks, some liquid cash equivalent holding should be kept for buying on market falls, and gold allocation can help in managing folio in bear markets.

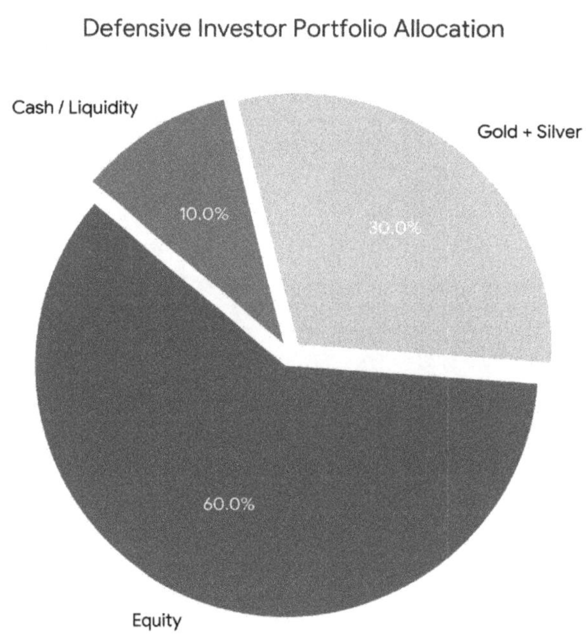

Discipline and patience are the key to managing a portfolio, avoiding high risk investments and using cash efficiently along with asset rotation based on geopolitics and economics is required for generating wealth steadily as money is within the system but rotating in different asset classes balancing them when one is over run or other is too bearish.

Each year market falls by 10-15% sometimes market fall by 20-25% creating a bear market, defensive investors should be taking advantages of these major falls by investing more money in equity at each big fall either by using cash or selling some bonds or even gold in case of a major crash like in 2000, 2008 and 2020, etc. Can generate enormous wealth for defensive investors.

Knowing our nature as investor, view on market is important to make aware decisions and avoid investing with a FOMO (Fear of Moving Out) which generally creates losses due to wrong time of entry in equity it can also make us lose our conviction over a particular stock story making us to sell earlier before the story has played out well.

Investors should be looking at market fall as an opportunity to buy at a falling index and sell at higher prices. But fear or greed often makes execution or portfolio to be managed in the opposite direction which might seem like a common sense or rational decision.

Chapter 3

Theories in stock investing

Theories of the market represent different perspectives on how markets function and how investors can consistently outperform them. These theories analyze the nature of the market, investor psychology, geopolitics, economics, and trends, providing a framework for strategic portfolio management.

1) Efficient Market Theory (EMT)

Efficient Market Hypothesis (EMH), developed primarily by economist Eugene Fama, suggests that stocks always trade at their fair value.
The price of a stock reflects all available information, meaning it's impossible to consistently achieve higher-than-average returns through publicly available information. Therefore, additional returns can only be made by making riskier investments like buying mid, small, and micro-cap stocks.

This hypothesis is in support with passive portfolio such as low-cost index funds will achieve the best long-term results while this statement is true for most investors but some but some investors like Warren Buffet, Peter Lynch, Jim Simons and many others have shown exceptional skills in beating the average market returns.

Graham also argues EMH theory that markets are not always efficient as there may be some hidden story within stock that becomes public later and adjusts prices for it.
Also, as per Mr. Market analogy every day it states different prices for stocks. It might be over optimistic or pessimistic, leading to inefficiencies that investors can take advantage of in the long run.

2) Price Has Memory

Stock prices have memory this theory contradicts efficient market theory but sometimes we see it greatly influence prices of stocks. This concept suggests that stocks do not follow an entirely random path but instead exhibit behavior and patterns that may repeat over time. Simply, historical price levels and patterns impact future prices. The same theory also works on index and mutual funds.

Techniques and concepts supporting price has memory

1. **Mean Reversion Theory**

If a stock is moving up or down then prices tend to revert to the moving average or regress to mean. Traders often use MA 20, 50 and 200 for taking long, short or exciting positions. This also means that a stock that is rising rapidly will go down back to the moving average or if it is falling it will bounce back to touch or near the moving average.

Since 2016, the 200 Moving Average (Red Line) has acted as a critical level of dynamic support for

Reliance. The stock exhibits a classic 'mean reversion' behavior: when the price extends too far above the average, it eventually cools off and returns to the red line. Conversely, whenever the price tests this support level, buyers step in, propelling the stock to new highs.

2. Support and Resistance Levels

Technical analysts or TV anchors often give price levels of support and resistance.
Support level is where buyers are interested to own the stock, also called demand zone.

Resistance level is where selling interest is strong enough to prevent further rises.
(If stock does not have memory, then why does stock maintain support and resistance levels) Usually the pending orders of investors create these levels, also called supply zone. For investors knowing the demand zone and supply zone is important to plan entry or exit for a few trading techniques supporting the concept of price memory.

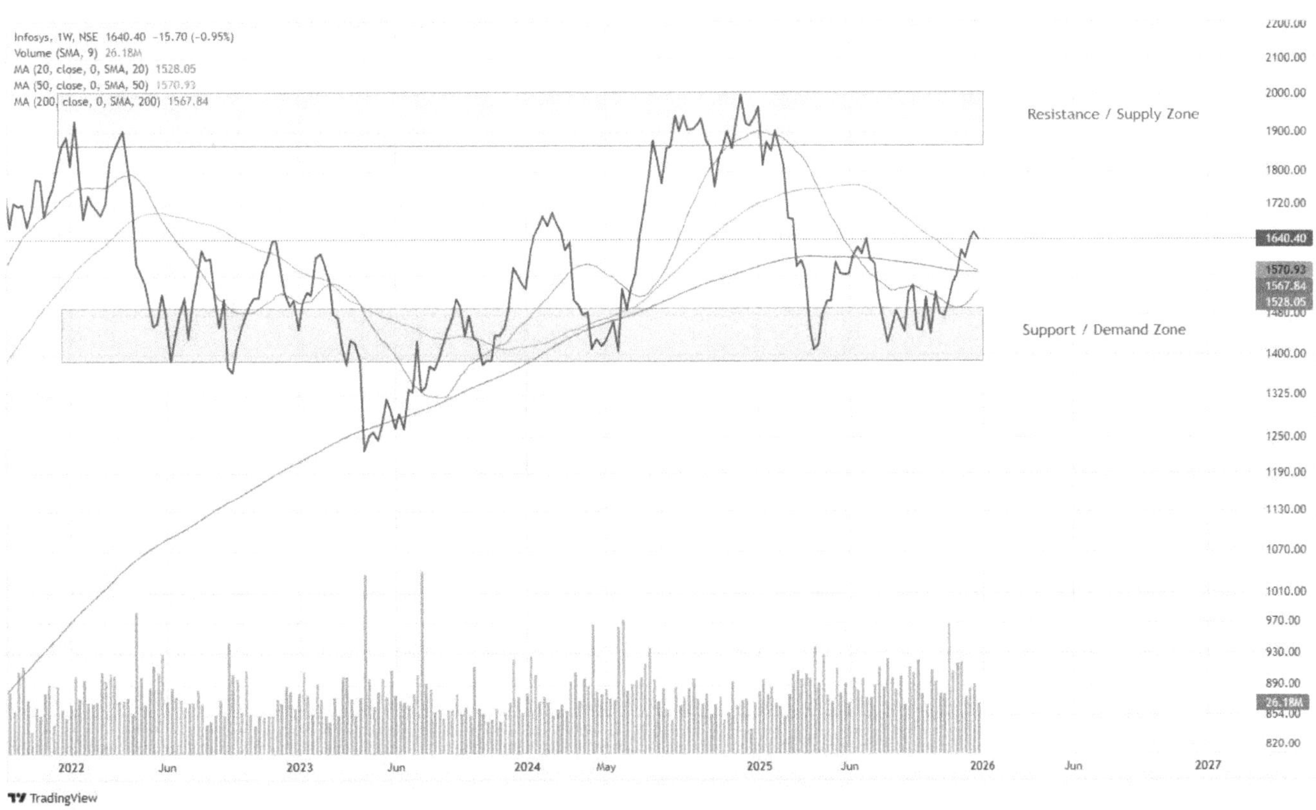

This weekly chart of Infosys illustrates a defined Market Structure driven by Supply and Demand zones.

The area highlighted in green represents a strong Demand Zone (Support), ranging approximately between 1,360 and 1,480, where buying interest historically renews, preventing further decline. Conversely, the red area marks a Supply Zone (Resistance), situated between 1,850 and 1,950, where selling pressure intensifies and caps upward momentum. The stock's oscillation between these two distinct zones highlights a consolidation phase, where traders often look to 'buy at support' near the 1,400 level and 'sell at resistance' near the 1,900 level until a decisive breakout occurs.

3. Momentum Investing

When a stock is moving up and we see a long-term chart of 5-10 years, the stock has a long history of rising prices and is likely to continue rising in the near term. Here, the stock price has memory of a direction which is either a positive or negative trend to reinforce buying or selling, which leads to continued movement in the same direction. Momentum investing is the strategy of buying stocks that are going up and selling stocks that are going down, in the belief that a stock's recent trend will likely continue.

Buy as long as 100 MA acting as dynamic support

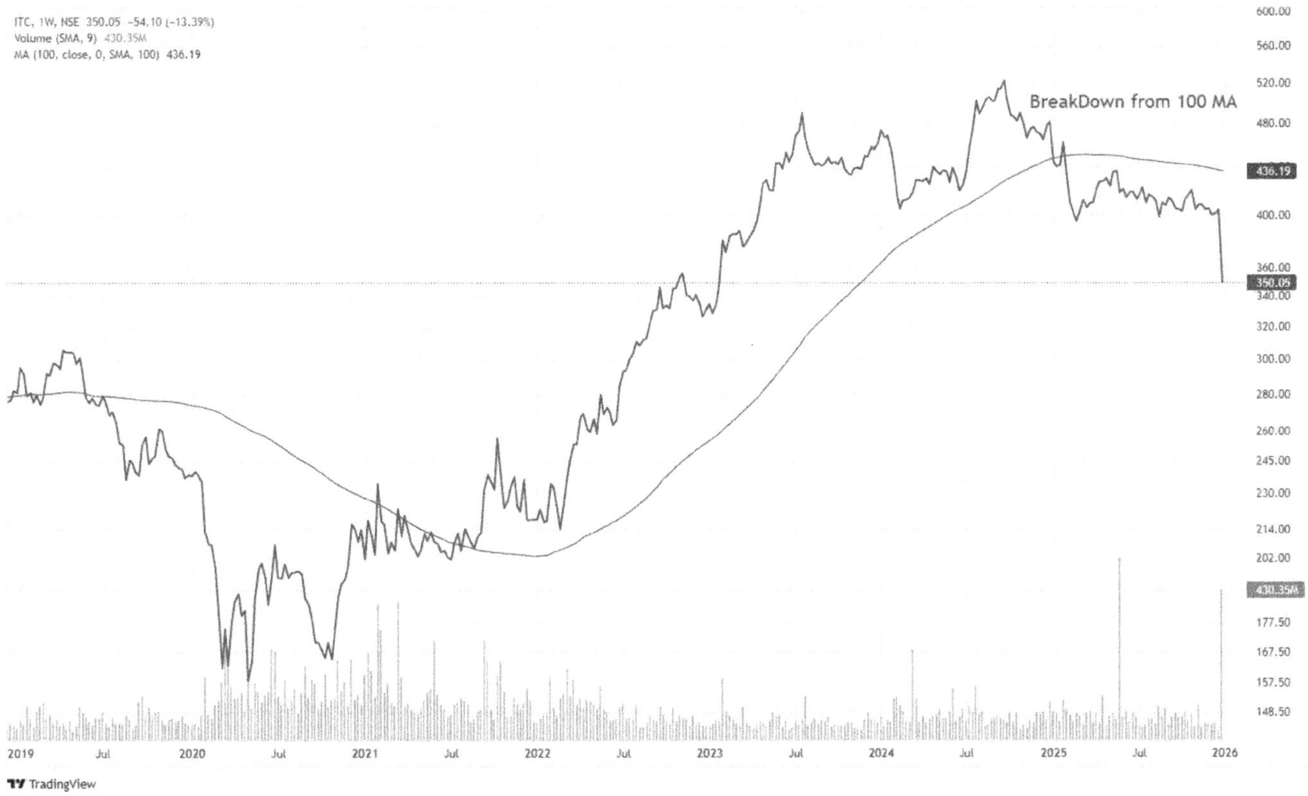

Sell as 100 MA dynamic support breakdown

4. Behavior and Psychology of Investor

Investor behavior and psychology are crucial because they explain why markets are not always rational. Investor biases, such as fear and greed, can lead to herd mentality and market bubbles, causing asset prices to deviate from their true value. Most of the retail investors start investing when stock starts falling and feel comfortable investing more assuming it will return to previous high.

If stock falls from 100 to 80, then investors see 100 as real value of stock influencing buy or sell decision creating a memory for old price and stock may reach previous high due to behavior of investors. This is also known as **anchoring bias**.

This technique is better used in index-based investing where chances of reaching previous highs are more, creating an opportunity of buying or making SIPs (Systematic Investment Plans) for additional returns. Price memory technique is useful to generate high returns by taking riskier positions whereas below 2 techniques are useful for generating more returns by taking relatively lower risks when applied on index.

i. V20 strategy

Great companies, blue-chip stocks with lots of cash selected when they fall significantly from the top while fundamentals remain like previous years can be bought to generate a good portfolio. These stocks should be sold when the current price is near the previous all-time high, creating a V pattern on the chart.

Since the stock has memories of previous all-time highs, it should hit there again in the long term when fundamentals support or headwinds come.

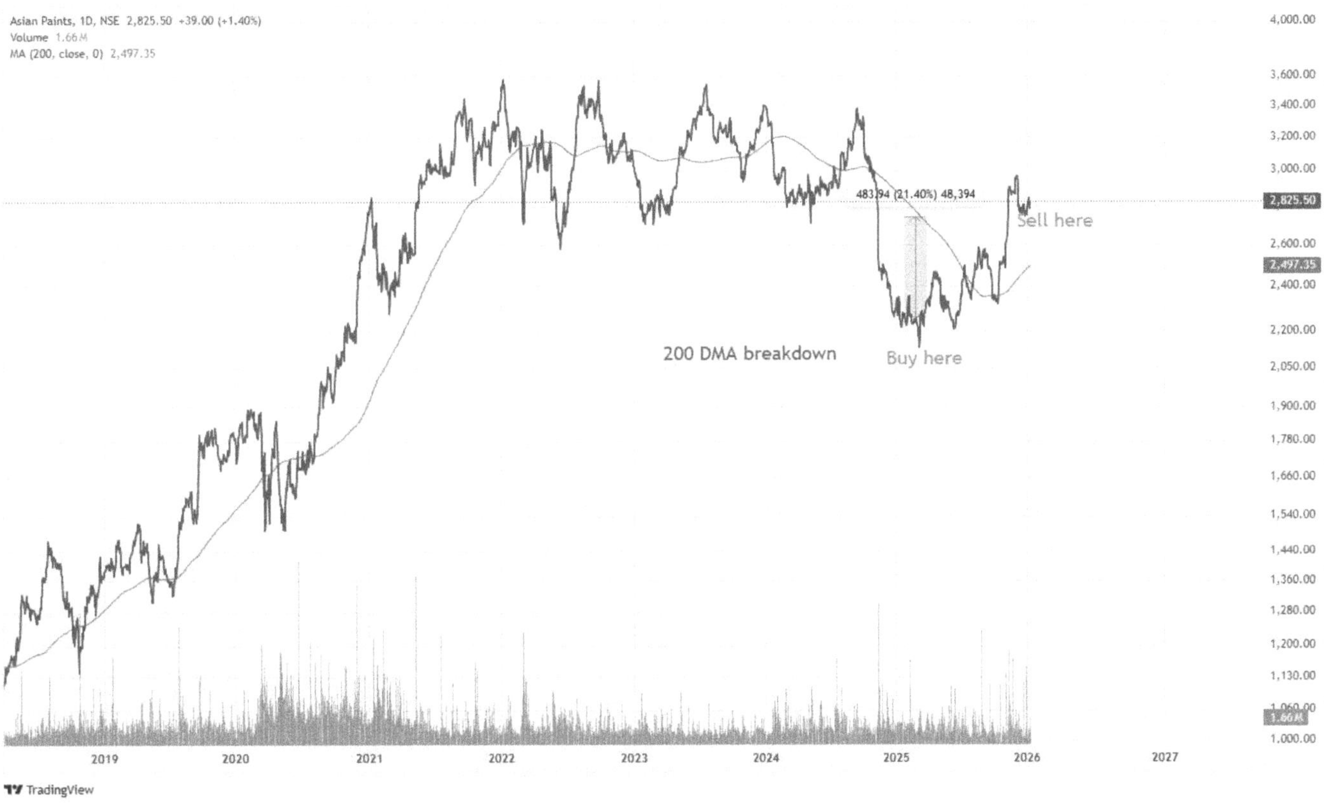

V20 strategy

For this strategy select stock from Nifty 50 or Nifty next 50, which is having average to good sales and profit growth over 3-5 years, P/E is also close to Nifty 50 P/E and is significantly down from all time highs. Then check for 200 MA if below more than 20% from 200 MA then stock can be bought here if pattern for reversal shows with target of 200 MA.

ii. WW recovery

When Nifty 50 or some good stocks ETF/mutual funds falls sharply and rate becomes stable which is equal to previous demand zone (or bottom) made in long term chart of 1-2 years, it is likely to recover back to previous high forming a W pattern on chart can be used to buy equity in multiple W patterns or range bound trading and sell them after a good price rebound nearing previous highs.

Nifty W pattern recovery

Formation of multiple WWs show consolidation pattern; most probable trade after this is markets don't go down usually after consolidation. Each fall after the W pattern is a buying opportunity in the dip. After this W pattern consolidation market has given a good upward rally.

3) Dow Theory

Dow Theory is a foundational framework of technical analysis that interprets stock market behavior and trends developed by Charles H. Dow, published between 1900 and 1902 in the wall street journal.

1. The Market Discounts Everything

Dow believed the stock market reflected all available information. This means that earnings reports, economic indicators, geopolitical events, and even investor's psychology are already priced in the market.

2. Market movements have three trends

i. **Primary Trends**:

This trend is the long-term trend that usually lasts a year or more. This trend is characterized by a sustained movement in one direction, either in an upward or downward direction.

Primary Trend, in upward direction from 5 years

ii. **Secondary Trends**:

These are counter-movements within the primary trend, lasting weeks to months. They are like waves within the tide, representing correction (retracements) of 33-66% of previous primary trend movement.

Secondary Trends, first downwards then upwards direction for 1 year

iii. **Minor Trends**:

Short term fluctuations, typically last days or weeks. This moves in the same direction as the primary trend and is often caused by short term fluctuations in supply and demand.

Minor Trends, rangebound market for 3 months

3. **Trends are confirmed by volume**
   Volumes (often representing emotions of the market) serve as a supporting indicator. A trend is more likely to be sustained if there is a high volume of trading activity in the direction of trend. Low volume during a trend may indicate that trend is weak and may not be sustained.

Volumes at different points showing the top, bottom and reversal, bottoming out and then breakout

4. **Indices must confirm each other**
   Dow stressed the importance of multiple indices moving in tandem. This means that signals occurring on one index must match or correspond with signals on the other. If one index such as Nifty 50 shows a primary trend, but another remains in a primary downtrend, traders should not assume that a new trend has begun.

Indices move in tandem with the Nifty 50 benchmark. This synchronized upward trend across diverse sectors validates the strength and sustainability of the primary market direction.

5. Trends persist until reversal

A trend remains until clear evidence suggests a reversal. Reversals are marked by significant shifts in price patterns, confirmed by volume and behavior across indices. This principle encourages investors to ‘ride the trend’ and avoid premature exits.

Biocon was in uptrend from 2016 to 2020 after which it started taking resistance from the redline creating lower lows and lower highs downtrend which continued until its breakout from red line with high volumes showing signs of reversal and creating a new uptrend again, from the point of reversal (Green Arrow) until now it gave 60% returns going from 250₹ back to 400₹ showing that trends persist until reversal.

4) Price Action Theory

Price action refers to movement of a stock or assets price over time, usually represented in the form of price charts. The theory is that all information needed to make an investment decision is reflected in the price itself.

Unlike traditional trading strategies, price action doesn't rely on external tools or indicators. It works on understanding how the market reacts to price changes and how psychological factors (like fear and greed) influence investor behavior.

- Why does price action work and whom it is for?

There are multiple entities investing in the market institutes, mutual funds, pension funds, global funds or ETFs, government banks, insurance companies, corporates, HNIs, retail and other participants.

All the chart patterns are formed by institutes buying/selling or entities putting in large amounts of money creating chart patterns or price/candles we see in the chart. We can track movements of big money using long term patterns in stock, volumes, price movement, and candlestick patterns. Large volumes show high interest in a stock or high public emotions; chart also makes large price movements usually after such volume spikes.

All patterns are based on the theory of demand/supply that a large buyer or seller that previously bought or sold at a particular price will again put in money forming at similar prices forming **demand zone and supply zone,** small investors can use this to make money by trading on these patterns.
Some stocks from total allocation can be sold to make up for interest or investment when stock is range-bound, usually in the short term.

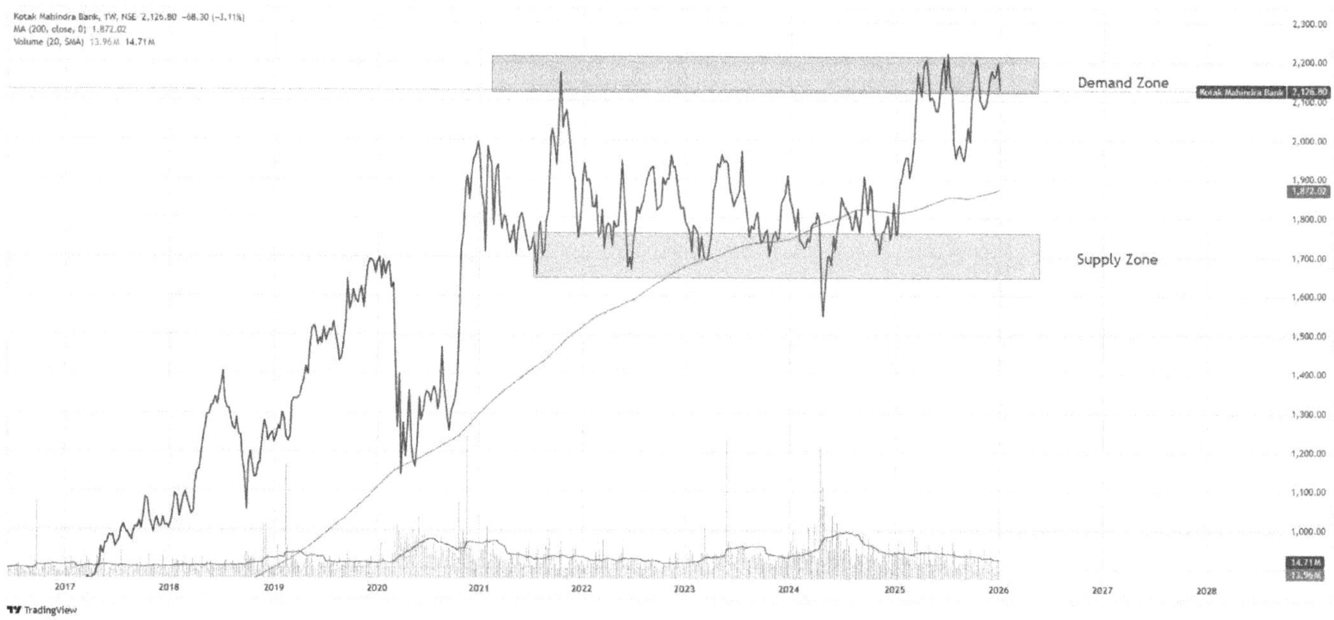

Demand and Supply Zone

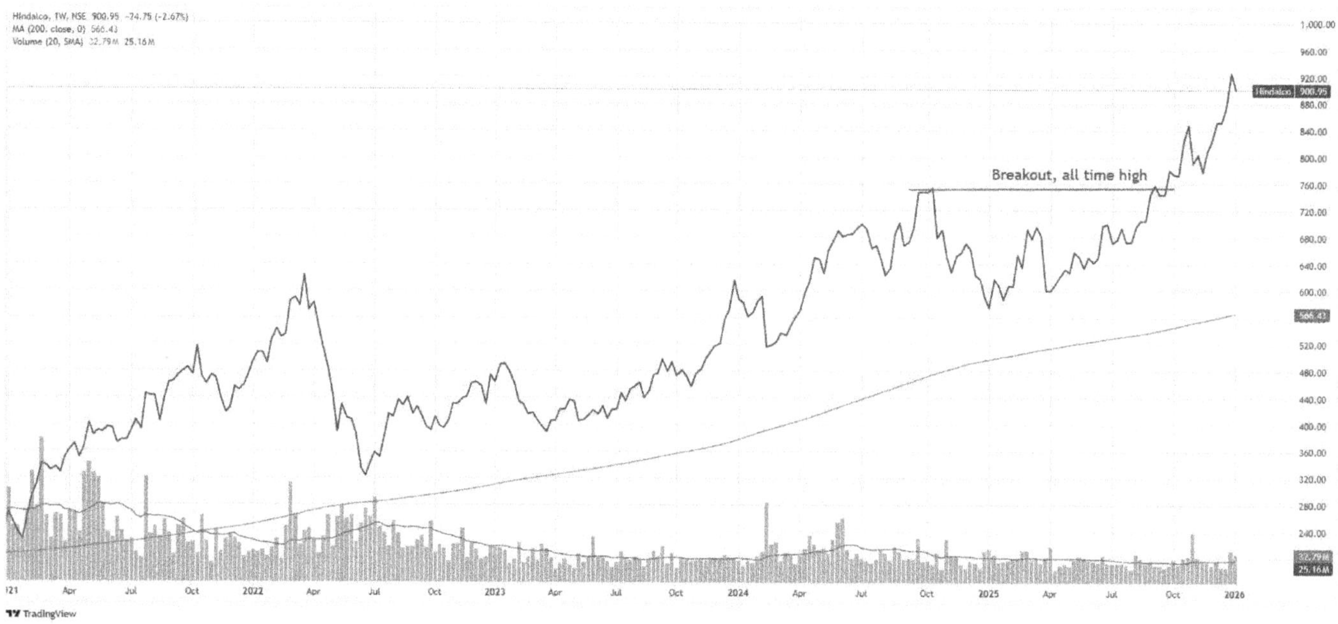

Breakout Chart

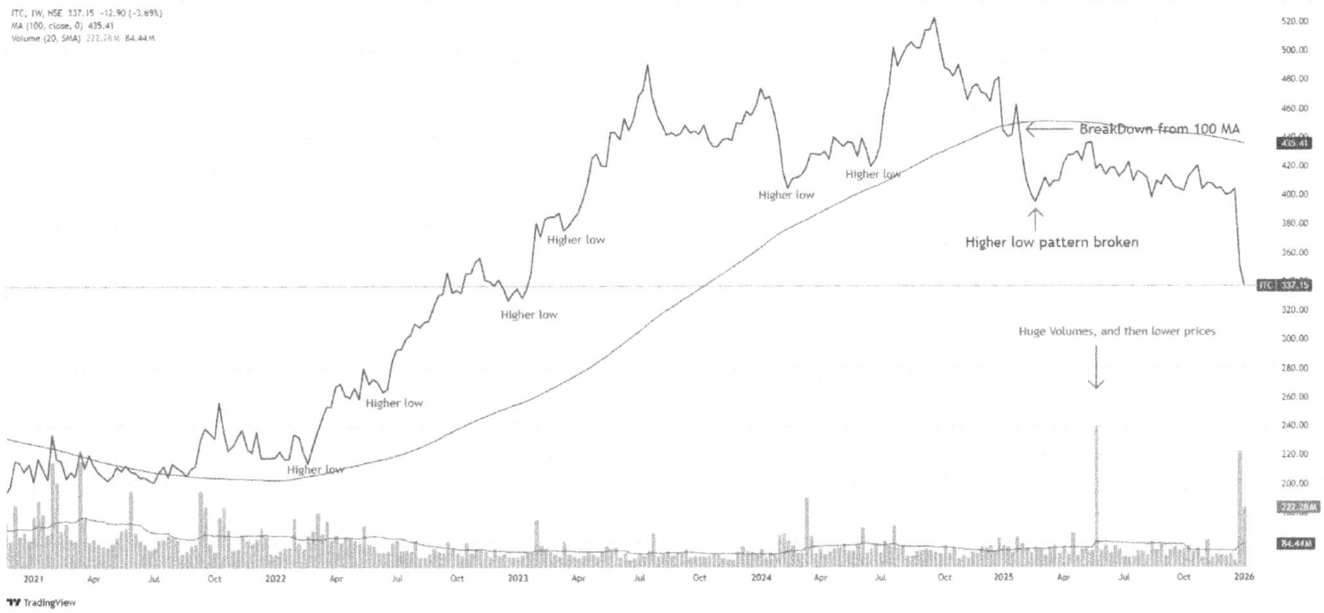

Breakdown chart

Candlestick charts are often used to analyze the stocks. Many candles show different pictures, but only three candles are most common.

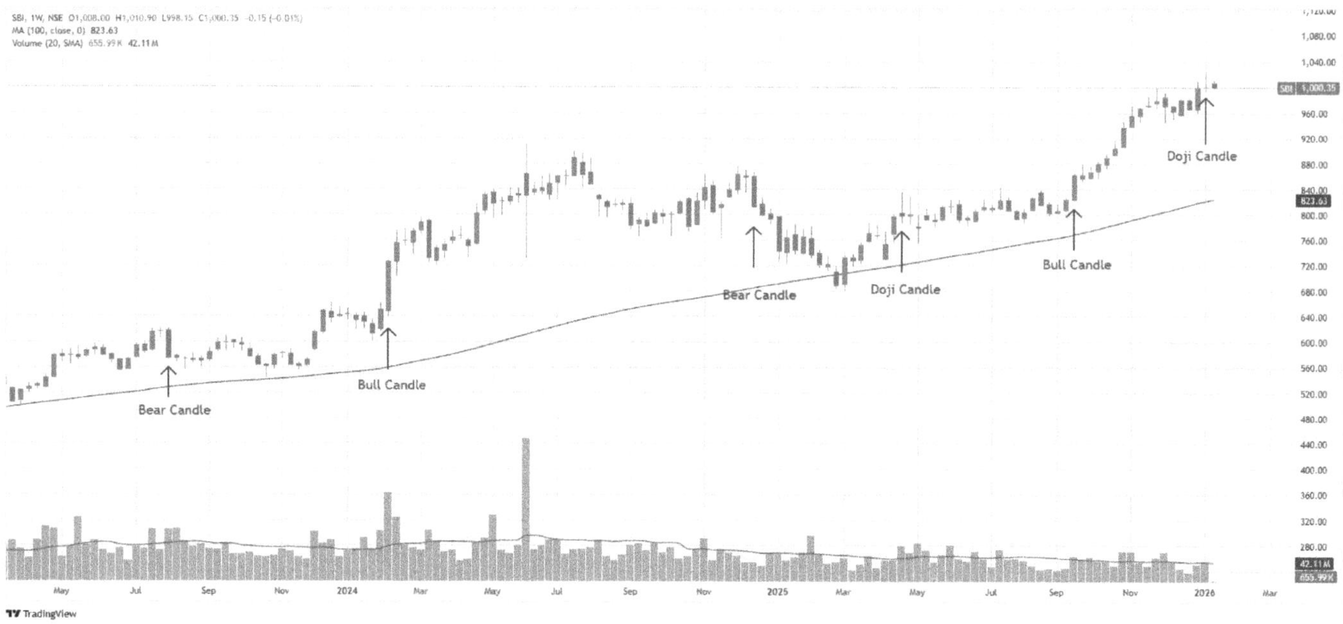

Bull, Bear and Doji Candles Chart

Some patterns that help in getting an idea of what side of the market is going on.

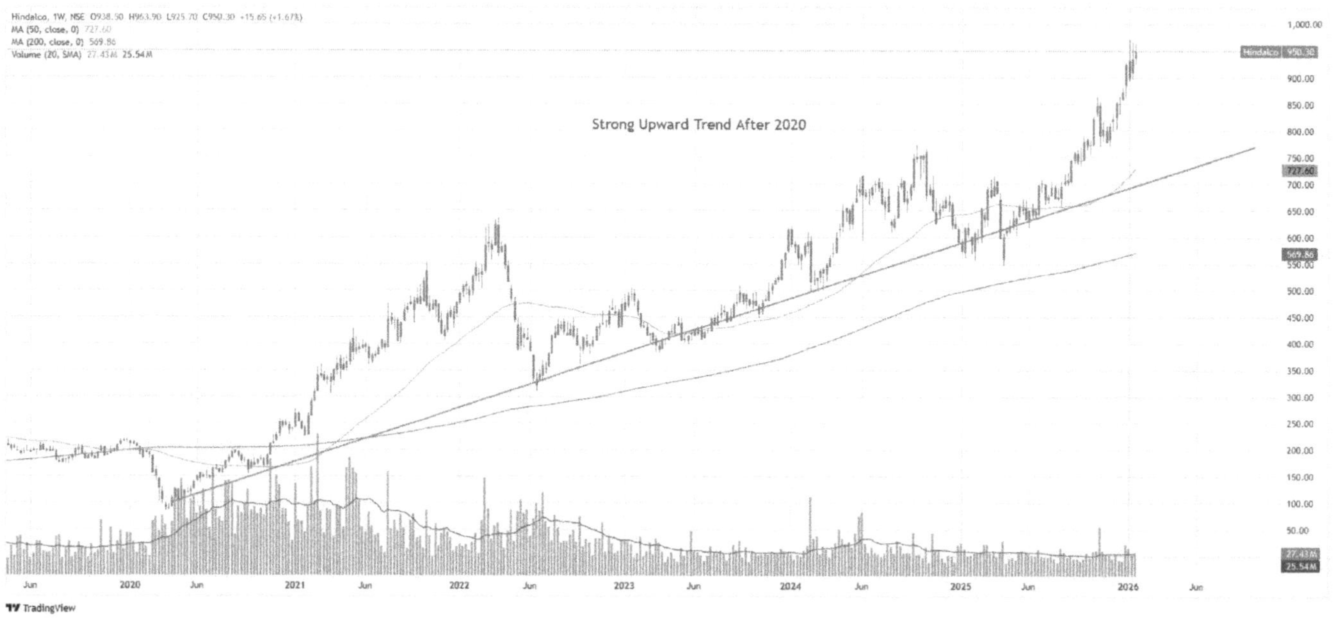

Strong upward trend

Hindalco after 2020 is showing strong upward trend where 200MA (red line) is acting as dynamic support for the stock in the long term for traders buying when prices go above 50MA with volumes and selling when falls below 50 MA until price falls below the green line (strong upward trend is broken).

Rounding Bottom Pattern

Nifty PSU BANK ETF has repeatedly shown rounding bottom patterns after 2020 with each bottom formation time being less than previous.

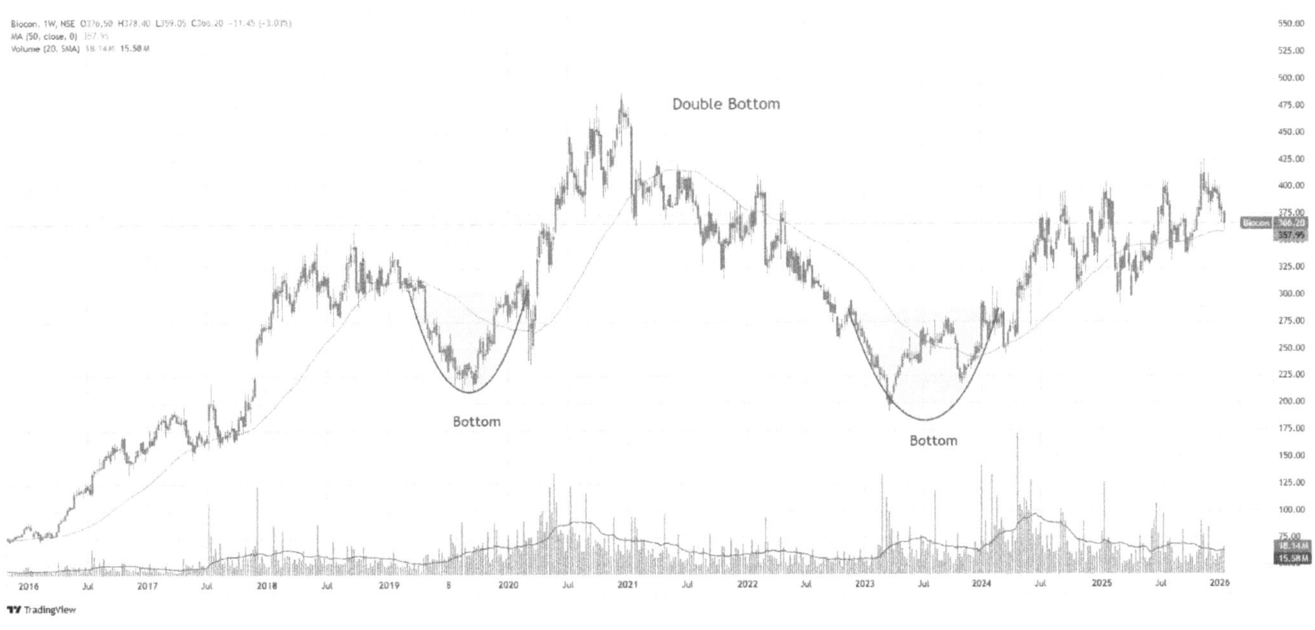

Double Bottom

Double bottom pattern after 4 years in Biocon

Inverse Head and Shoulder

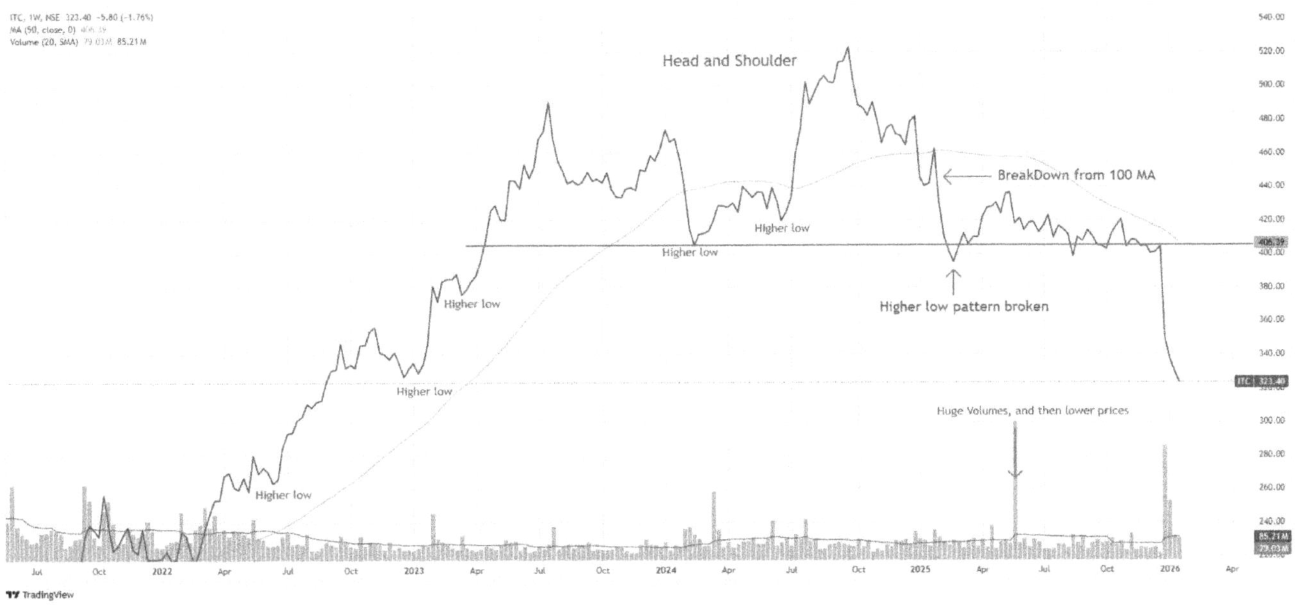

Head and Shoulder Pattern

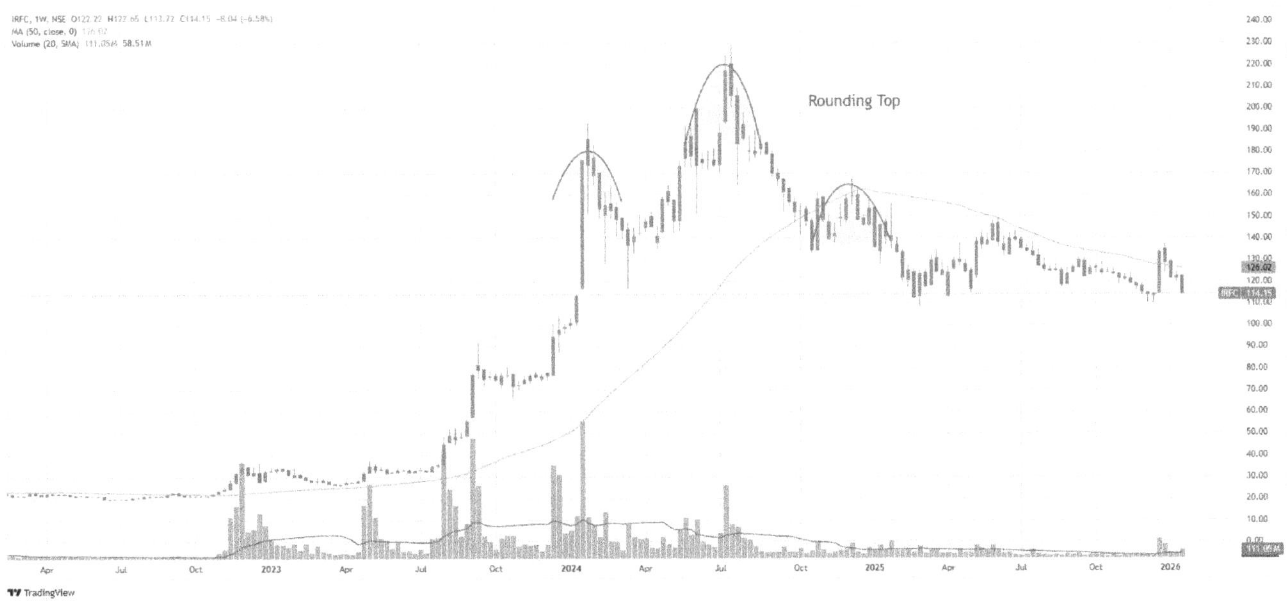

Rounding Top

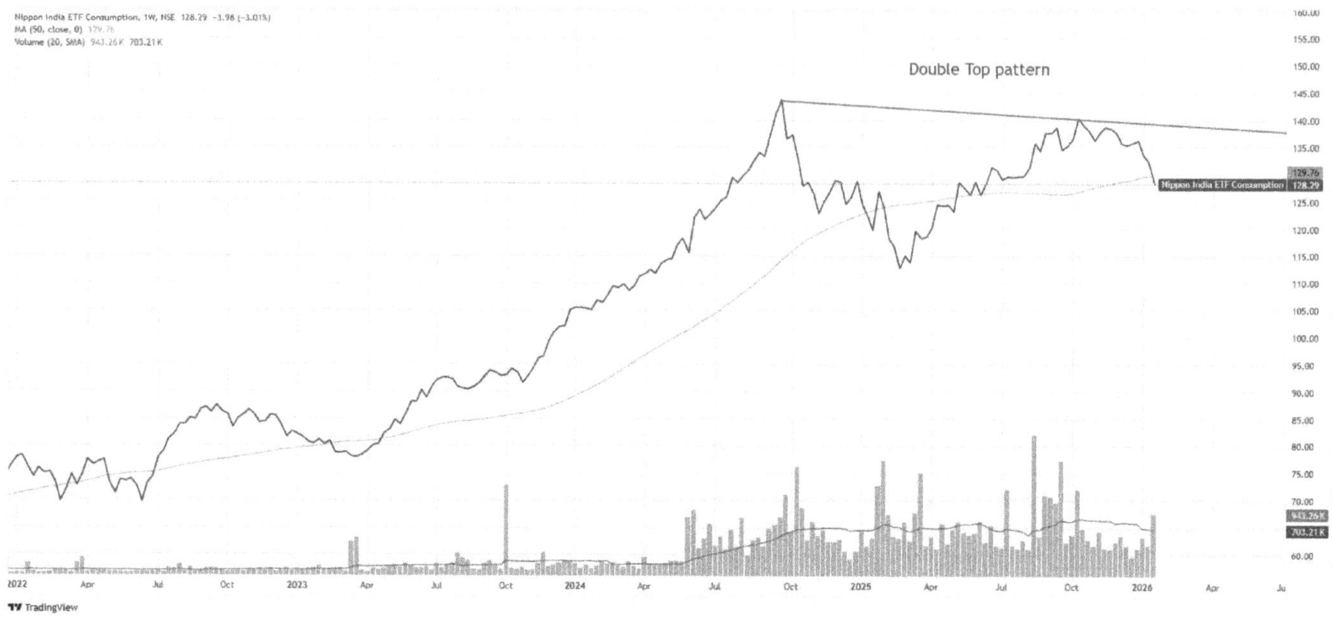

Double Top

Here, Double Top has formed on Nippon India Consumption ETF with the red line marked as resistance line

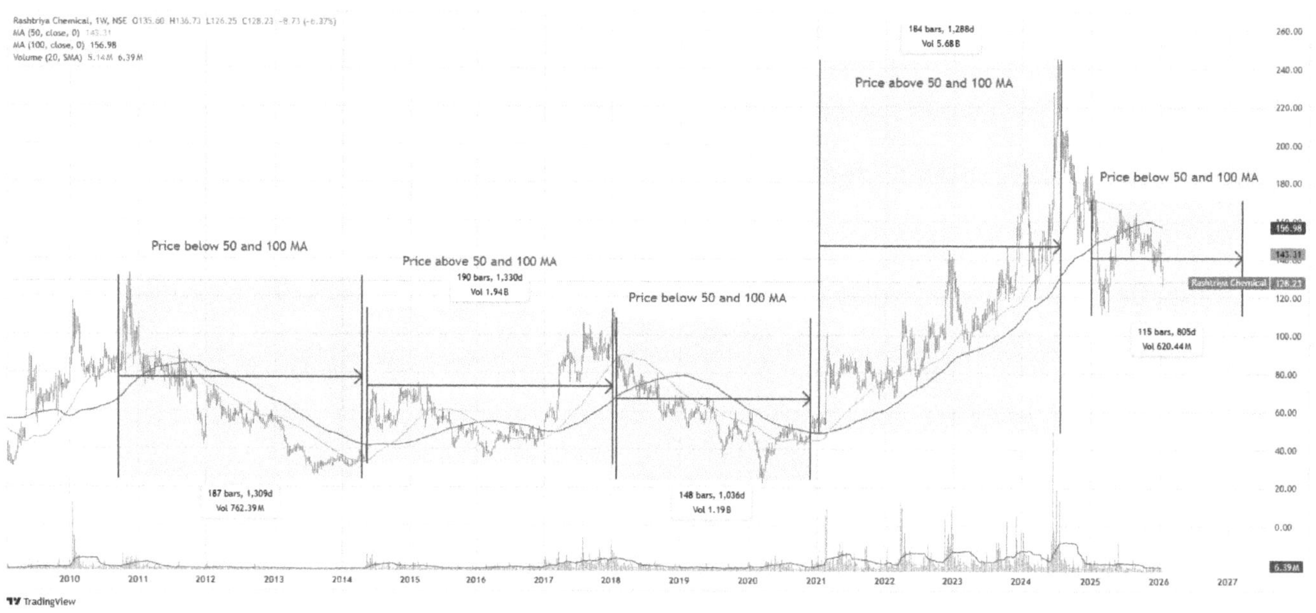

Moving averages acting as support and resistance

The Red Area shows stock prices below moving averages of 50 MA and 200 MA on weekly charts, not a good time to enter the stock. If already owned, profit should be booked or sold below 50 MA. The Green Area shows stock prices above moving averages of 50 MA and 200 MA on weekly charts, a good time to buy or build positions.

Swing Trades: -

For aggressive investors 20 days moving average (MAs) and 50 MAs are more important, when they have selected a group of stocks or index to trade each price touch to MA is buying opportunity and selling when price is falling breaking both the MAs. When choosing a new stock, 200 MA is important to see stock using it as support or resistance showing breakouts, buying or selling.

PCBL chart

Swing trading apply 5 points of diagram while keeping eye on Nifty 50, smallcap index and company results

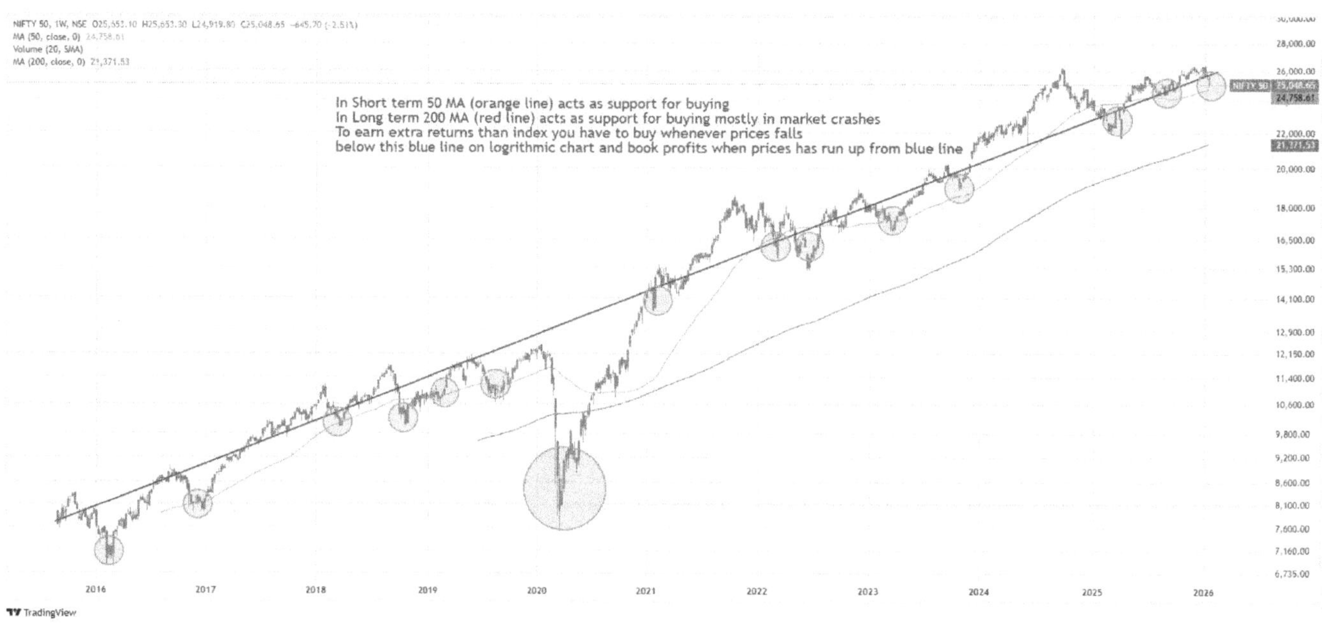

Nifty 50 trading for defensive investors

For defensive investors 50MA and 200MA are important when index like Nifty50 touches or goes below 200MA it is a great buying opportunity, for a gain of 10-15% extra one can put money at this pattern and keep on adding whenever price touches 50MA until trend or channel of buying is broken or market shows trend of sideways market.

5) CANSLIM Theory

A popular investment strategy developed by William J. O' Neil combines fundamental and technical analysis to identify growth stocks with the potential for significant returns.
This works like a screen for stocks to filter for high returns.

C – Current Earnings Per Share (EPS) Growth, company with recent quarterly EPS. Strong earnings are often a precursor to stock price increasing
A – Annual Earnings Growth, Look for stock with annual earnings growth of at least 20-25% over the last 3-5 years. This indicates a strong and growing company.

N – New Products, Services or Management

Companies innovating new products, services or leadership. Innovations often drive stock price growth

S – Supply and Demand

Stocks with high trading volume or limited shares available. Demand higher than supply often led to price appreciation. Companies buying their own stocks can be used here. Also, small companies often produce returns higher than larger companies with better fundamentals.

L - Leader or Laggard?

Laggard's stocks within the same industry are forgotten for years with no major price appreciation from multiple years, but good fundamentals and growth are chosen.

I - Institutional sponsorship

Stocks with increasing ownership by mutual funds or institutional investors. Institutions often have resources and research to choose winners.

M - Market Direction

The market should be in an overall bullish trend. Even strong stocks struggle in bear markets, that's why bull markets are important for CANSLIM.

CANSLIM is good for defensive investors because of its nature of holding laggards neglected by the market. Fundamentally , however , stock can outperform in a bull market but needs patience.

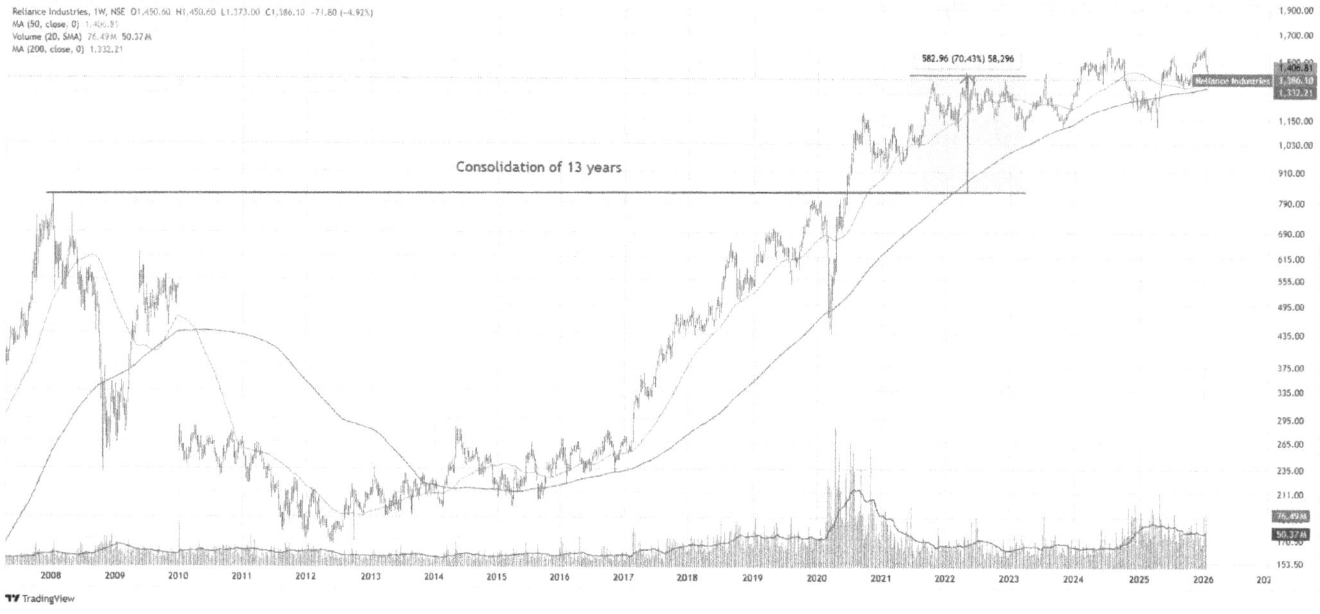

Reliance Industries

Leader of India's conglomerate, majority of revenues comes from oil consolidated for 13 years then breakout in June 2020 gaining 70% from 800 to 1400 within 1 year while results became better over the years

screener FEED SCREENS TOOLS

Reliance Industr | Chart | Analysis | Peers | Quarters | Profit & Loss | Balance Sheet | Cash Flow | Ratios | Investors | Documents

Profit & Loss

RELATED PARTY | PRODUCT SEGMENTS

Consolidated Figures in Rs. Crores / View Standalone

	Mar 2014	Mar 2015	Mar 2016	Mar 2017	Mar 2018	Mar 2019	Mar 2020	Mar 2021	Mar 2022	Mar 2023	Mar 2024	Mar 2025	TTM
Sales +	433,521	374,372	272,583	303,954	390,823	568,337	596,679	466,307	694,673	876,396	899,041	962,820	1,024,548
Expenses +	398,586	336,923	230,802	257,647	326,508	484,087	507,413	385,517	586,092	734,078	736,543	797,222	845,908
Operating Profit	**34,935**	**37,449**	**41,781**	**46,307**	**64,315**	**84,250**	**89,266**	**80,790**	**108,581**	**142,318**	**162,498**	**165,598**	**178,640**
OPM %	8%	10%	15%	15%	16%	15%	15%	17%	16%	16%	18%	17%	17%
Other Income +	8,865	8,528	12,212	9,222	9,869	8,406	8,570	22,432	19,600	12,020	15,792	17,824	29,420
Interest	3,836	3,316	3,691	3,849	8,052	16,495	22,027	21,189	14,584	19,571	23,118	24,269	26,631
Depreciation	11,201	11,547	11,565	11,646	16,706	20,934	22,203	26,572	29,782	40,303	50,832	53,136	56,359
Profit before tax	**28,763**	**31,114**	**38,737**	**40,034**	**49,426**	**55,227**	**53,606**	**55,461**	**83,815**	**94,464**	**104,340**	**106,017**	**125,070**
Tax %	22%	24%	23%	25%	27%	28%	26%	3%	19%	22%	25%	24%	
Net Profit +	**22,548**	**23,640**	**29,861**	**29,833**	**36,080**	**39,837**	**39,880**	**53,739**	**67,845**	**74,088**	**79,020**	**81,309**	**97,776**
EPS in Rs	16.31	17.07	21.51	21.55	26.69	29.28	29.10	38.75	44.87	49.29	51.45	51.47	61.49
Dividend Payout %	12%	12%	10%	11%	10%	10%	10%	9%	9%	9%	10%	11%	

Compounded Sales Growth		Compounded Profit Growth		Stock Price CAGR		Return on Equity	
10 Years:	10%	10 Years:	12%	10 Years:	19%	10 Years:	9%
5 Years:	10%	5 Years:	10%	5 Years:	10%	5 Years:	8%
3 Years:	11%	3 Years:	5%	3 Years:	9%	3 Years:	9%
TTM:	9%	TTM:	11%	1 Year:	11%	Last Year:	8%

Reliance Industries revenue and profit CAGR of 10+ % from last 10 years

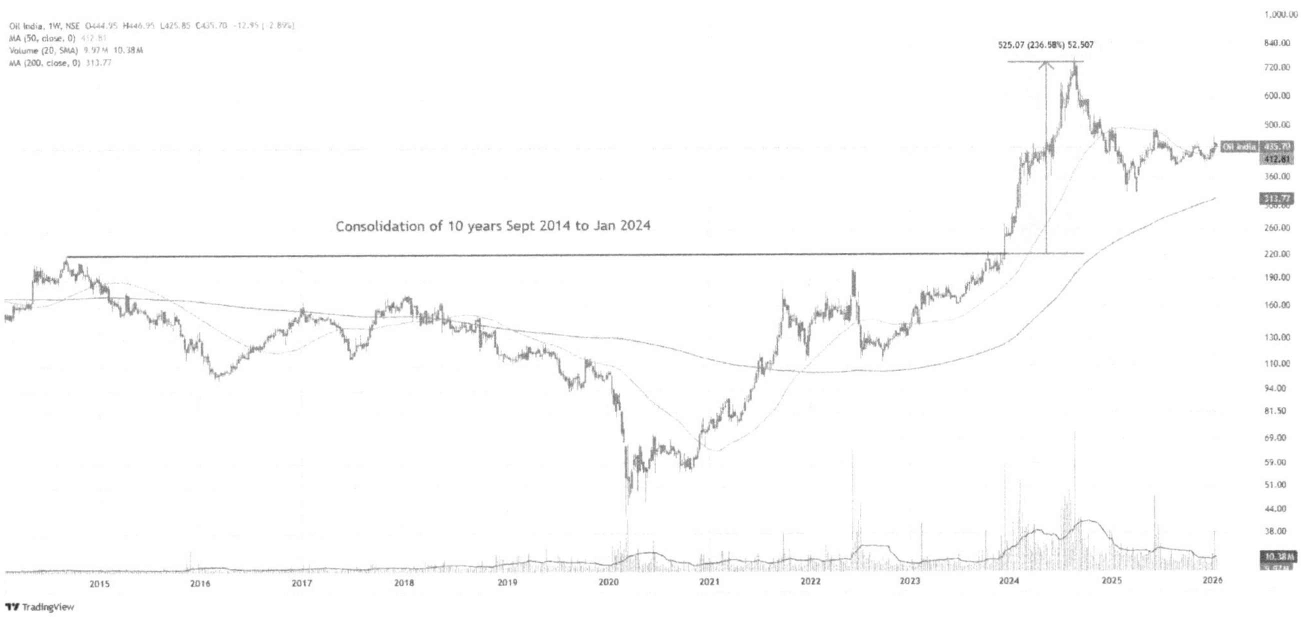

Oil India

Consolidation of 10 years then breakout gave returns of more than 235% after the breakout

Profit & Loss

Consolidated Figures in Rs. Crores / View Standalone

	Mar 2014	Mar 2015	Mar 2016	Mar 2017	Mar 2018	Mar 2019	Mar 2020	Mar 2021	Mar 2022	Mar 2023	Mar 2024	Mar 2025	TTM
Sales +	9,690	9,978	9,821	9,566	10,698	13,780	18,612	17,616	25,906	36,084	31,749	31,703	33,468
Expenses +	6,044	6,346	6,235	6,446	6,770	8,190	13,297	11,928	15,405	20,829	19,245	20,546	23,684
Operating Profit	**3,646**	**3,633**	**3,586**	**3,120**	**3,928**	**5,591**	**5,315**	**5,689**	**10,500**	**15,255**	**12,504**	**11,158**	**9,785**
OPM %	38%	36%	37%	33%	37%	41%	29%	32%	41%	42%	39%	35%	29%
Other Income +	1,589	1,258	1,198	793	1,812	1,251	2,147	1,185	1,254	737	-566	1,666	2,385
Interest	71	349	389	441	554	624	647	660	940	901	964	1,069	1,052
Depreciation	822	865	1,070	1,180	1,327	1,541	1,786	1,844	1,824	1,947	2,129	2,318	2,456
Profit before tax	**4,342**	**3,677**	**3,324**	**2,292**	**3,859**	**4,677**	**5,030**	**4,369**	**8,990**	**13,144**	**8,846**	**9,436**	**8,662**
Tax %	33%	32%	37%	30%	29%	31%	0%	5%	25%	25%	21%	25%	
Net Profit +	**2,990**	**2,608**	**2,080**	**1,597**	**2,735**	**3,238**	**5,005**	**4,146**	**6,719**	**9,854**	**6,980**	**7,040**	**6,644**
EPS in Rs	16.58	14.46	11.53	8.85	16.06	19.91	28.90	21.69	34.56	53.66	38.95	40.27	36.72
Dividend Payout %	43%	46%	46%	72%	42%	34%	24%	15%	27%	25%	25%	29%	

Compounded Sales Growth	
10 Years:	12%
5 Years:	11%
3 Years:	7%
TTM:	-2%

Compounded Profit Growth	
10 Years:	10%
5 Years:	6%
3 Years:	6%
TTM:	-29%

Stock Price CAGR	
10 Years:	14%
5 Years:	42%
3 Years:	40%
1 Year:	3%

Return on Equity	
10 Years:	16%
5 Years:	18%
3 Years:	18%
Last Year:	13%

Oil India Sales CAGR 12% in last 10 years and profit CAGR 10% from last 10 years

The above charts follow the CANSLIM investment strategy being the leader of the industries. Long consolidation periods break out with great institutional ownership.

Screeners are available for CANSLIM filters on multiple websites just like the link below.

Screener CANSLIM

6) Emotional Machine

Think of the market as a machine where stocks are traded regularly. The machine produces returns based on earnings growth of constituents (stocks) and input is stakeholders' money.

Ironically, this machine has emotions which change with every tick on the screen. It is moody, often quoting higher prices some day and lower the other day. In the long run it acts like a machine only producing returns equivalent to Growth + Inflation + Speculation which is usually around 12-15% CAGR.

This analogy helps in understanding the nature of the market and keeps our money in the market for a long time because returns are proportional to time spent in the market, seeing the market as an emotional machine also gives more insights over trends, levels and seeking low risk high return investments.

Emotions drive market movements

At its core, financial markets reflect human behavior. Every price movement, whether a sharp rise or a sudden fall, is influenced by the emotions of its participants.

Greed, fear, hope, and despair form supply and demand zones.

Each price level is an equilibrium of supply (seller) and demand (buyers).

Support levels:

These are levels where demand overpowers supply, reflecting optimism and a collective belief in the asset value. Buyers fear missing out (FOMO) while sellers fear a potential rally.

Resistance Levels:

These represent zones where supply overtakes demand. Sellers dominate, driven by greed to book profits, while buyers hesitate, fearing losses.

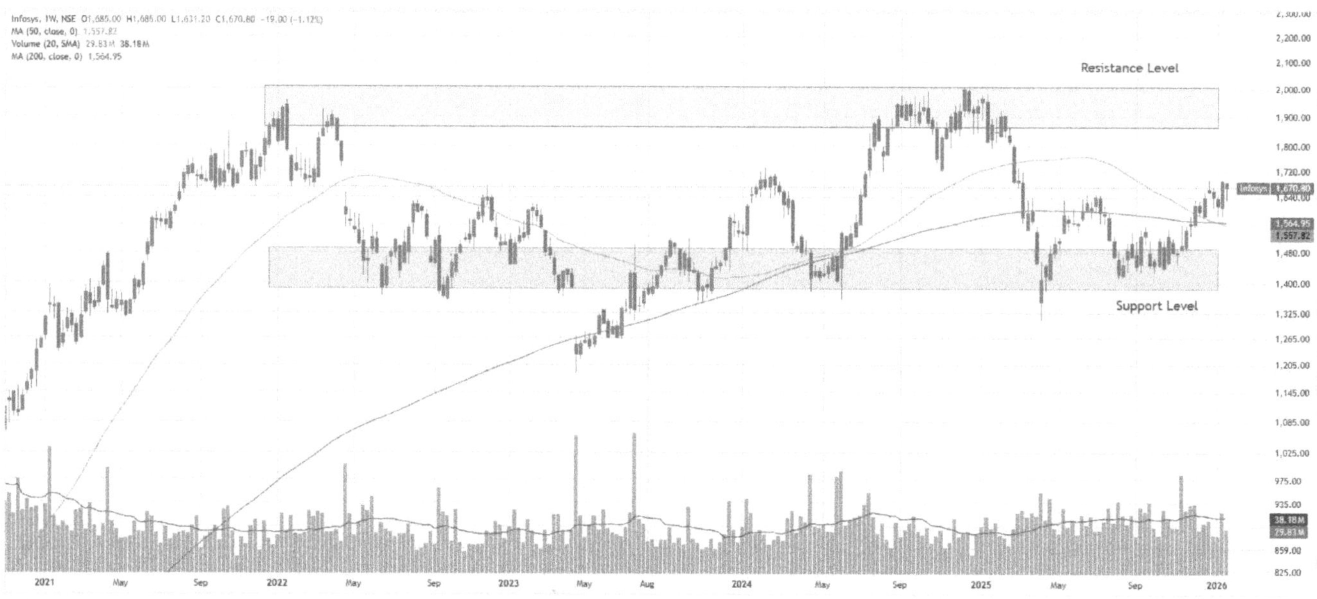

Support and Resistance Levels

*"**Be fearful when others are greedy and greedy when others are fearful.**"*

– Warren Buffett

Market often operates in cycles heavily influenced by crowd psychology; these cycles can be seen in 4 phases of market: -

i. **Accumulation Phase**

The accumulation phase occurs after a significant downtrend or a period of low volatility. In this phase, smart money (institutional investors) begins quietly building positions as the broader sentiment is still bearish or neutral. There is fear in the market and no clear reason why security is falling so much.

Accumulation Phase chart

200 MA close to price after a big downtrend and now 200 MA is becoming flat signalling institutes are

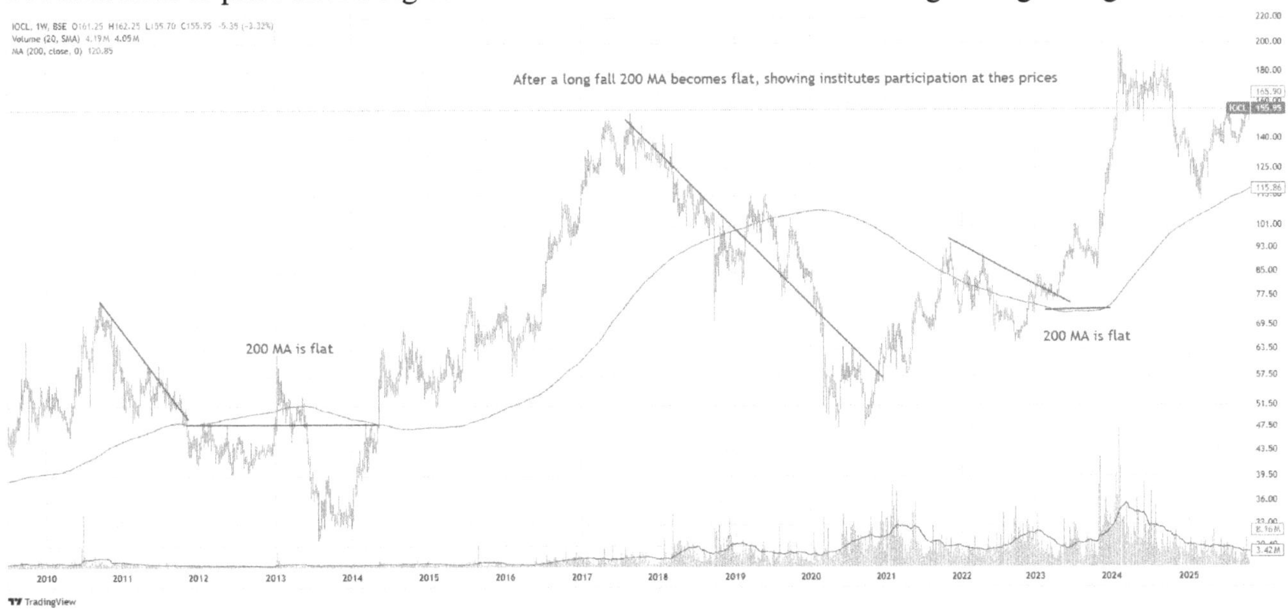

making positions at these low prices and upside can start after prices start taking support from moving averages

ii. Mark-Up Phase

The markup phase begins when the accumulation phase gives way to a clear uptrend. Often fueled by positive news and growing optimism.

- Higher highs and higher lows in price action
- Volume increases steadily as more participants enter the market
- Breakouts occur above resistance levels

Markup phase chart

Strong uptrend from 200 MA after consolidations, with 50 MA acting as a dynamic support for the price of stock. The price keeps bouncing off from this to create new highs until breakdowns

iii. Distribution Phase

In this phase, the trend begins to lose momentum as smart money starts to offload positions to late entrants (retail traders). Prices consolidate, and the The market shows indecision.

- Prices move sideways or form a topping pattern (head and shoulders top)
- Volume is high, reflecting active buying and selling
- Sentiment is overly optimistic

Distribution phase

After a good run up of stock, stock forming rounding top showing institutes are selling on these price levels and price starts reaching down to 200 MA, making the 200 MA flat signaling distribution phase after which downside can begin.

iv. Mark-Down Phase

In this phase, the market starts downtrend after the distribution phase. Selling pressure overwhelms buying interest, leading to sharp price declines.

- Lower highs and lower lows in price action
- Volume spikes during sell-off
- Breakdown occurs below key support levels

Markdown Phase chart

50 MA and 200 MA are falling along with the stock price. Each bounce towards MA of stock acts as resistance, and stock starts making lower lows.

Stocks and markets usually go through these phases. Understanding the phase the stock is currently at helps in understanding the momentum and price action for deciding when to buy or sell stocks since markets move in cycles.

This technical analysis shows the cycle we are at and the upcoming cycle according to prices along with indicators.

Understanding that the market is an 'emotional machine' in the short term—but in the long run must produce returns based on earnings growth—helps investors stay grounded. This perspective allows one to remain invested or even book great opportunities during adverse times, regardless of market sentiment.

Chapter 4

Making Money in the Market

The biggest thing in the market is making money. Everyone is here to make money. Most people can make money with patience and the right mindset.

We should not be too attached to the stock we own if we buy, and if it goes down we should not be associating our intelligence with price momentums.

Our psychology is mostly that if we buy some stocks and it goes up we are on top of the world as the most intelligent being on the planet and when it goes down we might think ourselves as stupid in the end it's about luck, the art of picking stock and patience. Most of the time we see stocks move up with absurd valuations; someone can make money more than everyone else with pure luck and no system but for how long? We should take a systematic and long-term approach to our portfolios.

In the end Jo Jeeta Wo Sikandar (the one who makes the most money wins & all other things are just theories).

Therefore, we will learn some practical techniques to make money which might work for you as well with blessings.

i. The law of average

The law of average is more universal law. Our body is accumulation and average of things we eat, our mind is average of all data we feed into it, all our emotions and experiences average, just like this financial markets are sum of all averaging of the money put into it, in form of debt or future/options or cash, also it is averaging of its participants, growth of economy, earnings of companies listed, etc.

This averaging helps us to find abnormality in the market whenever it is overheated or underwhelming it will revert to mean position from the extremes. So, every security (stock/index/fund) should return to its average over time following the universal law of average.

- Moving average of stocks helps in deciding buy or sell opportunities in charts. We can add this as an indicator on screener.in.

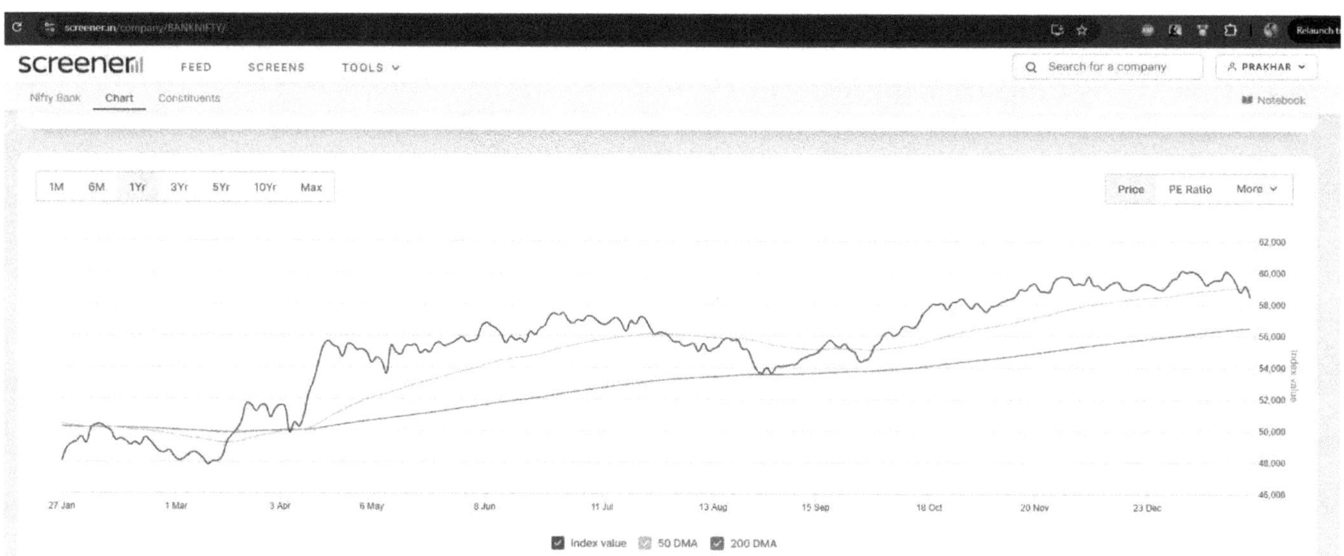

In tick 50 DMA, 200 DMA to see moving average lines yellow for 50 DMA, gray for 200 DMA.

On tradingview.com or Groww trading view chart you can put it on a stock index, etc. For 20MA, 50MA for short term generally, and 200MA, 300MA for long term.

- Whenever price touches 50MA or 200MA with the MA acting as support for the price it is a strong bullish pattern and we should be buying on every support of MA while the price taking resistance from MA is a bearish pattern, should be avoided for investment unless it has consolidated from a long time or showing superb earnings growth.
- On 4th Jan 2025, nifty touched 200 DMA at 23700 and acted as support for nifty so long-term investors can gain additional gains by buying at this point since it is down from all-time high for about 2000-2500 points, should get 10% fall benefit.
- The important thing to note is that this averaging is not ordinary; it is upward averaging. If you index for 5 years, 10 years, 20 years, you will see average lines moving up and always making new highs since

as a country and economy we are growing in a higher-high fashion. This implies just like our daily emotions don't matter in the long run and average out well in a higher high manner achieving great things in life markets, stocks, and economy has only a way up in the long run.

- Every index, stock if earnings are improving sentiment are good in long run should always break previous highs to create new highs, we can make money by this technique when emotions or economy or earnings are not doing well in short term but in long term things should average out in higher high manner, we should be buying on every bad moment and fear emotion of short term and generate wealth for long term.

ii. Price follows the earning

As Peter Lynch famously said stocks are not lottery tickets they are following earnings. Why does stock fall on poor earnings? Why do cyclical earnings affect stock prices? Why do growth stocks have a higher P/E ratio? The answer is the price follows earnings. If a stock doubles its income every year and currently it is trading for 100₹, 10 P/E, in 3-4 years . If earnings are doubled for this term in 4 years the P/E will be 0.625 (10/24). If the stock price doesn't change and stays at 100 ₹, what about the dividend? If it had a yield of 0.5% after four years with same dividend payout will be 0.5×2^4 =8% dividend and 0.625 P/E means if you buy this company whole business you will get all the money back in terms of profit within 0.625×12 months = 7.5 months and with dividend yield of 5% extra coming into your pocket. Sounds too good? Yeah, that's why we don't see these stocks in the market because everyone is looking for good deals and buying good businesses, that's how growth stocks work and have high or even exuberant P/E ratios of 100-400 sometimes because more growth means more attractive or higher demand. Therefore, prices follow earnings in the long run.

Companies that went from small-caps to mid-caps to large-caps were not due to high valuations or high demand that would be a bubble but only due because for years or even decades they consistently found ways to make more money by each passing year expanding capacity, buying businesses, investing, diversifying or creating more value.

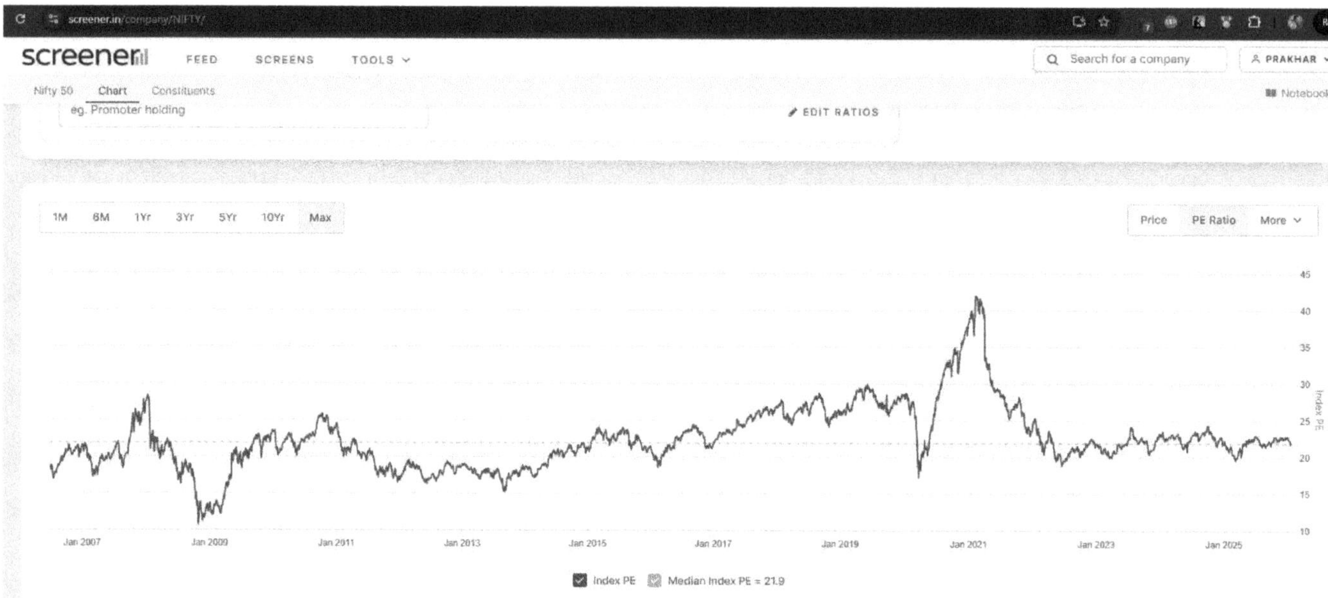

Nifty 50 P/E chart

Whenever the Nifty is above 24 P/E at the start of the year, returns of that year are likely to be less than 10% if earnings growth remains the same because P/E will expand beyond 25 which rarely happens. But if P/E is below 24 like 18 or 21 then on 21 P/E returns will be more than 10% because earnings are mostly bottomed out and likely to grow which led to P/E contraction. Additionally, valuation will bounce back to mean P/E of around 23-24. Both factors combined are more likely to generate good returns.

iii. Psychology in the market

Psychology plays a huge role in setting market mood. People keep getting too optimistic or too fearful based on market news. When markets are rising, investors often feel excited and optimistic, leading them to buy assets at inflated prices.

FOMO causes irrational investing, where people jump into stocks or cryptocurrencies simply because they see others making money. When the market crashes, fear takes over and investors sell their holdings at a loss to cut their losses.

Investors fear making mistakes, so they avoid taking necessary risks or holding onto bad investments too long. Mostly market returns work based on long term averages. If the market has fallen by 10-20% from the top and 3yrs CAGR from long term is 16% (on SIP), then in this fall 10-20% gain as a bonus take will recover and generate the same CAGR of 16% for next year as per long term average returns.

This is a rational approach for investing, but markets are often irrational in practice leading to bull and bear markets. To make money out of it should be bought when there is increased fear and sell on greed.

etmoney.com/mutual-funds/uti-nifty-50-index-fund-direct-growth/15397

ET Money

Trailing returns as on Jan 27, 2026

Period	This fund	Category average
1 Month	-3.4%	-3.05%
3 Months	-3.46%	-3.08%
6 Months	1.8%	2.2%
1 Year	10.85%	10.69%
2 Years	8.41%	8.17%
3 Years	13.54%	13.95%
4 Years	11.07%	11.19%
5 Years	13.48%	13.58%
7 Years	14.04%	13.61%
10 Years	14%	13.61%

View returns in detail

UTI NIFTY 50 Index Fund Returns

Nifty 50 average returns over 10 years are 12% CAGR in above image. They are around 14% whenever this 10-year returns go below 12% is a good time to buy. An easy way for it is to take note of 3yrs, 5yrs & 10yrs CAGR . When current returns are lower than long term average or fair valuation based on it is usually a good time to invest in equities.

iv. Growth and inflation quadrant

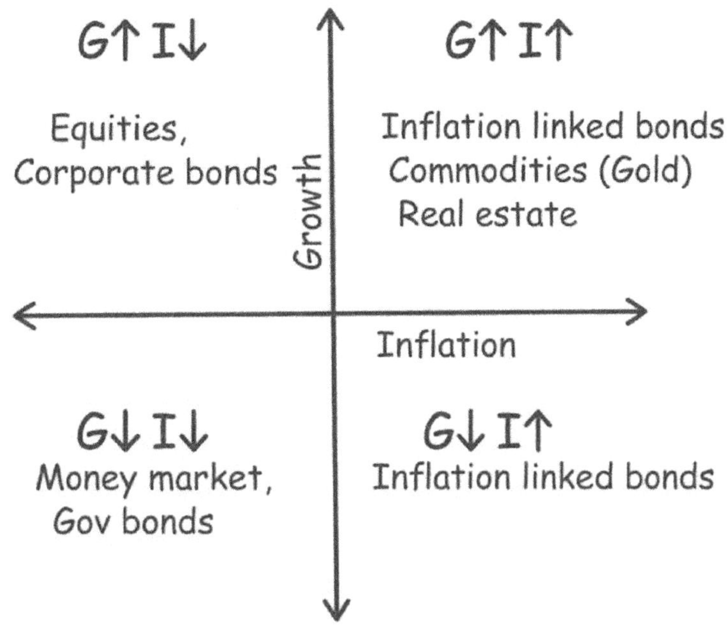

Growth and Inflation Quadrant

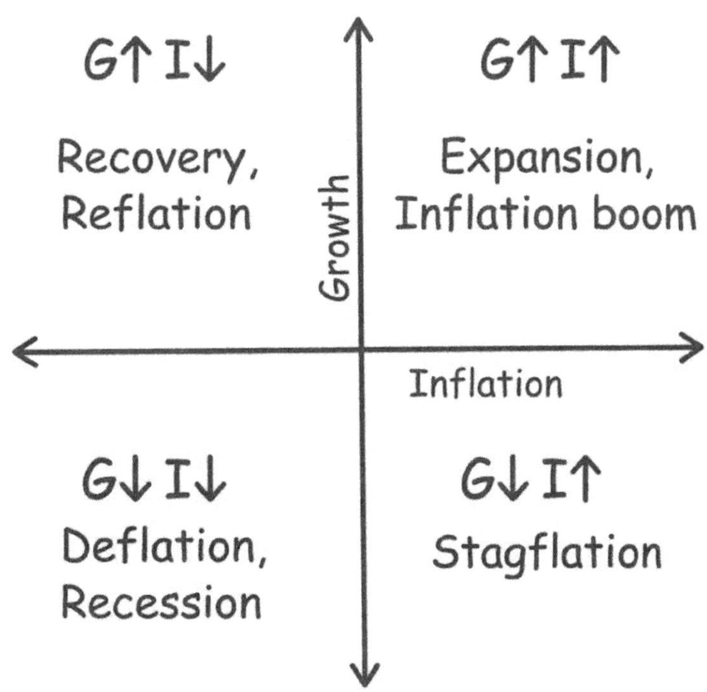

Four Economic Phases

Four Economic Phases: What to Buy?

This strategy helps you choose the right assets based on two key factors: **Growth (G)** and **Inflation (I)**.

1. Recovery & Reflation (G ↑ I ↓)

- **Scenario:** The economy is starting to grow, but inflation is falling.
- **What to Buy: Equities (Stocks)** and **Corporate Bonds**.

2. Expansion & Inflation Boom (G ↑ I ↑)

- **Scenario:** The economy is growing rapidly, and prices are rising.
- **What to Buy: Real Estate**, **Commodities (Gold)**, and **Inflation-linked Bonds**.

3. Deflation & Recession (G ↓ I ↓)

- **Scenario:** Economic growth is slowing and prices are falling.
- **What to Buy: Government Bonds** and **Money Market Funds**.

4. Stagflation (G ↓ I ↑)

- **Scenario:** Growth is slowing, but inflation remains high (a difficult phase).
- **What to Buy: Inflation-linked Bonds** (to protect purchasing power).

How to Apply This Strategy?

To effectively use this model, you must determine the current economic position:

- **Global View:** Identify which quadrant the **World Economy** currently fits into based on global reports.
- **India View:** Analyze domestic data to find India's quadrant:
    - Check **GDP Data** to see if Growth (G) is rising or falling.
    - Check **CPI Data** to see if Inflation (I) is rising or falling.

v. Negative correlations

Correlation in assets refers to the price movements of two or more assets. It measures how assets move relative to each other and is expressed as a correlation coefficient ranging from -1 to +1.

We can make a lot of money by investing in assets that are negatively correlated, meaning when the price of one increases the price of another asset decreases.

Commodities show a lot of volatility. The commodity producers and users show negative correlation or in simple words trade in opposite directions.

Crude oil, aviation, tyres and paints (When crude prices rise, input costs for airlines and paint companies increase, hurting their margins/stock prices.)

Interest rates, real estate and auto (When rates go up, loans become expensive, reducing demand for homes and cars.)

Rupee strength, IT and Pharma (When the Rupee gets stronger, export-heavy sectors like IT and Pharma earn less in local currency.)

Dollar index, gold and emerging markets (When the US Dollar strengthens, gold and emerging market equities (like India) typically fall due to capital outflows.)

Natural gas, fertilizer and ceramics (Gas is a major raw material; when prices spike, margins for fertilizer and ceramic tile makers drop.)

Metal prices, Metal Miners and Piping industry (When metal prices rise, miners benefit from higher selling prices and profits, while piping and manufacturing companies suffer from increased raw material costs, squeezing their margins.)

Crude Oil, Upstream and Downstream companies (When oil prices rise, upstream companies [like ONGC] earn more per barrel, while downstream OMCs [like BPCL, HPCL] often suffer because they can't fully pass on the higher cost to consumers.)

Rubber prices and Tyre companies (Natural rubber is the main raw material for tyres; when rubber prices jump, the profit margins of tyre manufacturers shrink significantly.)

Coal prices and Cement industry (Coal is used heavily for power and heating kilns in cement production. When coal prices rise, the cost of producing every bag of cement goes up, hurting profitability.

Exercise: Finding Uncorrelated Assets for a Resilient Portfolio

Task: Calculate the percentage of your portfolio currently relying on "Economic Drivers." If it is above 90%, you are overexposed to systemic market crashes.

You do not need complex software to find uncorrelated assets. Use the same comparison tool mentioned in the "Pairs Trading" section of this book.

1. Open your charting platform (e.g., TradingView or Groww).
2. Plot the Nifty 50 index on the chart.
3. Click the "+" icon to add a secondary asset (e.g., GoldBees, Liquid Funds, or 10-Year Gilt ETFs).
4. Observe the 5-year and 10-year chart:
    - **High Correlation:** Does the asset mirror the Nifty? (If yes, it provides little protection).
    - **Negative/Low Correlation:** Does the asset remain flat or rise when Nifty falls? (This is your "Buffer" candidate).

vi. Supply and Demand Zones

Supply and demand zones are critical concepts in trading, particularly in technical analysis, as they help traders identify potential areas where price movements might reverse or stall.

Supply and demand zones are formed from market imbalances where the volume of buyers exceeds sell orders or vice-versa triggering sharp price movements. These are mainly formed by institutional activity as large players like hedge funds or banks execute bulk orders that leave discernible footprints on price charts.

Supply zone - a price area where selling pressure exceeds buying pressure, causing prices to drop. These zones often act as resistance levels and are identified by sharp declines following a price rally.

Demand zone - a price area where buying pressure exceeds selling pressure, causing prices to rise. These zones often act as support levels and are identified by sharp rallies following a price drop. Whenever buying a stock or entering a new sector check support and demand levels, try to add positions on demand levels and sell at supply levels or add positions only when stock or sector is in blue sky zone or at all-time highs with a stoploss.

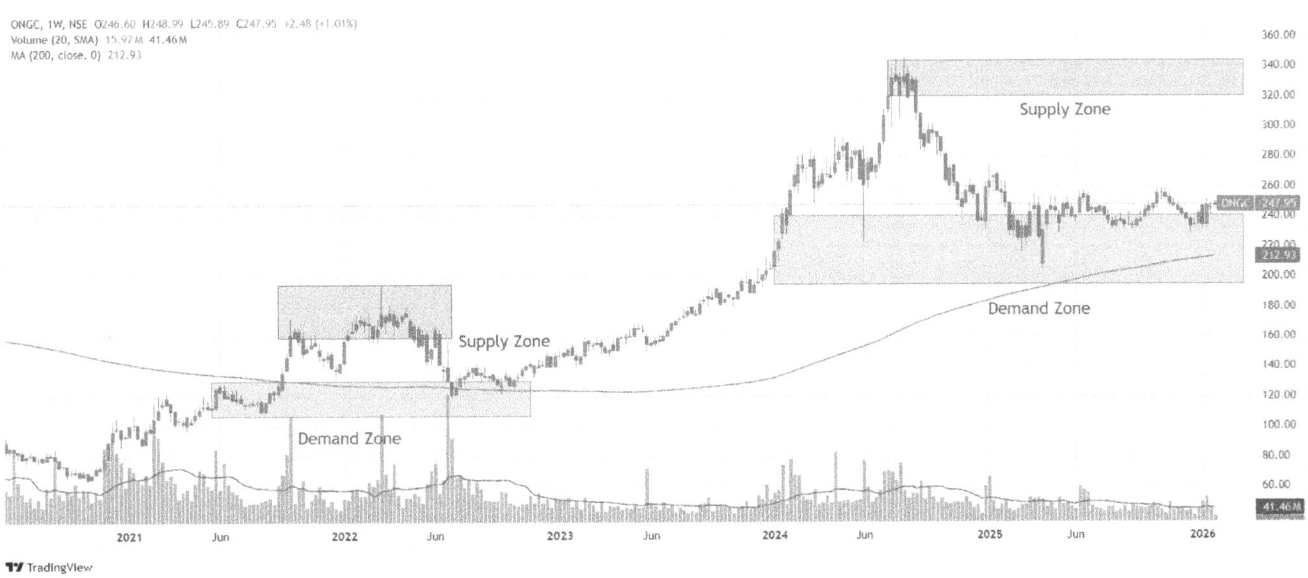

Supply and Demand Zone

Once a breakout occurs and prices go above supply zone by a large margin, the supply zone becomes new demand zone like in above image

vii. Always use index for sectoral buying S/R level

Each sector in the market is cyclic where large booms and busts happen from time to time. IT boom of 2000, pharma boom, metals boom after covid, PSUs boom and defence, many other sectors also boom and bust based on raw material prices like tyre industry, exports like sugar, textile, food grain, distillery companies and chemicals. We can compare these charts against Nifty 50. Whenever a sector is going above nifty, we can add positions and cut them when it reaches or touches nifty charts. On Tickertape, Moneycontrol and trading view we can compare these sectoral charts.

We can check sectoral funds and ETFs charts for 3, 5 or 10+ years where the chart shows prices for a sector are dormant for multiple years, but if we are hopeful of its revival, we can buy them until it reaches near Nifty returns.

For trading we can add positions whenever the sector is going above the Nifty. We can add positions and start cutting when there are signs of topping out.

PSU Banks vs Nifty 50

For a long time PSU banks underperformed Nifty but after 2020 PSU banks started outperforming as shown in below image.

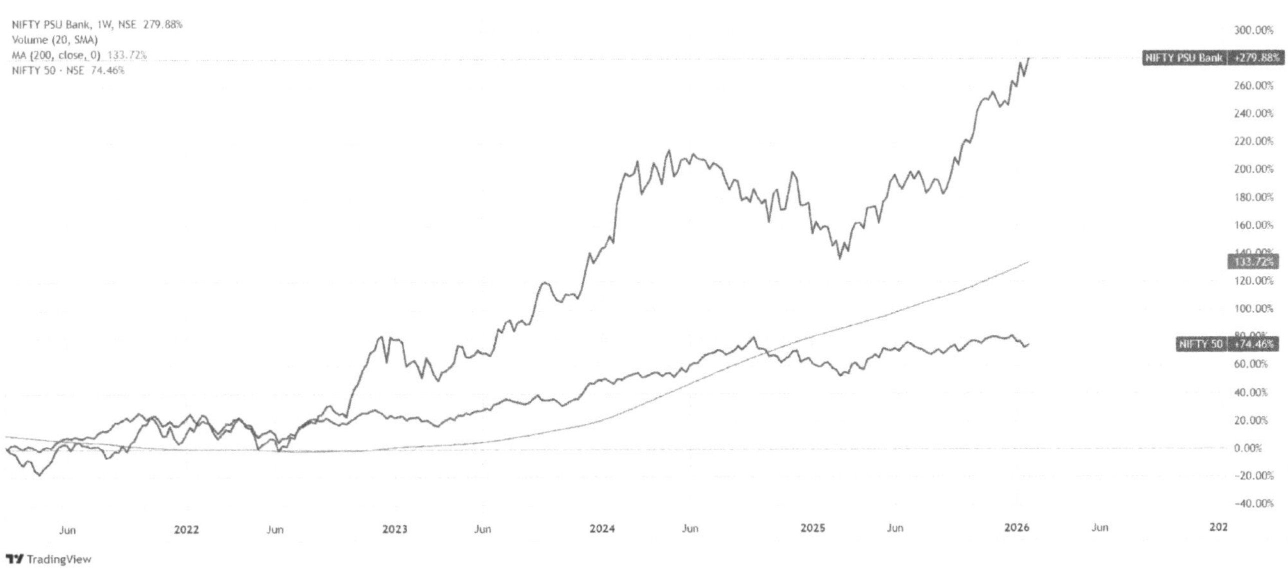

PSU Banks started outperforming Nifty by huge margin mostly due to asset quality improvements and change in Government policies

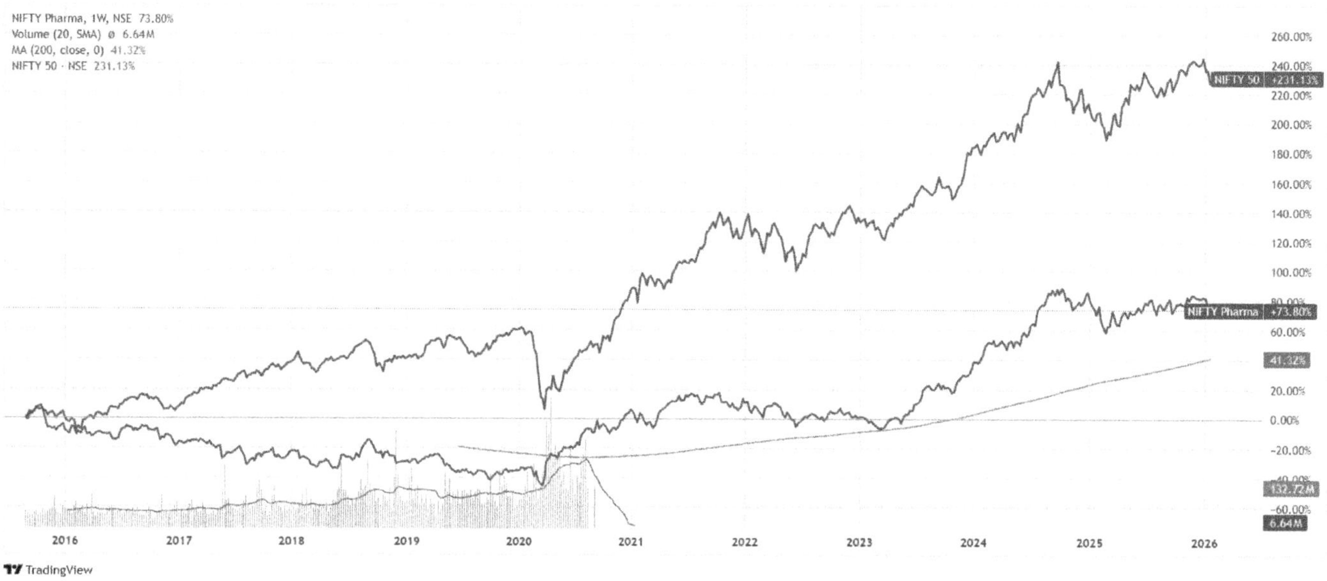

Pharma Index underperforming Nifty from a long time

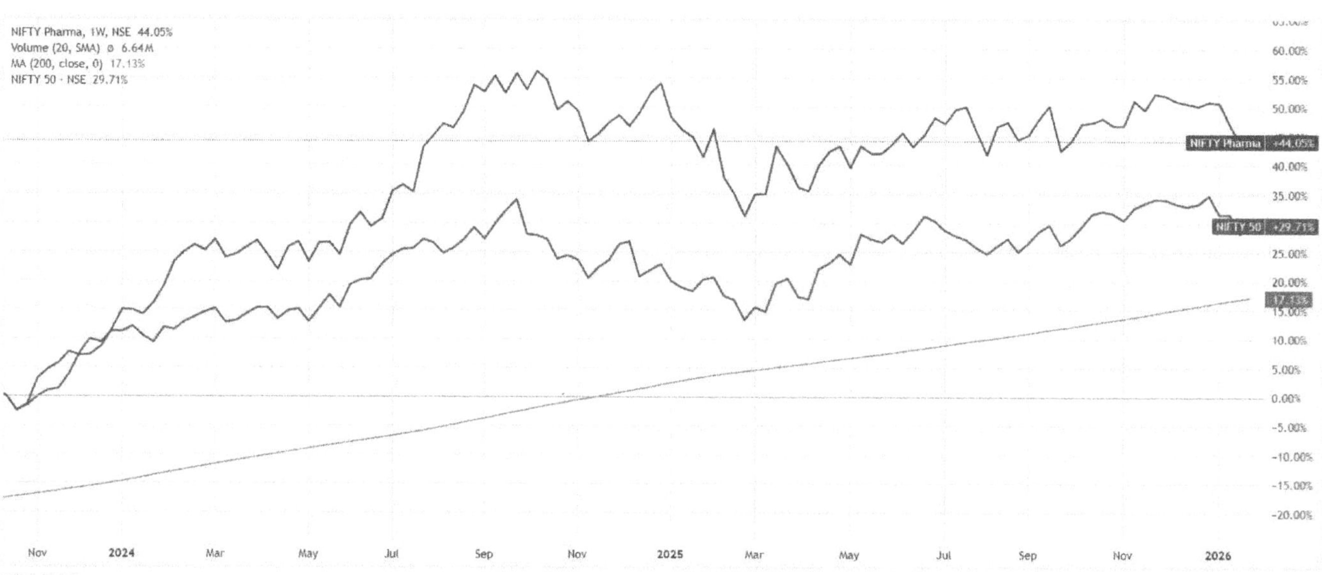

After 2023 Pharma Index Outperformed Nifty

Nifty Auto Index performed same as Nifty 50 from 10 years

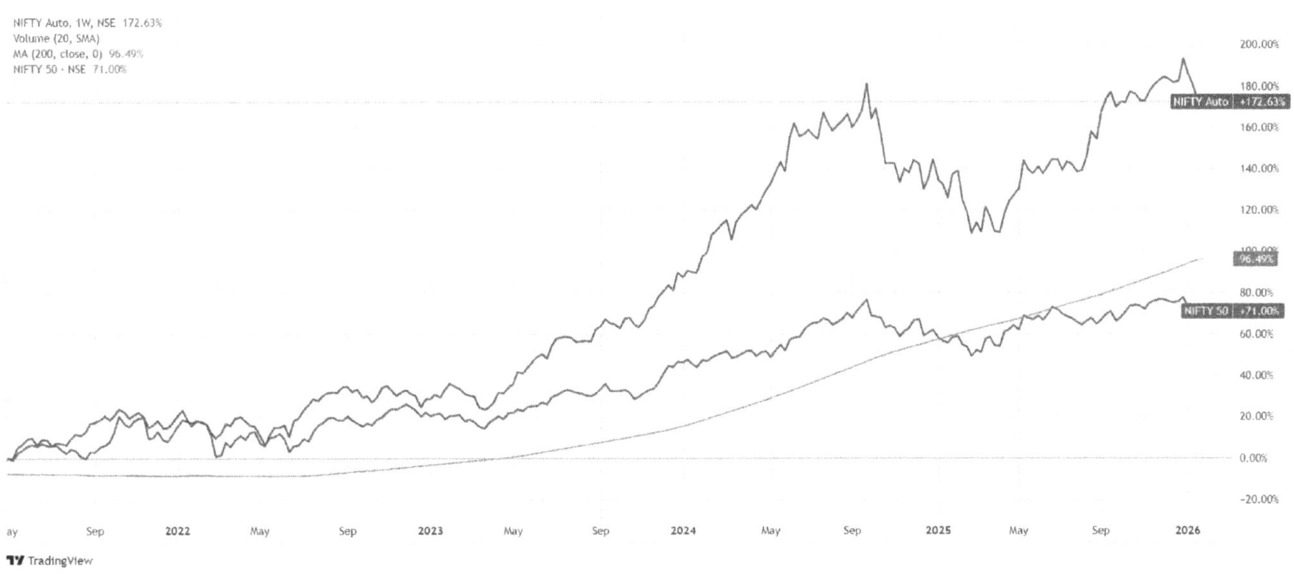

Nifty Auto outperforming Nifty 50 from 2021

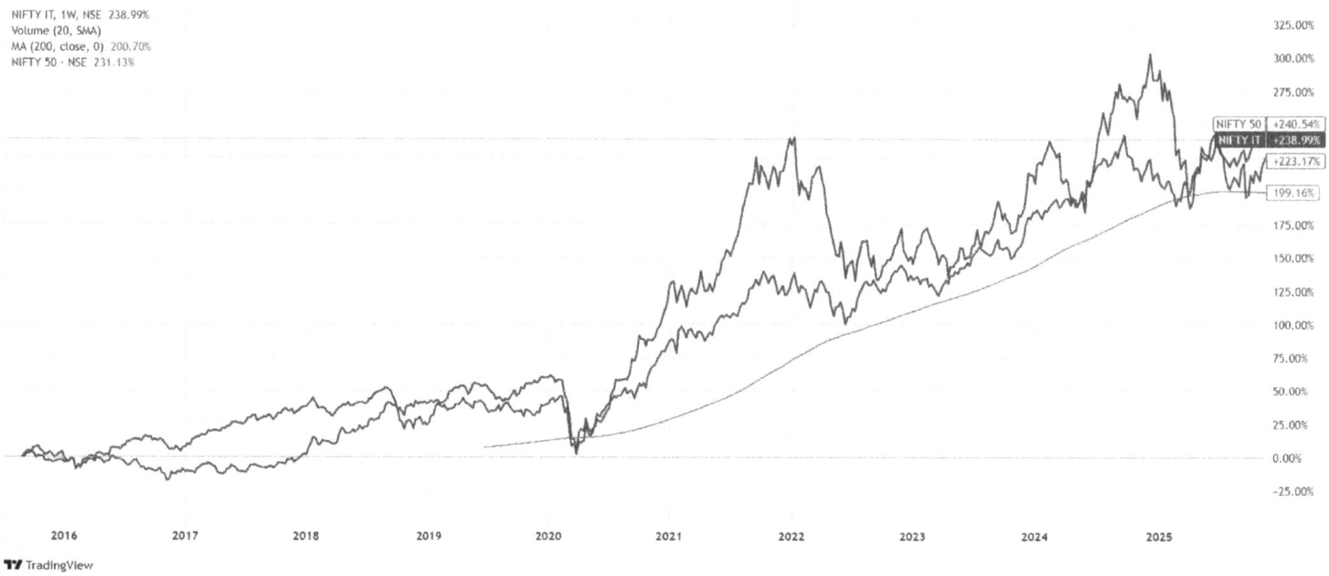

Nifty IT outperforming Nifty 50 in long run (especially after 2020)

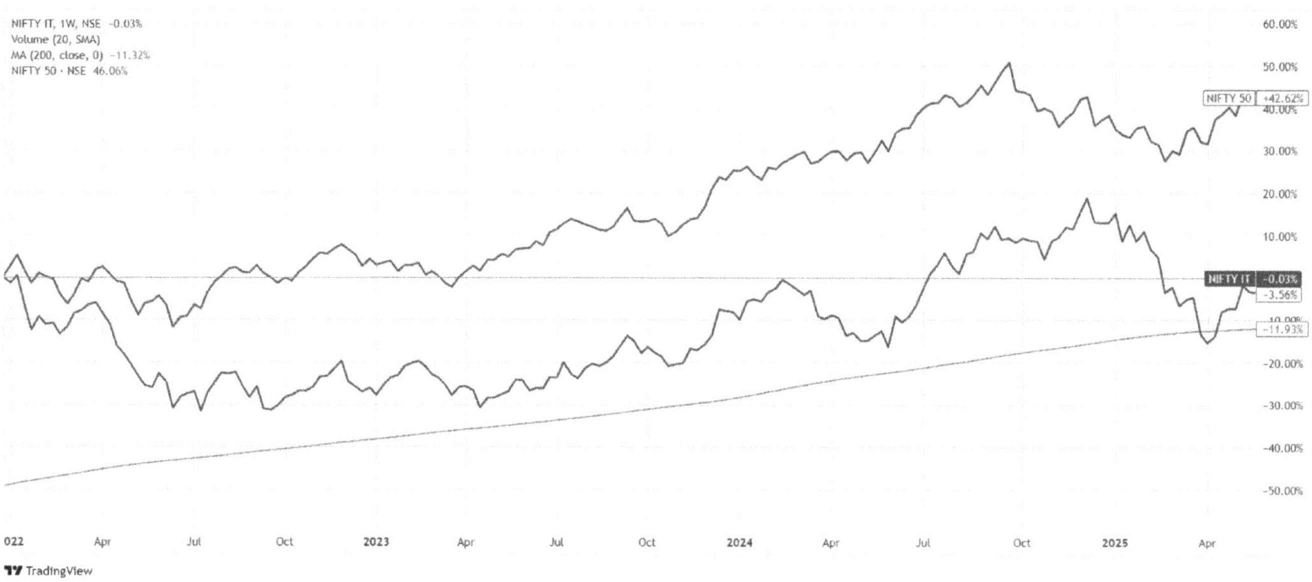

Nifty IT started underperforming Nifty 50 after 2022

viii. Look for deep discounts

Sometimes, the market behaves irrationally. It focuses so intensely on short-term fear or "boring" sectors that it leaves money on the table. This creates a specific opportunity known as **Deep Value Investing.** Sometimes stocks are available at low P/Es. The company might be holding cash greater than current value. You might be getting good companies with a finite future at high . Consistent dividend yield which might be higher than sovereign bond rates is a very good discount with capital appreciation happening till previous all-time highs.

- **Hindustan Zinc & IOC:** In cyclical downturns, companies like Hindustan Zinc have offered dividend yields of over 15%, while Indian Oil Corp (IOC) often trades at 8-10% yields. Investors effectively get paid to wait, buying a finite asset at a discount with a consistent cash return that beats fixed deposits.
- **MRPL in 2023:** Due to a spike in refining margins, MRPL traded at a P/E of roughly 1x–2x in its annual earnings. The market priced a record-breaking year as a "one-off" event, ignoring the structural value of the asset.
- **REC, PFC & PSU Banks, 2020:** During the peak of NPA (bad loan) fears, state-owned lenders traded at 0.2x to 0.4x for their book value. Investors were buying ₹100 loan assets for ₹20. As the cycle turned, these stocks became multi-baggers.
- **Mazagon Dock in 2020–2021:** Trading at a market capitalization of roughly ₹3,000 Cr while holding over ₹5,800 Cr in cash, the stock offered a rare "Negative Enterprise Value" scenario. The market dismissed this massive cash pile as merely "customer advances" rather than owned assets. Investors who recognized that this cash would convert to revenue effectively bought the business for free, plus a cash bonus, leading to a massive re-rating.

Check the quadrant from screener if the company has grown revenue consistently while price CAGR has been stagnant that stock can be at deep discount levels.

You can also create your own screen on screen.in to access these scripts when they are trading at discount levels.

IOCL 10 years profit growth is 12% while price CAGR is only 9% shows more room for price appreciation if profit continues to hold

Business with more cash is usually valued more

While the world obsesses over "Net Profit" (which can be manipulated with accounting tricks), smart investors look at **Operating Cash Flow (OCF)**—the actual cash entering the company's bank account from its core business.

A business with increasing OCF is a powerhouse. But how much should you pay? The market assigns different "multiples" based on the industry's stability.

1. Valuation Multiples (What is Market Paying?)

The industry values a company's OCF (Market Cap ÷ Operating Cash Flow) in three distinct buckets:

- **3x – 8x (The "Deep Value" / Cyclical Bucket):**
  - **Sectors:** Metals, Mining, Oil & Gas, and PSUs.
  - **Logic:** The market fears their profits are temporary (cyclical), so it assigns a low multiple. Buying here often yields massive returns if the cycle lasts longer than expected.
- **10x – 15x (The "Fair Value" / Manufacturing Bucket):**
  - **Sectors:** Auto, Pharma, and stable Manufacturing.
  - **Logic:** These companies have predictable cash flows, so the market pays a "fair" price.
- **30x+ (The "Expensive Safety" Bucket):**
  - **Sectors:** FMCG (like Nestle, Titan) and High-Growth Tech.
  - **Logic:** The market pays a huge premium for the certainty that cash flow will never drop.

2. Case Study: Nalco (The Leveraged Cash Play)

National Aluminium Company (NALCO) provides the perfect example for understanding the relationship between Stock Price and Cash Flow.

- **The Relation:** Nalco's stock price does not follow its "Net Profit" as closely as it follows its **Operating Cash Flow**.
  - **When OCF Rises:** As aluminum prices go up, Nalco's cash generation explodes. The stock price typically acts as a "leveraged" shadow of this cash flow, rising 3x–4x in response to a 2x rise in cash.
  - **When OCF Falls:** When the cycle turns and cash flow dips, the stock price crashes.
- **The Signal:** In 2020, Nalco's Market Cap fell so low that it was trading at barely **3x–4x** with its average operating cash flow. This was a clear "Deep Value" buy signal.

3. Case Study: Coal India & NMDC (The Cash Cows)

Just like Nalco, these mining giants trade at rock-bottom cash flow multiples because the market often assumes their business has "no future" due to environmental concerns.

- **Coal India:** Consistently trades at a Price-to-OCF multiple of **5x – 7x**.
  - **The Reality:** Despite being priced for decline, its operating cash flow keeps rising due to India's energy needs. This massive cash pile allows them to pay 5–7% dividend yields, effectively returning your capital while you hold the stock.
- **NMDC (Iron Ore):** Historically trades at **3x – 5x** Operating Cash Flow.
  - **The Opportunity:** When iron ore prices spike, NMDC generates so much cash in a single year that it can amount to 20–25% of its entire market cap. The market often ignores this until the cash hits the bank, causing a sudden re-rating.

Summary Checklist for Cash Flow Investing:

1. **Is Operating Cash Flow increasing?** (Business is healthy).
2. **Is the Stock Trading at < 8x OCF?** (Potential Cyclical/Deep Value bargain).
3. **Is the Stock Trading at > 30x OCF?** (Be careful; you are paying for perfection).

ix. Find a stable sector stock and find similar more volatile peer

Suppose two stocks are trading both with similar results and similar business. Stock A is more volatile, and stock B is less volatile. Over time, you keep investing at regular intervals like SIP. Stock A produces more returns than stock B because you will get more quantity when price is less, and this will generate more returns if both stocks perform or give some point-to-point return. To make this strategy work, find a sector with consistent growth outlook over multiple years like the capital market (AMCs, depositories, RTAs) or chemical, pharma, hospitals etc. For example ABSLAMC and Nippon AMC. From 2024 to 2025, both gave good generous returns. Multiple times ABSL and Nippon showed large gaps in prices, often around 50-100, even more sometimes . So whenever ABSL exceeds price levels, you buy a more stable Nippon by selling ABSL . And when ABSL falls below Nippon without bad results or news we can buy ABSL until it reaches price levels of Nippon and then sell ABSL to buy and hold the more stable leader Nippon (according to ROE and market share) for capital appreciation. This is also called a pairs trading strategy.

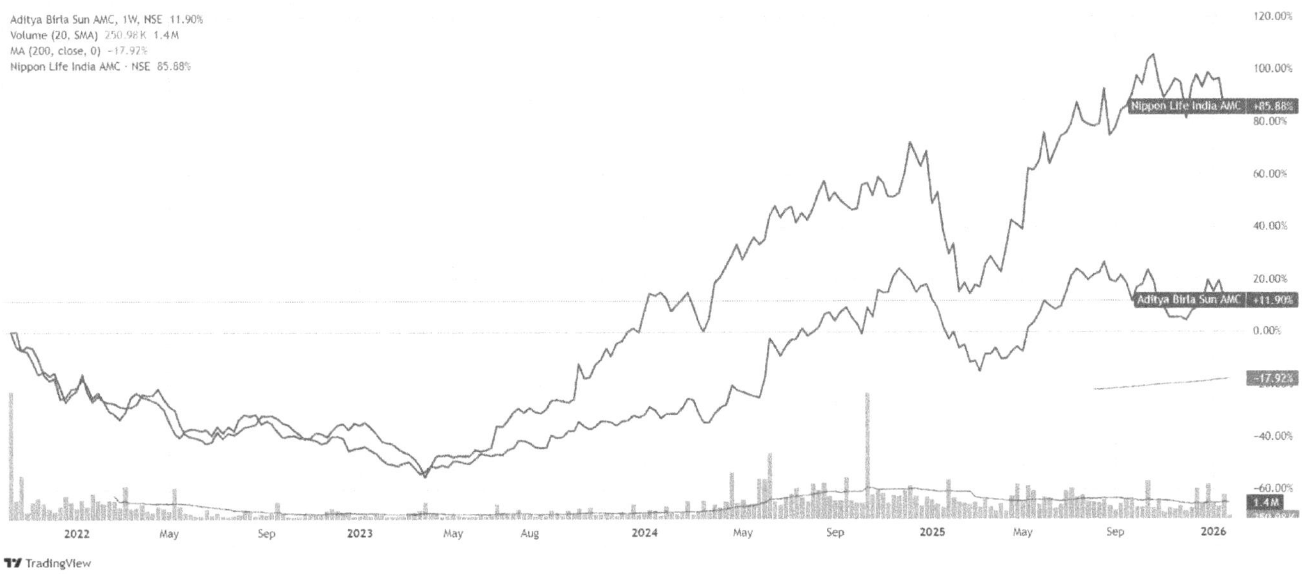

Overall Nippon AMC has outperformed ABSL AMC due to higher ROE % but sometimes the ABSL AMC also matches prices of Nippon for short time

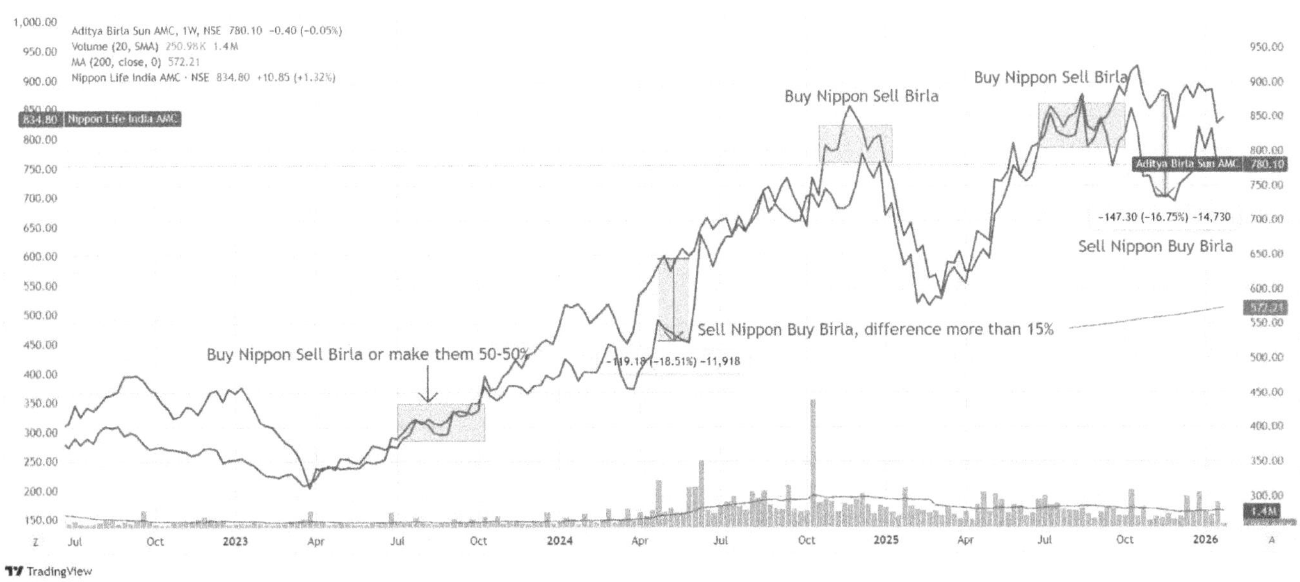

Buy/Sell opportunities in ABSL AMC and Nippon AMC

Whenever the price of Birla comes above or matches Nippon, we can make each 50% in the holdings or change all Birla to Nippon and when the difference between their prices increase like more than 15% then again rebalance by selling Nippon and buy Birla or converting all holdings of Nippon to Birla. This pairs trading works in companies within the same sector and similar ROEs.

Other examples for pairs trading are IOC and BPCL, Oil India and ONGC, Nalco and Hindalco, Kotak and HDFC bank, IGL and MGL and many others. Check their charts using comparisons on groww or tradingview.

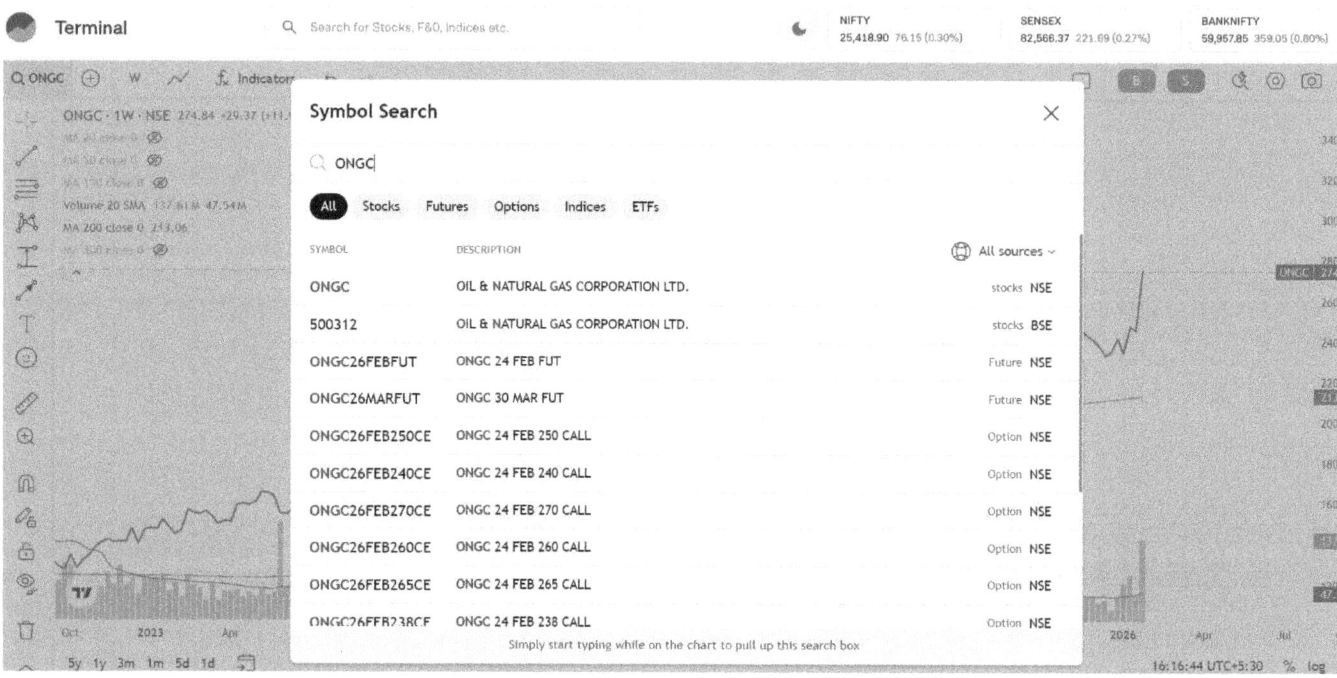

Search for stock like ONGC then click on it

Then click on plus icon on top left beside ONGC

Search and click on the stock you want to compare with; the chart will be plotted.

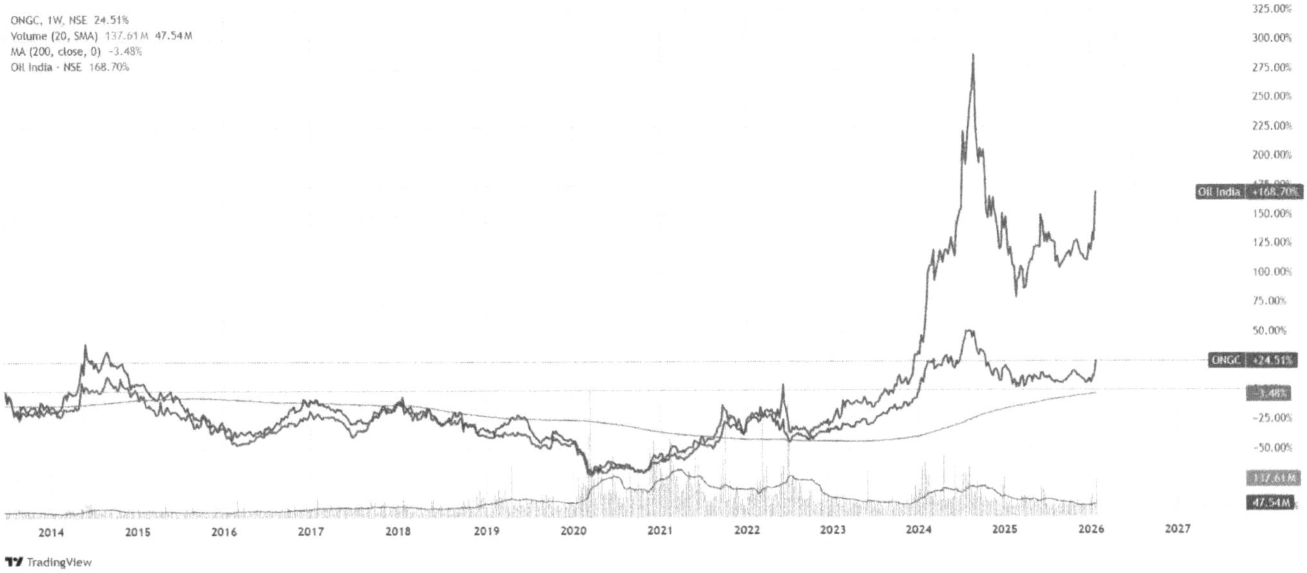

x. Market works on price probability and risk reward ratio

When the GDP of a country is increasing, inflation is within check. Long-term charts of assets like gold, silver and index in local currency (like Nifty chart in ₹) will be increasing at a specific CAGR. Especially when real GDP is strong from long term history which has been true for India for decades.

So, if we use indicators like 50 EMA and our Nifty, gold or silver which keep on increasing is touching or near 50 EMA then the most probable outcome is in the long run it will again increase creating new highs. In this case we can do a SIP for it which looks good as per chart and use cash to buy whenever it falls. When the rate is low, you get less risk and more rewards.

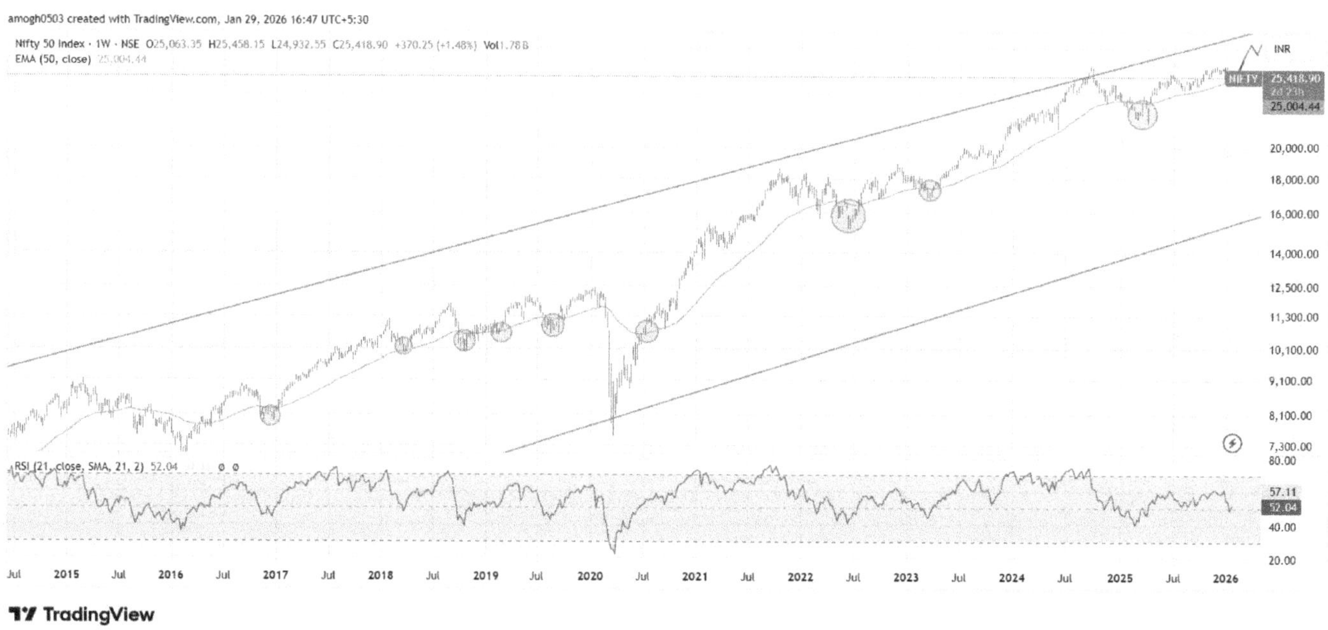

Nifty 50 with 50 EMA and RSI 21 days weekly candle chart

Nifty 50 below 50 EMA in long-term is a good buy level only except 2020 which was better to buy at bottom (RSI < 20), the risk of Nifty prices falling below 50 EMA is low unless there is a global markets crash, and the probability of prices going up from here is very high.

Therefore, the risk reward ratio is better below 50 EMA on Nifty and has worked well in the long run.

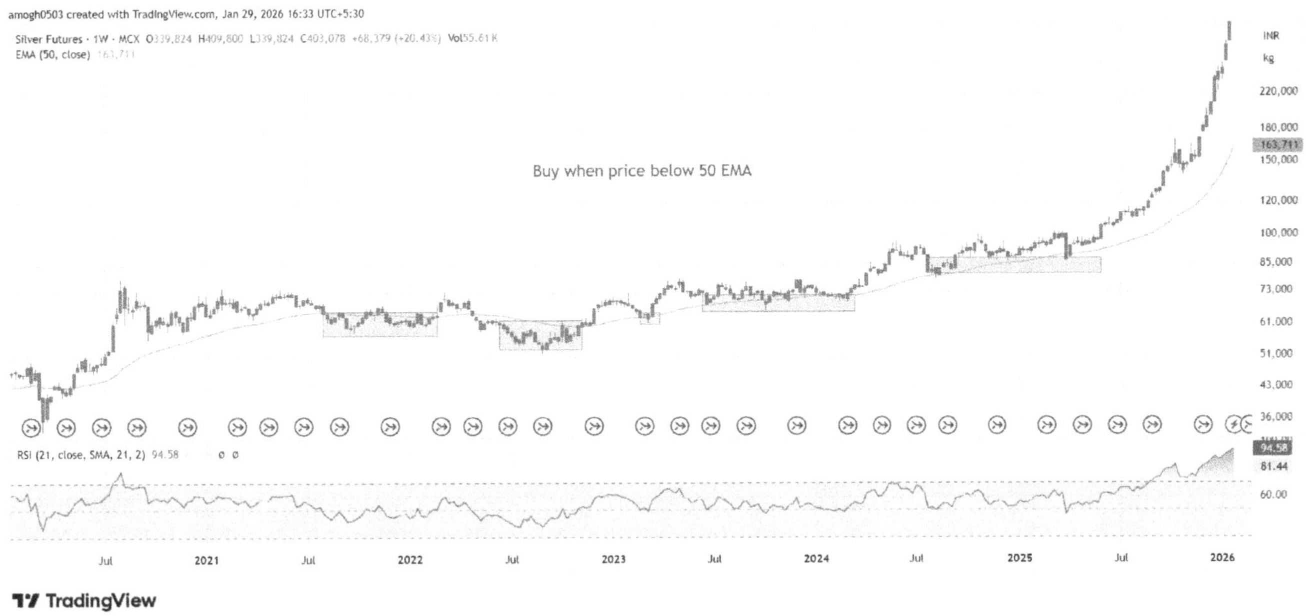

Silver after 2020, after 2025 silver went parabolic up, this trade becomes invalid in situations like this but from 2021 to 2025 it worked well

Most falls of silver have been sharp 5% or more in single days, which makes a great lumpsum opportunity whenever it has reached nearly 50 EMA. When it nears the EMA, keep buying more . On every 1-2% fall you put 10K (or more as per your risk reward preference) max you put is around 10 times which means silver is 10-20% below EMA after a sharp move, not slow falls, and is in an oversold zone. It has again made new highs. So, entry near EMA at every 2% fall you increase buying by 10-20% then selling near previous highs all or near half quantity has worked well, if you are bullish on it can be used with SIP too or also on NIFTY/gold other stable growing securities.

xi. VLRTCE framework

Valuation - Liquidity - Risk Appetite - Time - Compression - Expansion. The Quant Mutual Fund has been using it for a long time and can be useful for picking stocks.

Valuation: You can find stocks at high dividend yield, low P/E or high growth/high ROE at reasonable pricing or in long term charts at multi year low Price/Sales, Price/Book Value, Price/Earnings, etc.

Liquidity: Average trading volume for a day, week or year. Due to good results or higher interest because of increasing order book stock might trade at volumes highest in years.

Risk Appetite: Markets sometimes produce low risk high reward opportunities like nifty, or top companies' falls.

Time: Timing can be in the cyclical sector, prices of commodity fluctuation or rate hike, cut or pause events. If you can, time rewards are huge.

Compression: This is an extension of the VLRT framework when P/E or valuation of stock is changed. Decreasing prices of stocks can be due to the business cycle, lower revenue, or increased competition. Resulting in reduction of P/E that it was getting for a few years before.

Expansion: Vice versa, when stock is showing good results continuously for years and is expected to do well in many coming years, not only price increases like with 3x earning increasing price increased 3 times keeping P/E ratio same. It will also experience P/E expansion. That's why the market has huge booms and busts for P/E compression and expansion.

Timing can be perfected in cyclical stocks using valuations at historic low, high volumes showing reversals, low risk due to falls without impact on business. So, this model should be viewed together and can be applied to high growth or strong fundamental stocks.

Finding stocks that has good valuation i.e. available at cheap rates historically, liquidity is coming to it which will lead to re-rating of stock (high volumes), risk seems low like moving average is flattened or started rising, since the stock is also cheap risk is less here, and continue good result can make its P/E higher due to expected coming good years for company which can make P/E expand that's how we can use **VLRTCE** framework to select stocks.

VLRT should be seen together as stock has lots of valuable assets, but when will the price reflect it? Liquidity is needed to reach correct valuations.

Suppose stock has grown stupidly to newer highs which do not match valuations at all when will it fall? Maybe when the volume increases.

Will you be taking more risk or less will be decided by historical valuations of peers or history of stock.

Timing can be perfected in cyclical stocks using valuations at historical low, high volumes showing reversals, low risk due to falls without impact on business.

So, this model should be viewed together and can be applied to high growth or strong fundamental stocks.

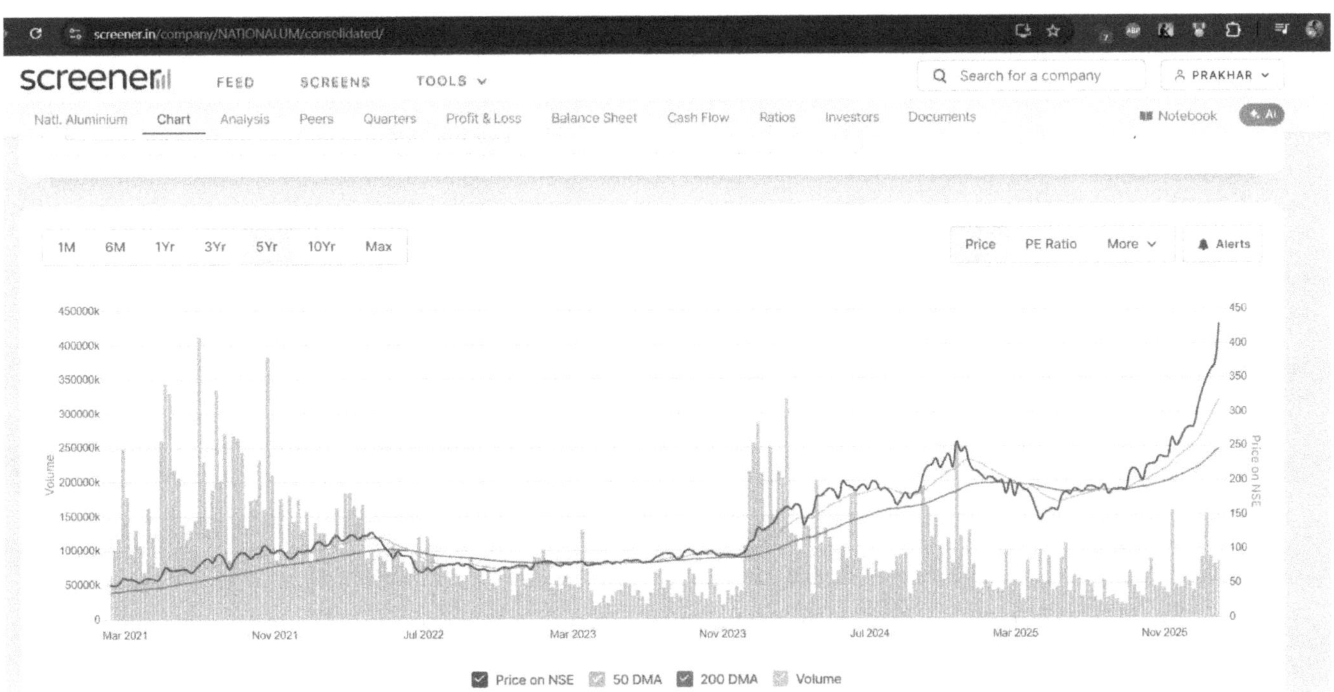

November 2024 National Aluminium touched all time high price 256₹

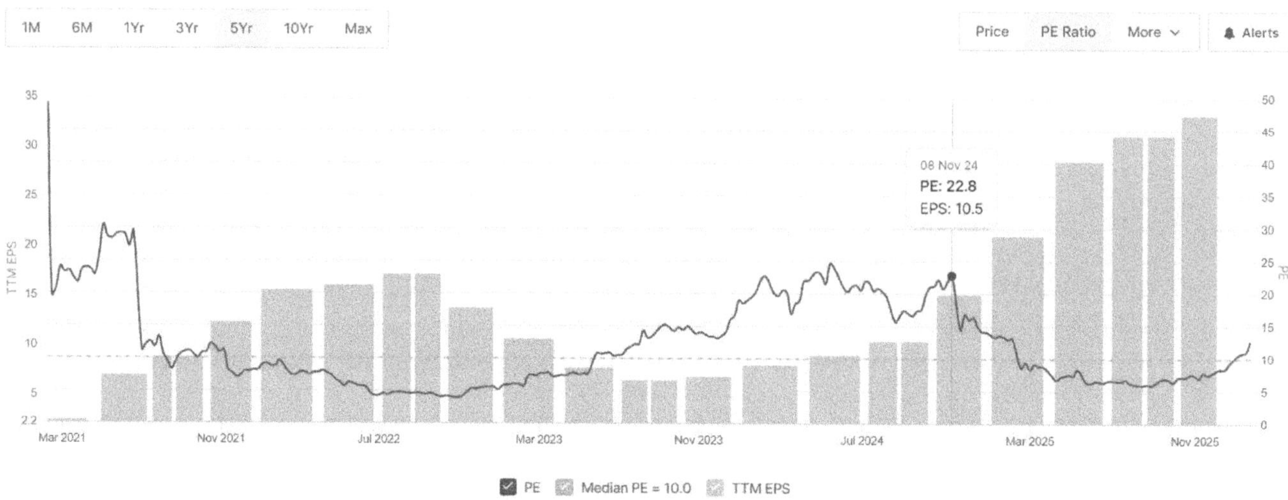

Nalco PE chart

National Aluminium (Nalco) PE was at 22.8. After that, stock fell to 150 in April 2025 while PE at 7 while earnings kept increasing, then the prices started going up after aluminium commodity bottomed out and started performing well reaching 430 ₹ in Jan 2026 while PE remained at 13 and earnings yet increasing.

This is an example of PE **compression** even on good results each quarter now this PE can again go back to 16 the 10 years average PE or even shoot up to 23 PE which was the previous high.

The period of March 2023 Nalco was at 80₹ and earnings falling as you can see in above chart earnings fell from July 2022 to bottoming out in Nov 2023 while the price of Nalco stock bottomed around March 2023 and stock made new all-time high of 164₹ in March 2024 while earnings were still picking up not yet all-time high and PE shootout to 23 around 50 % above the average of 16 PE. This is an example of PE **expansion**, then even after all time high earnings stock fell due to PE expansion and fell to PE of 6 in Aug 2025 well below 16 PE average of long term.

PE expansion and compression can make bumper profits in a stock, but you need to be careful in timing them. This reversion to mean PE creates big moves on the chart.

xii. How about getting all monopoly or duopoly

The Fortress Portfolio: How to Win the Monopoly Game

The stock market is a moody machine. Prices fluctuate wildly based on supply and demand, fear and greed. One day the market is euphoric, the next it is panicking. As an investor, if you try to predict these moods, you will lose. But if you change *what* you buy, the mood swings stop mattering.

Standard advice says a portfolio of 20 to 30 stocks is good for diversification. But if you fill out that list with average companies, you just get average results and average risks. "Fortress Strategy" is different. We fill our portfolio exclusively with **Monopolies and Duopolies**.

These are companies where there is only one player (Monopoly) or two dominant players (Duopoly). In a normal market, competition kills profits. But for these companies, competition is virtually non-existent. When the market dips, they don't go out of business because they *are* the business.

Building the "Moat 30" Portfolio

To execute this, we don't just buy random stocks; we buy the gatekeepers of the Indian economy. We can divide our "Moat 30" into three logical buckets based on how they make money.

1. The Sovereign Kings (The Resource Giants)

These are mostly government-backed giants that own raw materials. You can't build a nation without them.

- **Coal India** controls over 80% of the coal we use for electricity.
- **Hindustan Zinc** is a global giant in zinc (essential for steel).
- **MOIL** dominates manganese ore.
- **NMDC** is the iron ore king.
- **PowerGrid** transmits almost all the electricity in India.

These companies are cash machines. They don't need to advertise; they just dig and sell. Because they are monopolies, they have massive pricing power. Even if the economy slows, we still need electricity and steel.

2. The Daily Habits (Consumer Champions)

These are the companies that own the customer's mind.

- **ITC** is the undisputed king of cigarettes.
- **Pidilite (Fevicol)** has no real competition. It is a synonym for glue.
- **Asian Paints** nearly half the homes in India.
- **Nestle India** has a near-total monopoly on baby food (Cerelac).
- **IRCTC** is the only way you can book a train ticket online.
- **Marico** (Parachute oil) and **Zydus Wellness** (Sugar Free) dominate their niches.

These stocks are compounding machines. Inflation doesn't hurt them; they just raise their prices, and we keep buying because there is no alternative.

3. The Hidden Toll Collectors & Cycle Riders

These are the businesses that take a cut off every transaction or ride massive commodity waves.

- **MCX** and **IEX** are platforms where commodities and energy are traded. You can't trade without paying them a fee.
- **CDSL** holds your shares; **CAMS** processes your mutual funds. They are duopolies that grow automatically as Indians invest more.
- **HAL** makes our fighter jets; **BEL** makes the radars. The government has no choice but to buy them.
- Then you have the cyclical giants like **Graphite India**, **HEG**, **NOCIL**, and **Paradeep Phosphates**. These companies process raw materials where prices can sometimes jump to 10x. When the cycle turns, their profits explode.

The "Twin Engine" Yield: How You Make Money

The beauty of this portfolio is that it works on two engines at the same time.

Engine 1: The Rent (High Dividends)

The Sovereign Kings (like Coal India, Hindustan Zinc, ONGC) are mature businesses. They don't need to build new factories every year, so they share their massive profits with you. Historically, these stocks have offered dividend yields of 5% to 10%. This is like getting rent from a property. In many cases, if you hold them for 10 years, the dividends alone pay back your entire initial investment. You essentially end up owning the stock for free.

Engine 2: The Growth (Capital Appreciation)

The Consumer Champions (like Asian Paints, Titan, Pidilite) are growth engines. They reinvest their money to grow. Over the last 15 years, these stocks have compounded wealth from 15% to 20% annually. They turn small sums into fortunes over time.

The Strategy: Accumulate on Dips

This is not a "get rich quick" scheme; it is a "get rich sure" scheme. Since the country is growing, the demand for power, housing, travel, and finance will mathematically go up. A monopoly captures 100% of that growth.

The strategy is simple:

1. Create your list of these 30 fortress stocks.
2. Wait for the "moody machine" to panic. When there is bad news or a market crash, these stocks will fall temporarily.
3. Use those dips to buy.
4. Take the dividends from the "Kings" (Coal India/HZL) and reinvest them into the "Champions" (Asian Paints/Pidilite).

If well researched and managed, this portfolio offers the safety of a bond (through dividends) and the explosion of a growth stock (through monopolies). It is the ultimate sleep-well-at-night portfolio.

xiii. Catching the Turnaround

In the stock market, everyone loves "Growth." We are taught to find companies that grow their profits by 15% or 20% every year. It feels safe. It feels predictable. But there is another strategy that is often ignored because it looks scary, yet it holds the potential for life-changing returns: **The Turnaround.**

Buying a steady growth stock is like betting on a healthy athlete to win a race. Buying a turnaround stock is like betting on an injured champion who is just starting to walk again. If they recover, the rewards are not just 20% or 30%; they can be 10x or 20x.

The Math of the Comeback

Why do turnarounds offer such explosive returns? It comes down to simple math and a concept called "Price Memory."

Imagine a great company's stock was trading at ₹100. Due to bad decisions, heavy debt, or a market crisis, the stock crashes by 90%. It is now trading at ₹10.

- **The Loss:** For older investors, this is a disaster.
- **The Opportunity:** For a new investor entering at ₹10, the potential is massive.

If the company fixes its problems and the stock price eventually goes back to its old high of ₹100, the stock must rise 10 times (1000%) from the bottom. The old investors just recovered their money, but the turnaround investor made a fortune. This is why hunting for "fallen angels" is so rewarding.

What to Look For: The Signs of Life

You cannot just buy any company that has crashed. That is called "catching a falling knife," and it will cut your hands. You need to identify companies that are actively fixing their mess.

Look for these specific triggers:

1. **Selling "Bleeding" Assets:** Is the company selling off a subsidiary that was losing money?
2. **Debt Reduction:** Are they repaying loans aggressively? (e.g., Usha Martin, Suzlon).
3. **Management Change:** Did a new CEO come to clean the house?

4. **Demergers:** Are they separating good business from bad? (e.g., Arvind).
   Note: Never buy on promises alone. Ensure the company has shown good revenue and, more importantly, profits for the last few quarters. You want to see the numbers turn black before you put your money down.

Case Study: The Tale of Two Housing Finance Companies

To understand the difference between "Growth" and "Turnaround," let's look at two major players in the housing finance sector: **LIC Housing Finance** and **PNB Housing Finance.**

The Growth Candidate: LIC Housing Finance

LIC Housing is the steady giant. It has the backing of LIC, cheap access to funds, and a massive distribution network. It is a "safe" bet. Over the years, it has grown its book value steadily. If you invested in LIC Housing, you likely slept well at night, earning decent, consistent returns. It is a classic compounder.

The Turnaround Candidate: PNB Housing Finance

PNB Housing, on the other hand, went through a crisis. A few years ago, it faced serious issues with asset quality and corporate governance. The stock was hammered, crashing from highs of over ₹1,000 to below ₹400. The market wrote it off.

But then, the cleanup began.

- **New Strategy:** They shifted focus to "Retail" loans (safer) instead of "Corporate" loans (risky).
- **Capital Infusion:** They raised fresh money through a rights issue to strengthen their balance sheet.
- **Profit Jump:** The quarterly numbers started showing consistent profit growth.

The Result:

While LIC Housing moved up slowly and steadily, PNB Housing exploded. From its lows, PNB Housing doubled and tripled in value much faster than its peers. Why? Because the market re-rated it from a "risky" company to a "stable" company. That shift in perception, combined with rising profits, creates the "multibagger" effect.

In Jan 2021 LIC housing and PNB Housing both were available at 1 Price to Book value, meaning both were valued equally at that time, using this as a point of start we can compare both the stocks and their relative performance.

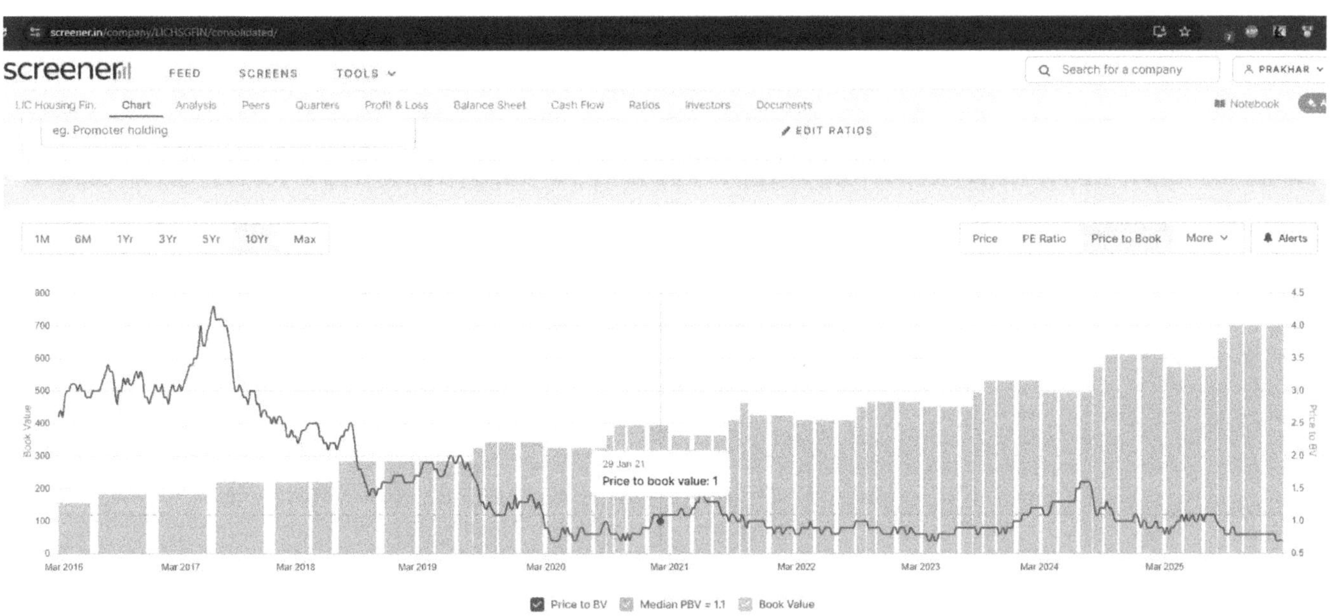

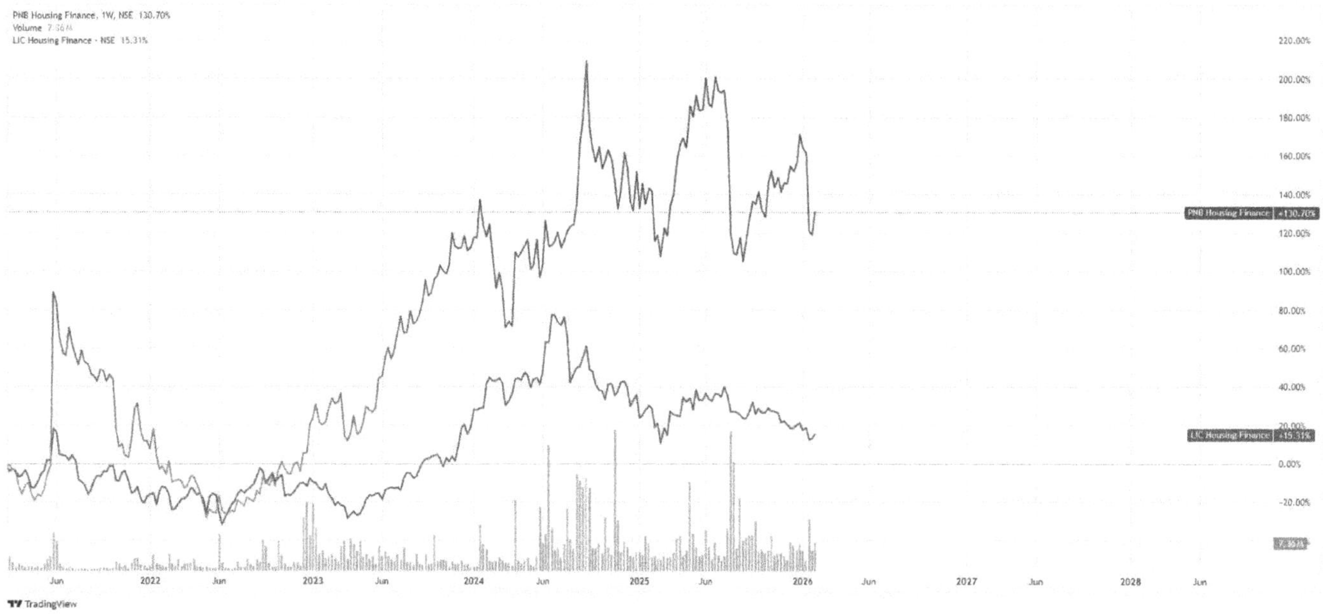

PNB Housing increased by 130% to high of 200% were as LIC Housing increased by 15% to high of 75% in 5 years to Jan 2026

Mostly because PNB Housing has better Return on Assets 2.52% currently while LIC Housing has 1.8%. But in 2021, PNB Housing had significantly less financing margin than LIC Housing and had fallen from 1400 ₹ to 300 ₹ due to bad results and increasing NPAs. The turnaround of PNB Housing in NPAs and financing margin made its price shine over LIC Housing even when LIC Housing consistently kept giving better results. This is the power of turnaround stocks if you can catch them at the right time.

Other Success Stories

The Indian market is full of such examples for those who looked closely:

- **Suzlon:** Once crushed by debt, it restructured, reduced its loans, and rode the new wave of green energy demand.
- **Usha Martin:** Sold its steel division to Tata Steel to clear debt and focused purely on its core wire rope business, unlocking massive value.
- **Arvind:** Demerged its branded apparel business (Arvind Fashions) and engineering business (Anup Engineering), allowing each part to grow faster.

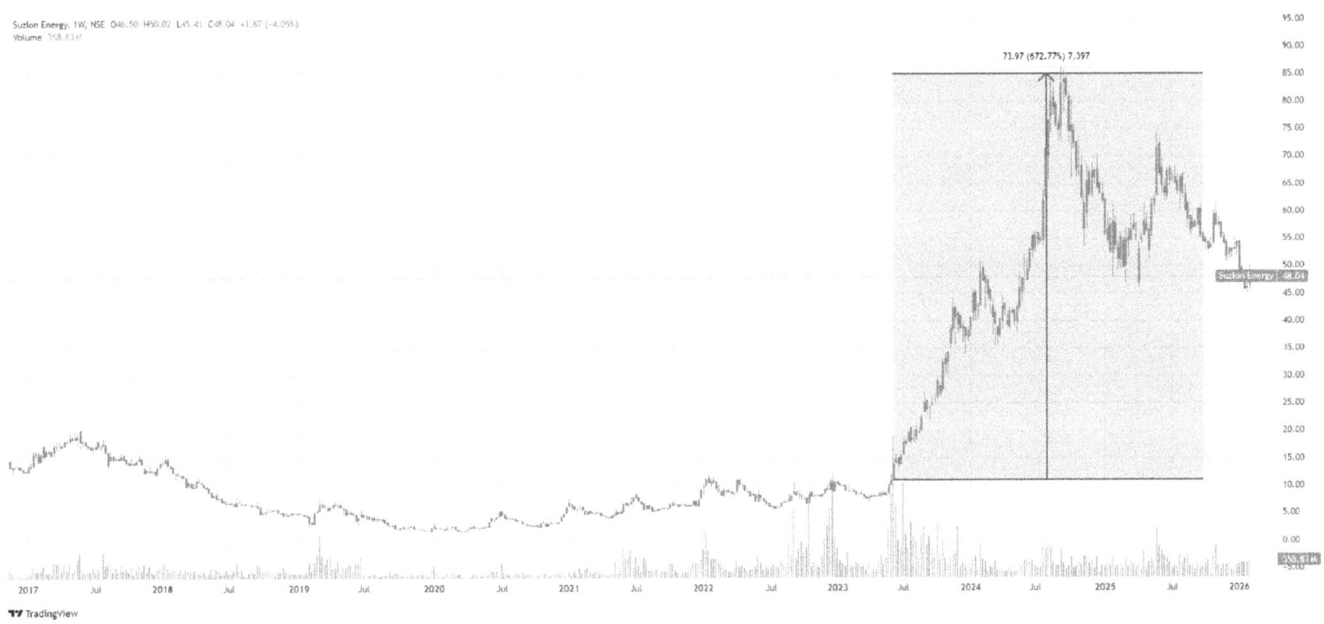

Turn around of Suzlon made 7-8 times returns

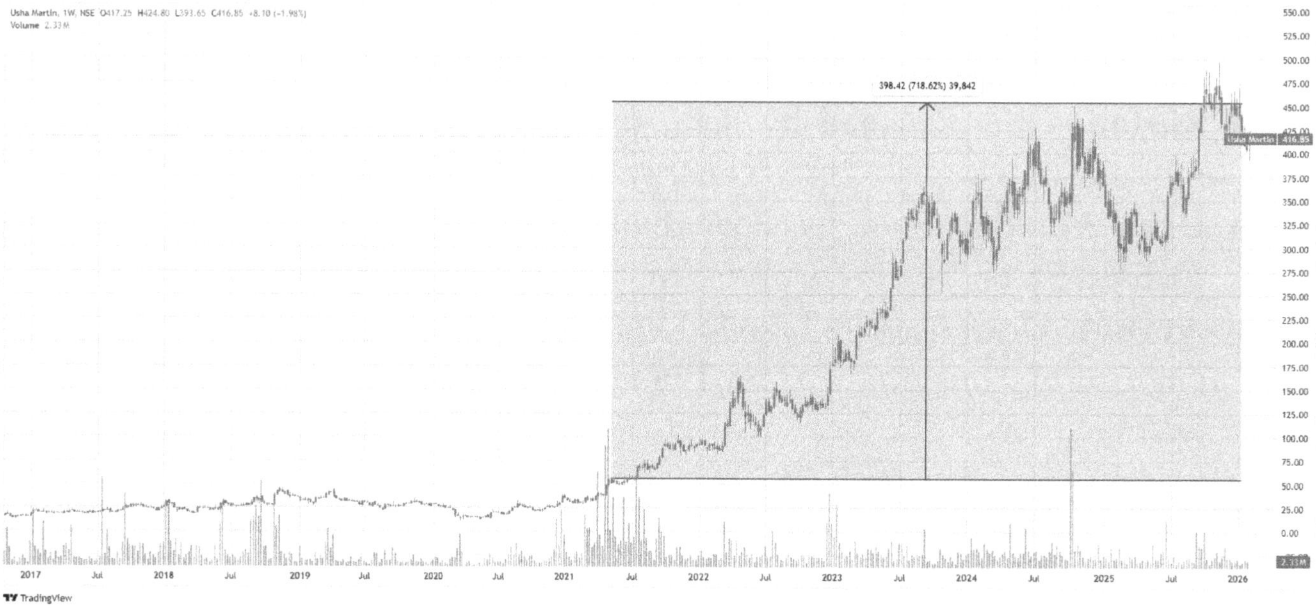

Usha Martin gave 8-9 times returns

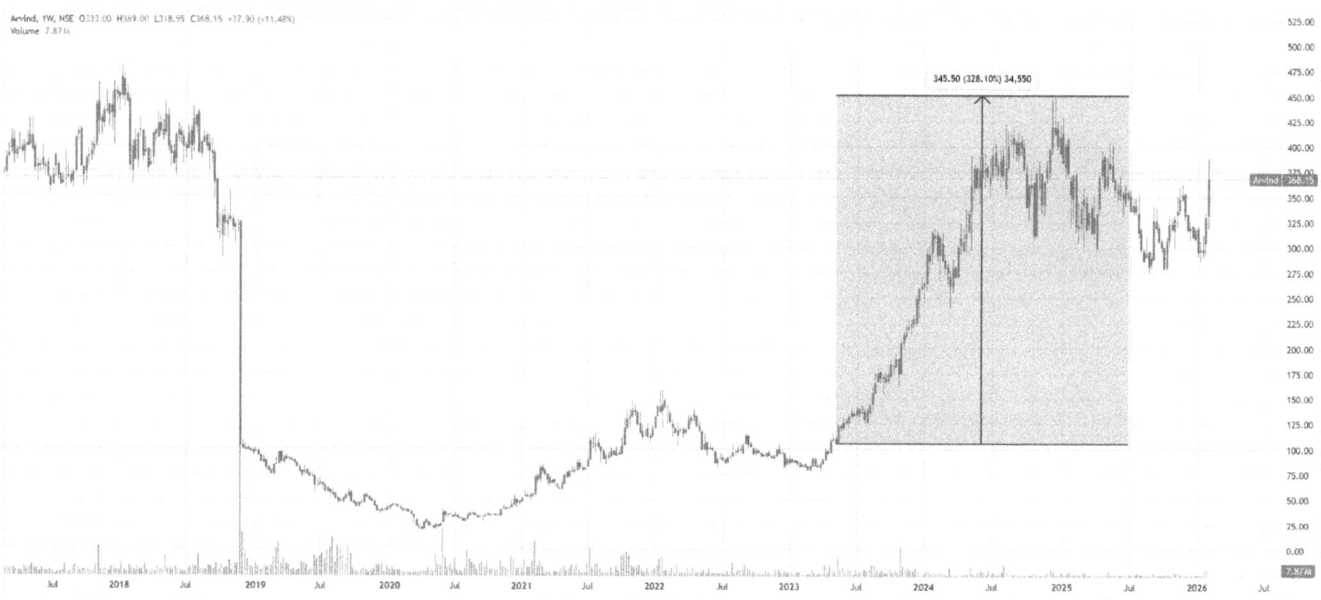

Arvind gave 4 times returns

Investing in turnarounds is risky, but the risk can be managed. Don't buy blindly. Wait until quarterly results confirm the bad days are over. When a good old brand restructures, sells bad assets, and starts posting profits again, pay close attention. The journey from bottom to old peak is where the biggest wealth in the stock market is made.

xiv. Strategies to pick stocks at cheap rates

Finding a cheap stock isn't just about looking at a low P/E ratio. It's about spotting a change before the rest of the market sees it. Over the years, I have realized that the biggest multi-baggers come from five specific triggers. If you can catch these early, you aren't just buying a stock; you are buying a future trend at a discount.

1) Government Planning: The Policy Play

- Since 2014, India has seen major political stability, and with that came aggressive policy changes. The government doesn't hide its plans; they announce them in budgets and speeches. The market just takes time to believe them. That gap is your opportunity.
- **The Banking Turnaround (The 4R Framework):** Remember the gloomy days when PSU banks were drowning in bad loans (NPAs)? The government introduced the "4R Framework"—Recognition, Resolution, Recapitalization, and Reform. They cleaned up the balance sheets. Back then, stocks like SBI, Bank of Baroda, and Canara Bank were available at dirt-cheap valuations, trading well below their book value. Those who understood the 4R policy knew that once the books were clean, profits would return. And they did. The CPSE index and PSU Bank index rallied hard after 2020.

- **Green Energy Push:** Look at the targets set during the G20 climate conference. India promised to go green. Companies like **Suzlon** (wind), **SJVN** (hydro/solar), and **Waaree** were ignored for years. But the government's relentless focus on achieving renewable targets ahead of time changed their fortunes. The policy created the demand, and the stocks followed.

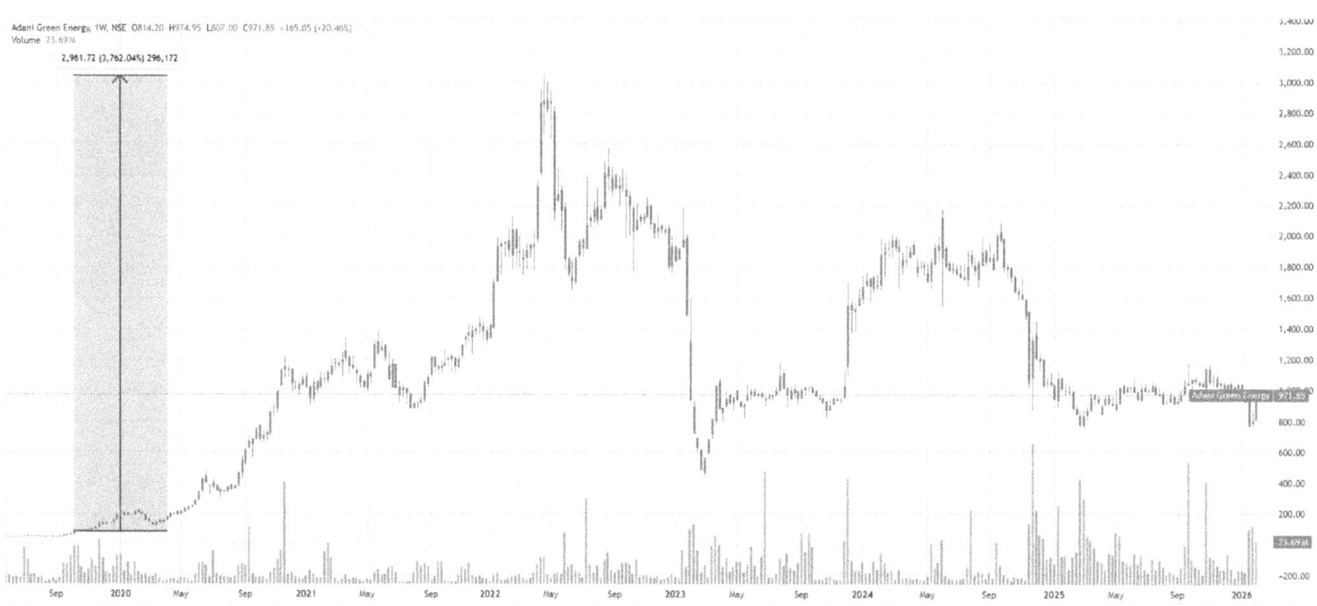

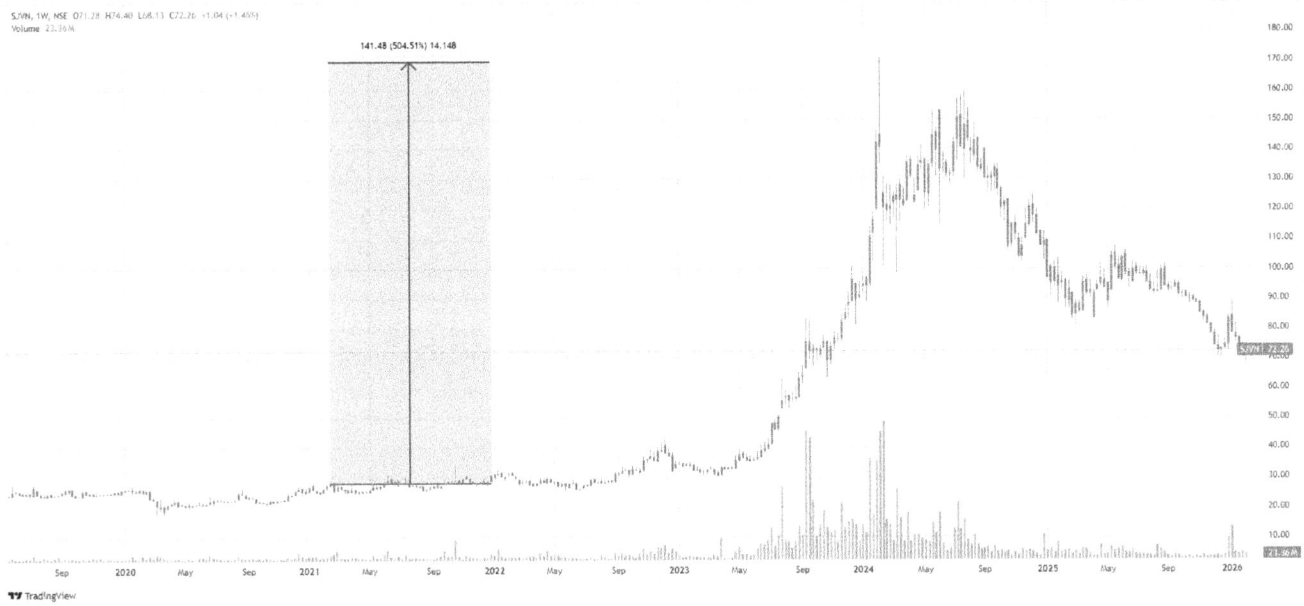

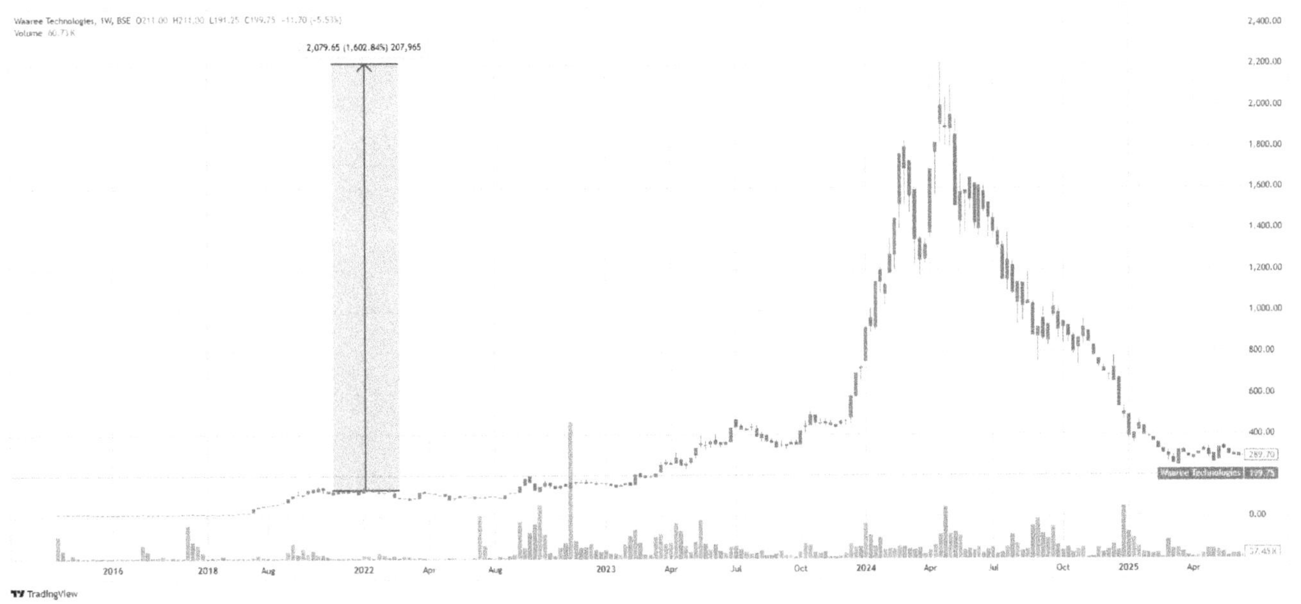

Green energy has given multibagger returns

- **Other Policy Triggers:**
- **Insurance:** Increasing the FDI cap allowed foreign money to flow into companies like **GIC, NIACL, and SBI Life**.
- **KYC Norms:** The push for uniform KYC in finance (2014-15) simplified customer acquisition, setting the stage for a financial boom.

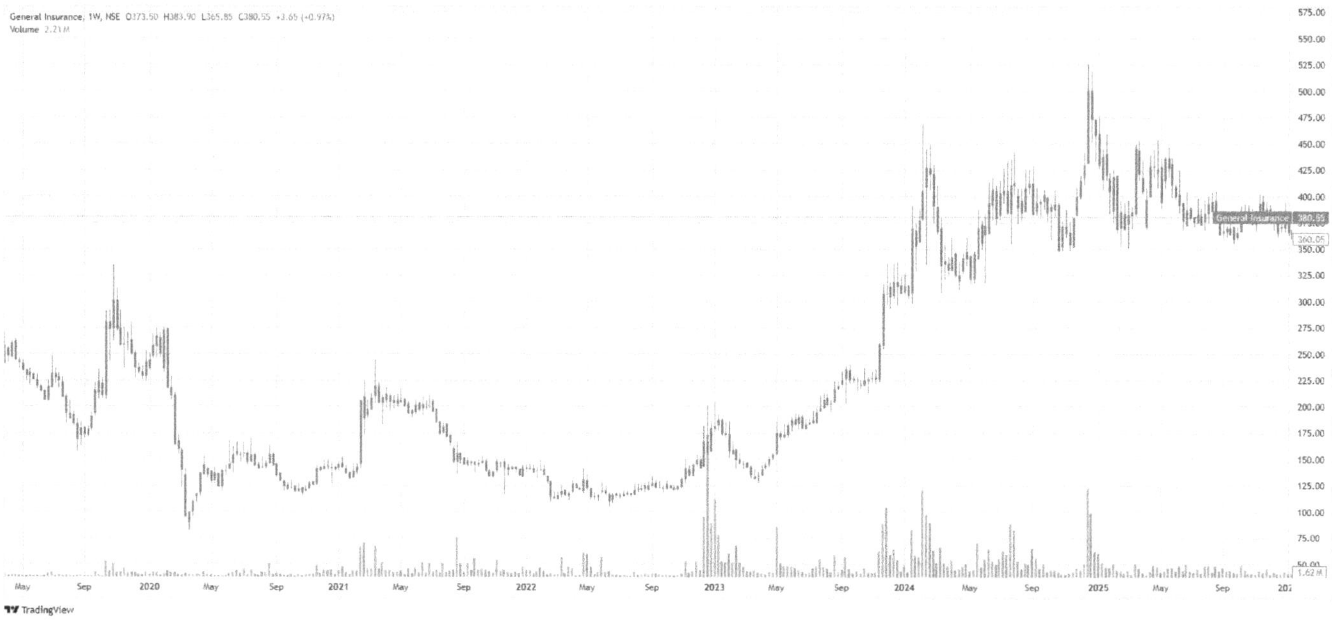

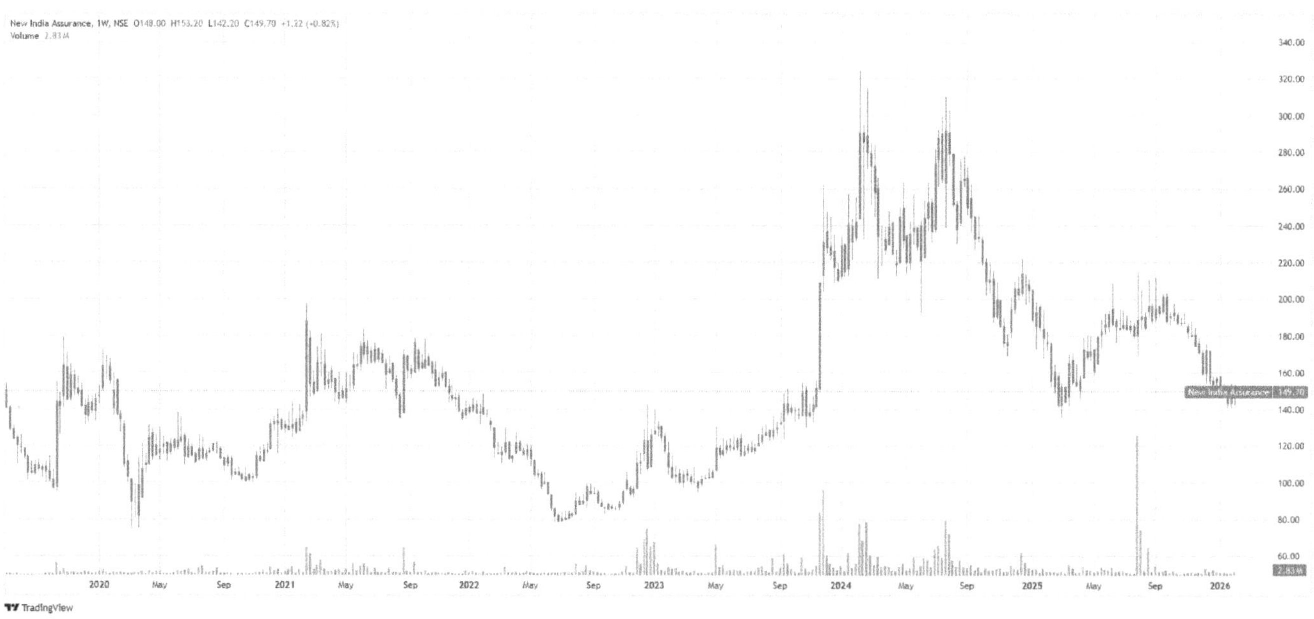

Insurance sectors performed well after FDI limits changed

2) System Upgrades: The Structural Shift

Sometimes, the government doesn't just change a rule; they upgrade the entire operating system of the country. These upgrades remove friction and explode volumes.

- **The Digital Revolution (UPI & T+1):** Digital India, UPI, and the shift to T+1 settlement changed how India transacts forever. It made buying shares and starting SIPs effortless. Who benefited? The gatekeepers of this system.

CDSL & CAMS: More Demat accounts and more SIPs mean more recurring revenue for them.

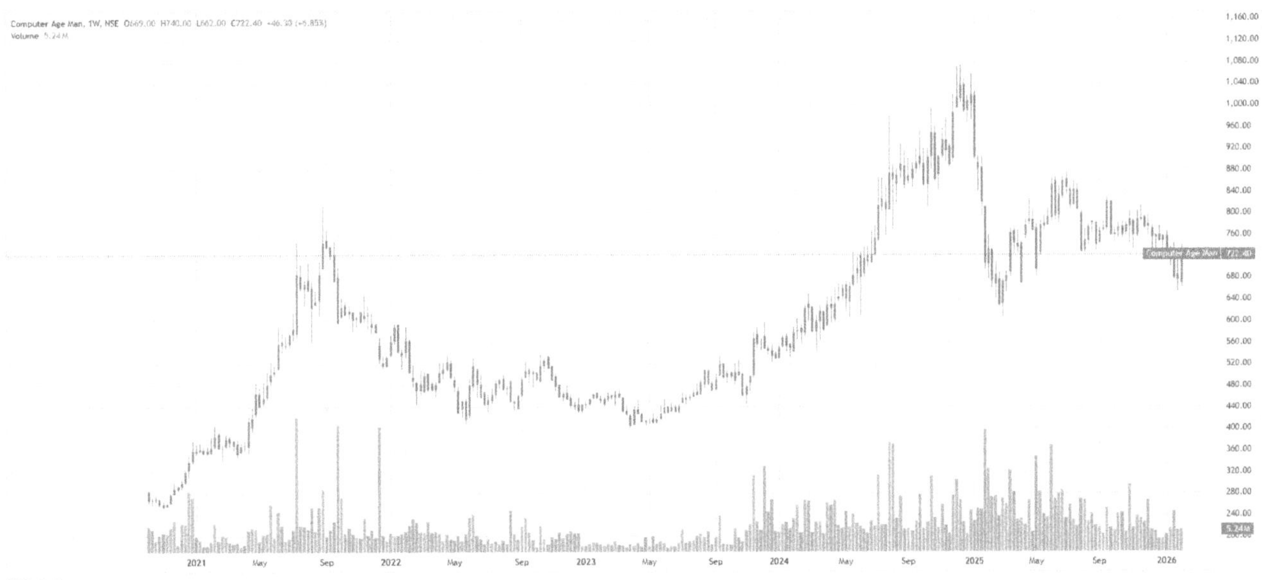

- **BSE, Zerodha & Angel One:** The discount broker revolution was only possible because of this digital infrastructure, this also increases exchange volumes.

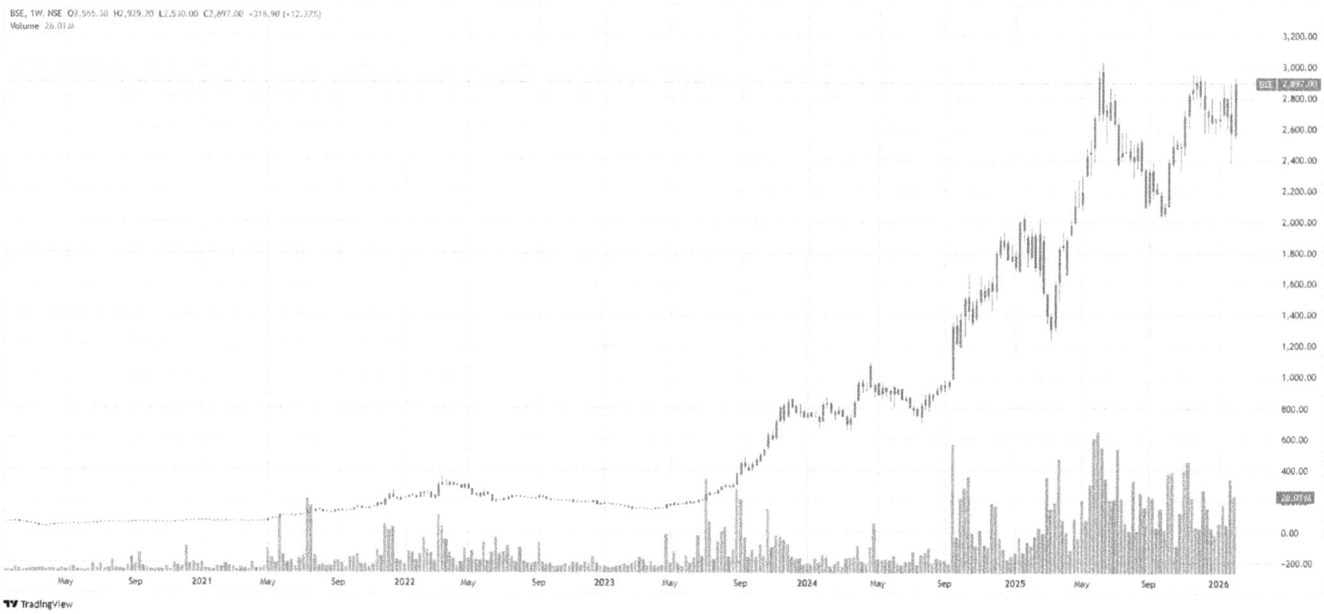
BSE, 1W, NSE O2,565.30 H2,929.20 L2,530.00 C2,897.00 +318.90 (+12.37%)
Volume 26.01M
TradingView

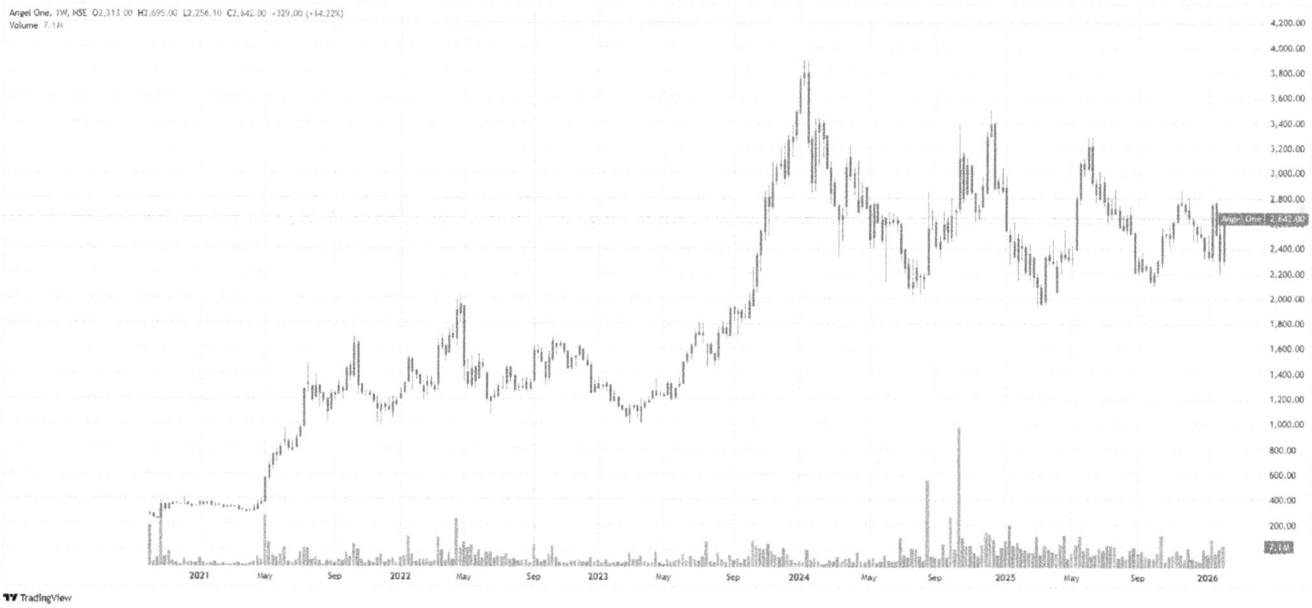
Angel One, 1W, NSE O2,313.00 H2,695.00 L2,256.10 C2,642.00 +329.00 (+14.22%)
Volume 7.1M
TradingView

- **MOFSL & HDFC AMC:** Asset managers saw inflows like never before.

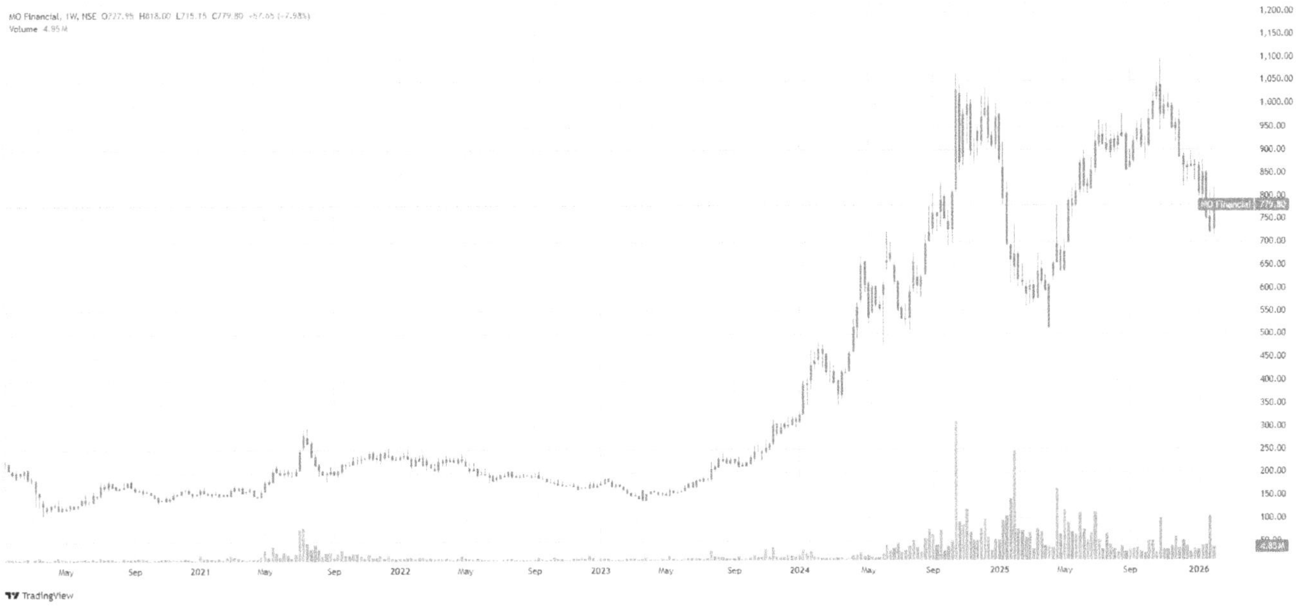

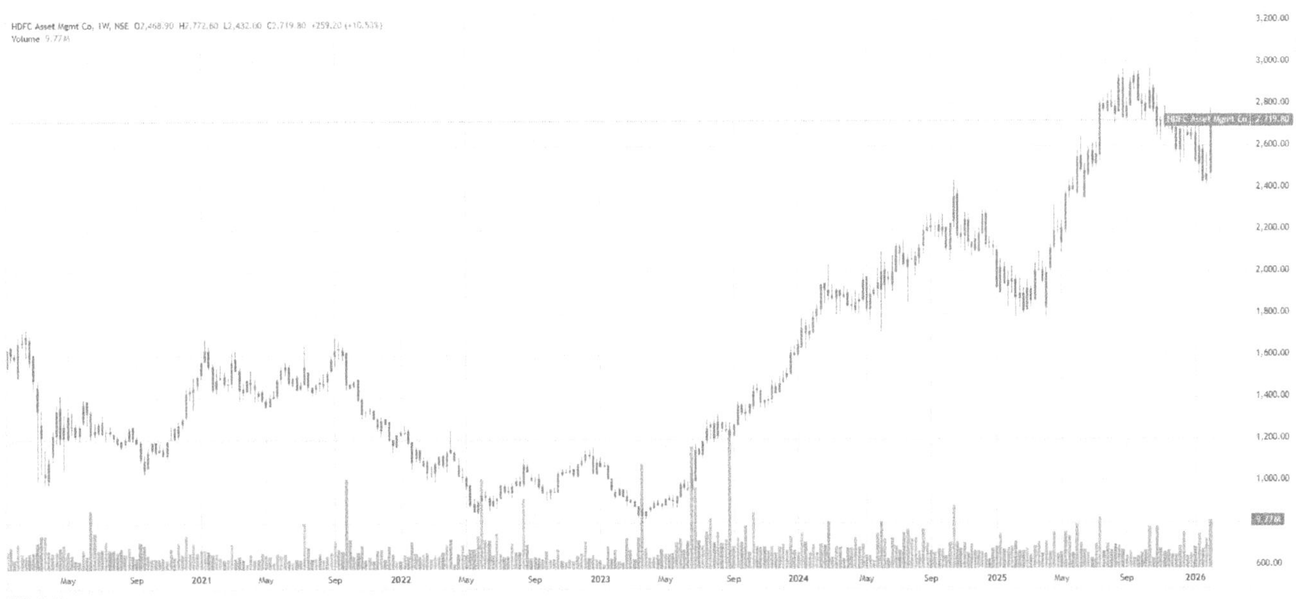

- **Ethanol Blending (E20 Policy):** To reduce crude oil imports, the government mandated mixing ethanol in petrol. Suddenly, sugar companies became energy companies. **Balrampur Chini, EID Parry, and Praj Industries** (who make the ethanol plants) saw a structural shift in demand.

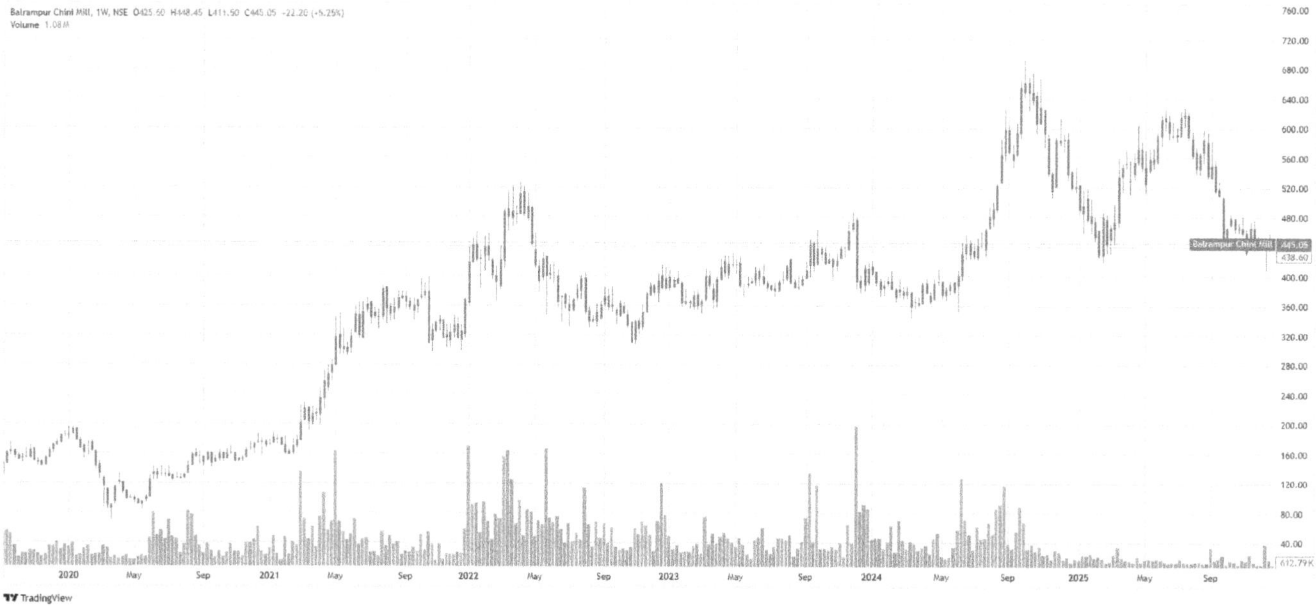

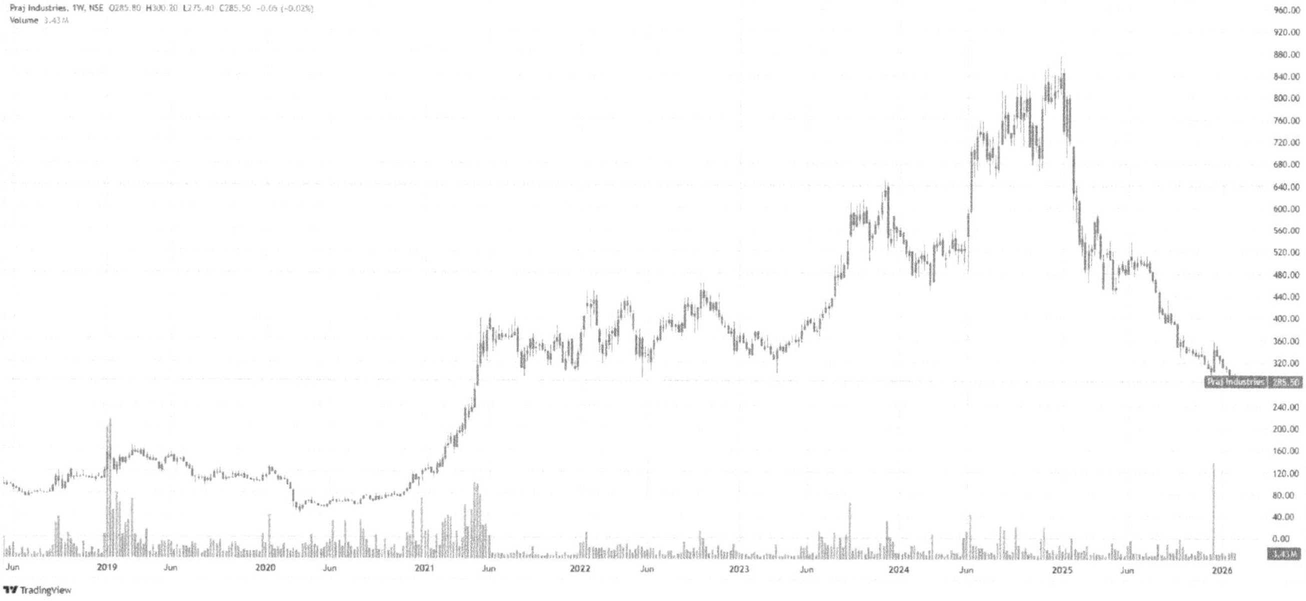

- **Piped Gas Policy:** The mission to connect every house with gas pipelines benefited **Gujarat Gas, IGL, and HPCL**.

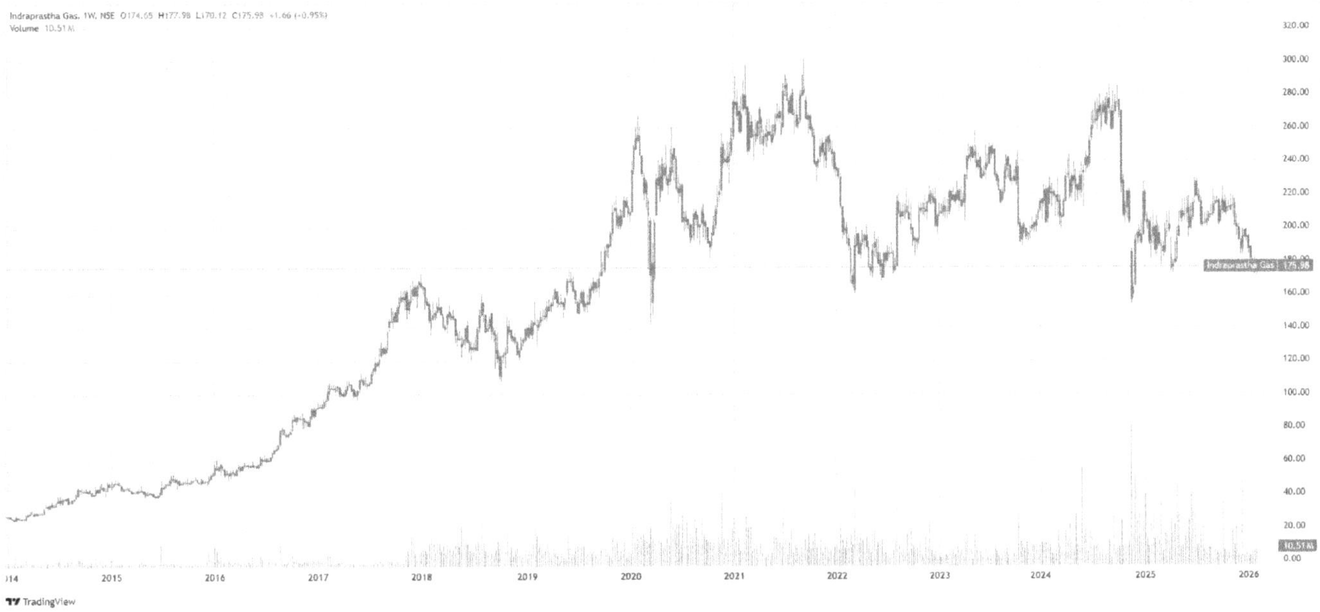

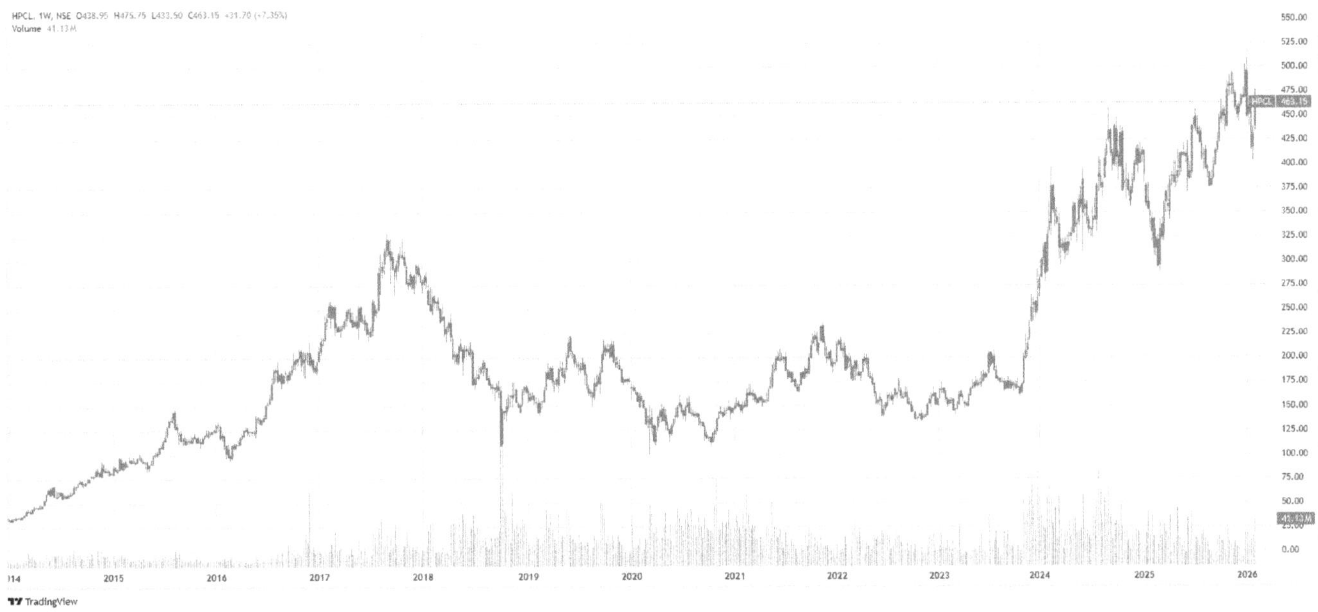

- **Defence (Atmanirbhar Bharat):** The government made a bold claim to make India a net exporter of defence equipment. The market doubted it, but the order books of **HAL, BEL, Mazagon Dock, and Paras Defence** started swelling. The result? Massive returns for believers.

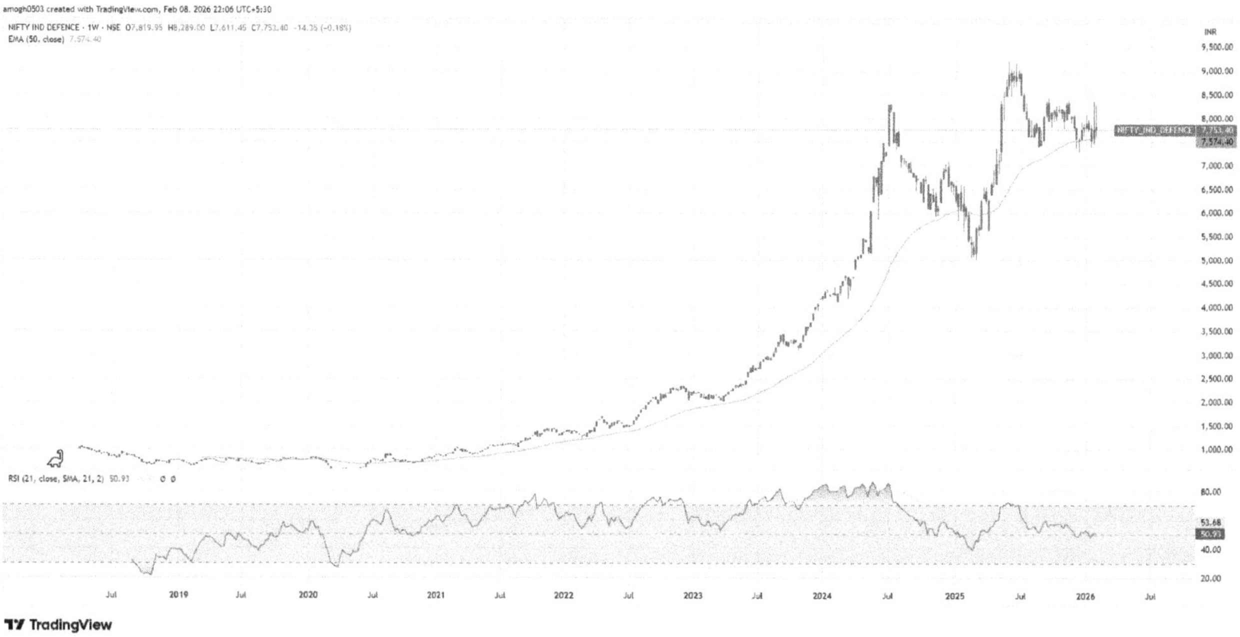

- **Railways:** The Dedicated Freight Corridor (DFC) was a heavy capex plan. It needed wagons, tracks, and finance. Enter **IRFC, RVNL, Jupiter Wagons, Titagarh** etc.

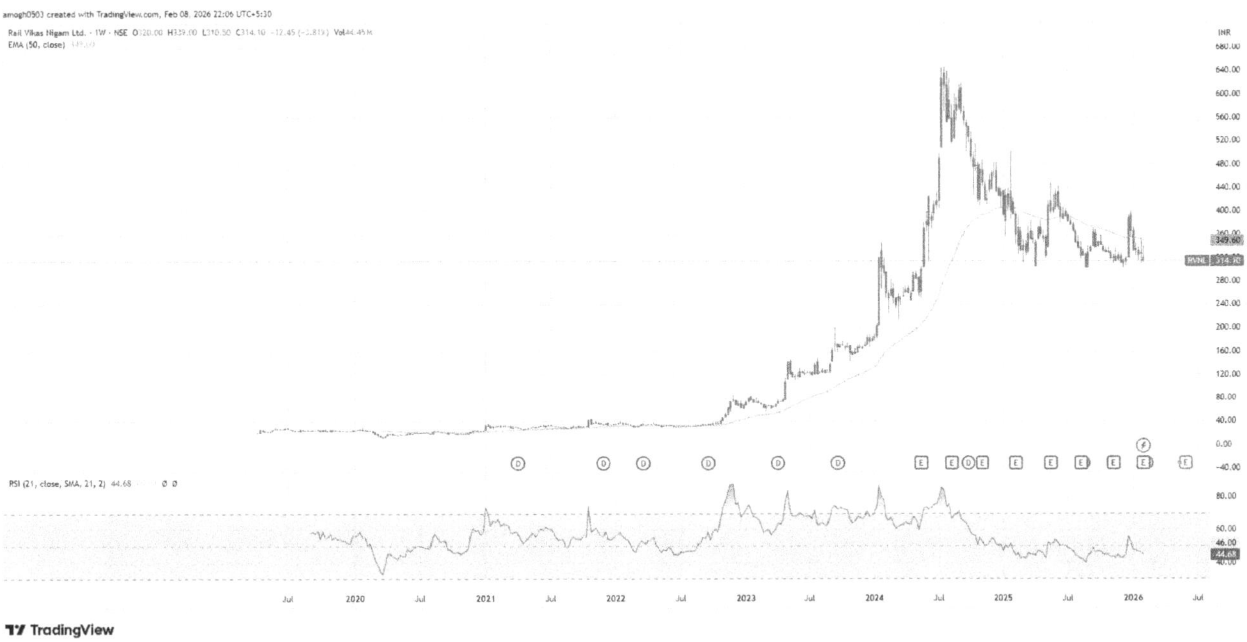

- **Fertilizers:** The aim to be a net-zero importer led to reviving old gas blocks for fertilizer plants. **FACT, RCF, NFL, and Paradeep Phosphates** rode this wave.

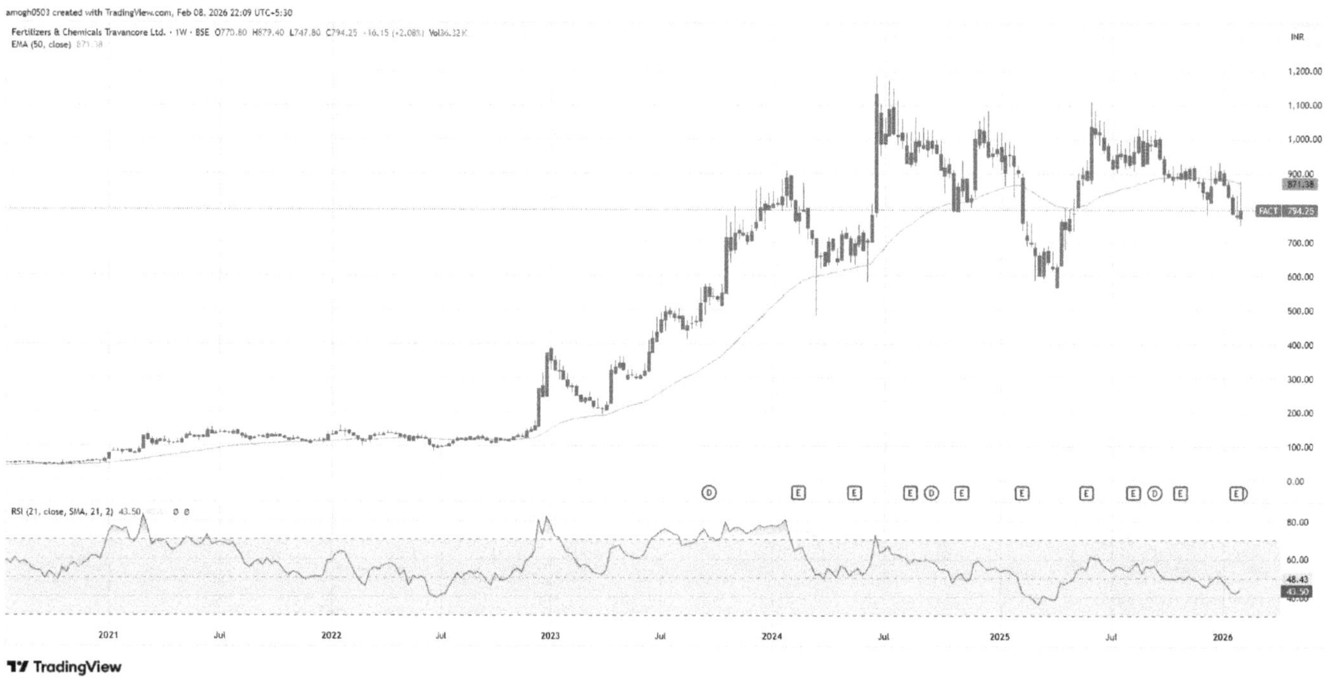

- **Critical Minerals:** The new mining policy to find rare earth metals in India is the next frontier for companies like **NMDC, NALCO, CMPDI, Pondy Oxides** and **Gravita India**.

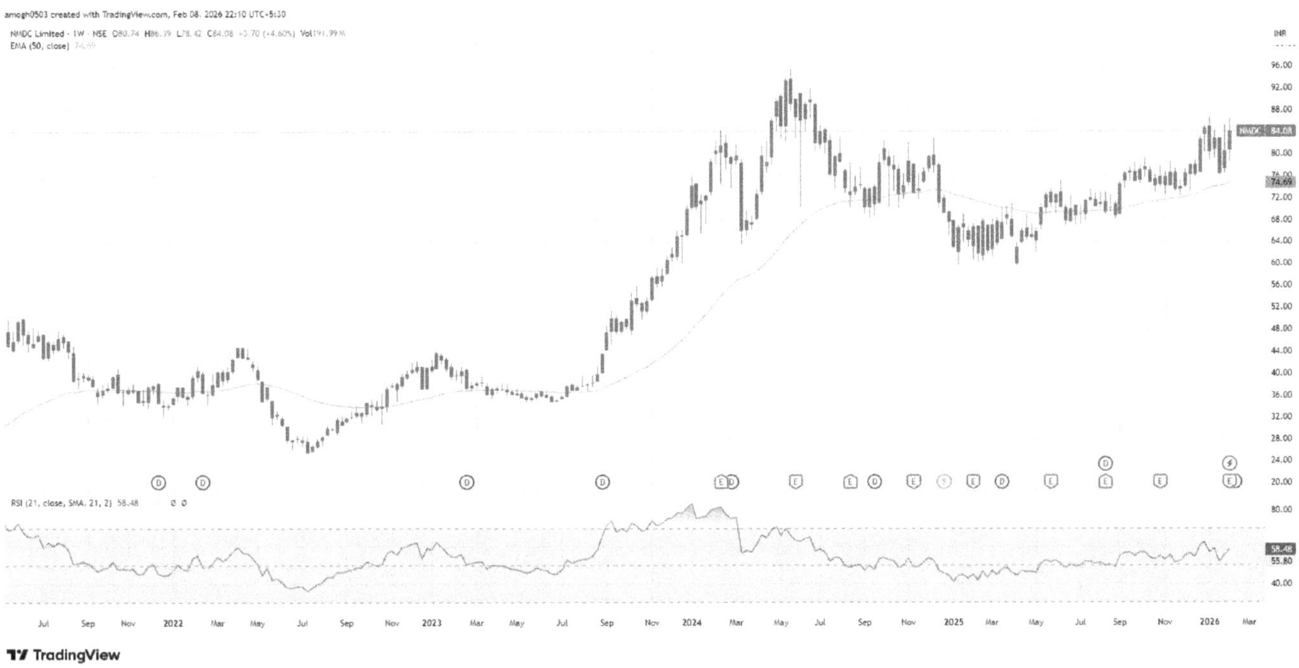

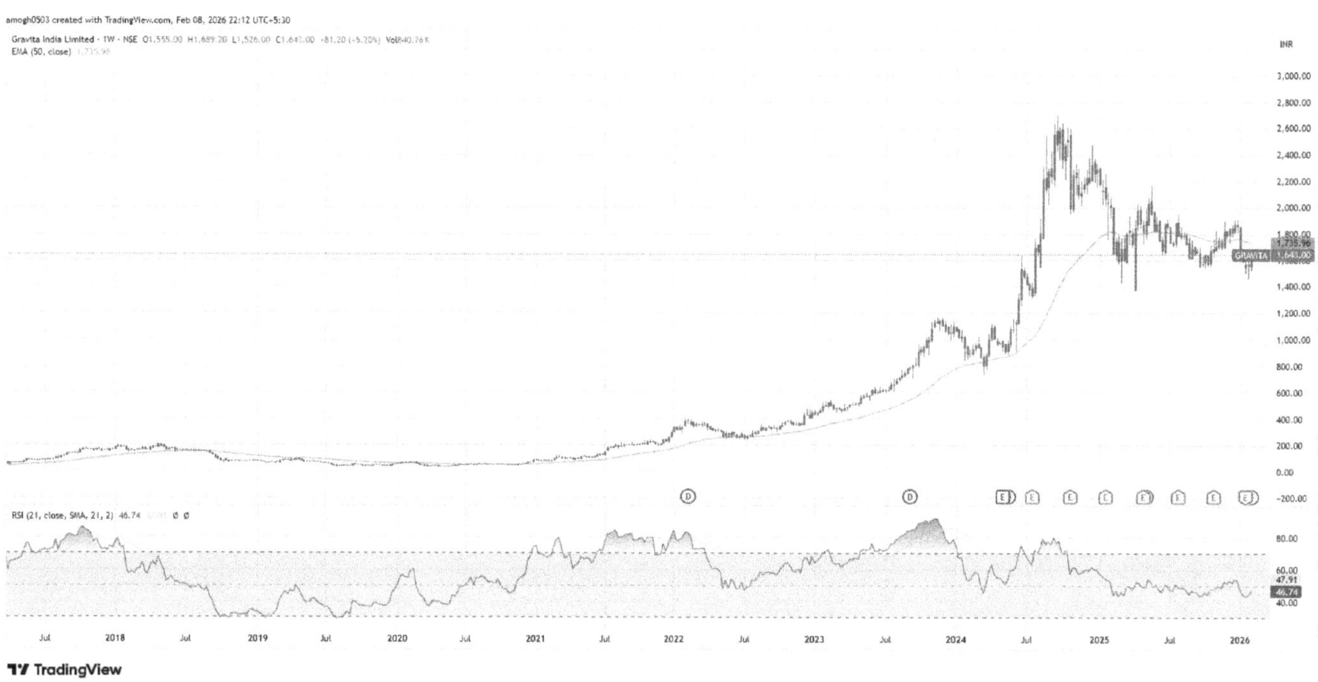

The Lesson: What is the government planning next? Finding the answer to this can be life's most fortunate event, a 10x to 100x opportunity. But be careful. Don't just buy the hype. Wait for the groundwork to start. Let the charts and quarterly results verify that the policy is translating into business.

3) Proxy Play: The Backdoor Entry

Sometimes, the direct sector leader is too expensive or too risky. This is where "Proxy Investing" works. Instead of betting on the gold miner, you bet on the guy selling the shovels.

How to do it:

1. Identify a fast-growing theme (e.g., Green Energy, EV, Infrastructure).
2. Find the critical supplier or service provider to that sector.
3. Analyse their dependency—the more entrenched they are, the better.

Examples: -

1. The "Capital Markets" Proxy (Instead of Brokers)

If you believe more Indians will enter the stock market (financialization of savings), you don't just have to buy volatile brokerage stocks. You can buy the monopolies that run the infrastructure.

- **The Play: CDSL** (Central Depository Services Ltd) or **CAMS** (Computer Age Management Services).
- **Why:** Every time a new Demat account is opened, or a Mutual Fund SIP is registered, these companies make money regardless of whether the market goes up or down. They are a proxy for *volume* and *participation.*

2. The "Real Estate" Proxy (Instead of Developers)

Real estate developers (like DLF or Godrej) carry high debt and inventory risk. A safer way to play the housing boom is through "Home Improvement" or building materials.

- **The Play: Polycab / KEI** (Wires & Cables) or **Astral / Prince Pipes** (Piping).
- **Why:** Every new house needs wires and pipes. These companies have cleaner balance sheets than developers and faster cash conversion cycles.
    - Alternative*:* **Kajaria Ceramics** (Tiles) or **Century Ply** (Plywood).

3. The "Infrastructure" Proxy (Instead of Construction)

This is likely where **Action Construction Equipment (ACE)** fits in. Instead of buying a construction company that might get stuck with delayed payments, you buy the company selling them the machines.

- **The Play: Action Construction Equipment (ACE).**
- **Why:** It sells cranes and heavy equipment. If India is building bridges, metros, and factories, ACE sells the equipment to *all* the contractors. They get paid upfront or on strict terms, avoiding the working capital issues of the actual builders.

4. The "EV & Auto" Proxy (Instead of Car Brands)

It is hard to predict if Tata Motors, M&M, or Maruti will win the EV race. However, they all need specific parts.

- **The Play: Sona BLW Precision** or **Uno Minda**.
- **Why:** Sona BLW supplies differential gears and EV components to almost all global and Indian players. You win regardless of which car brand sells the most.

5. The "Power" Proxy (Instead of Power Gen)

Buying power generation companies (like NTPC) can be slow. The real "action" is in the transmission of that power.

- **The Play: Apar Industries** (Conductors/Cables) or **Hitachi Energy** (Transformers).
- **Why:** As India upgrades its renewable energy grid, demand for premium conductors and transformers is skyrocketing. These stocks have shown massive relative strength compared to standard power utilities.

Similar plays in the market are Anant Raj, Actuaas Chemicals, etc.
Watch them for good returns on sectoral headwinds.

4) Cycle of Blue-chips (The Sleeping Giants)

Blue-chip companies usually don't have the explosive revenue growth of small caps. They are steady ships. But they go through cycles of popularity.

The Strategy: Look for a blue chip that is trading at a valuation (P/B or P/E) much lower than its 10-year average.

- Check if revenue is higher than previous years.
- Ensure the business has no fundamental negative threat (like Kodak facing digital cameras).
- **The Logic:** If a company like **Reliance or Godrej Industries** was trading at a Price-to-Book (P/B) of 10x historically, and today it is available at a P/B of 5x, yet its profits and revenues are at all-time highs—that is a divergence. The market is simply bored or distracted. If you buy at these lows, "Price Memory" kicks in. Eventually, the valuation creates a floor, and the stock reverts to its mean. As mentioned in the CANSLIM section, waiting for the technical breakout here adds safety to value.

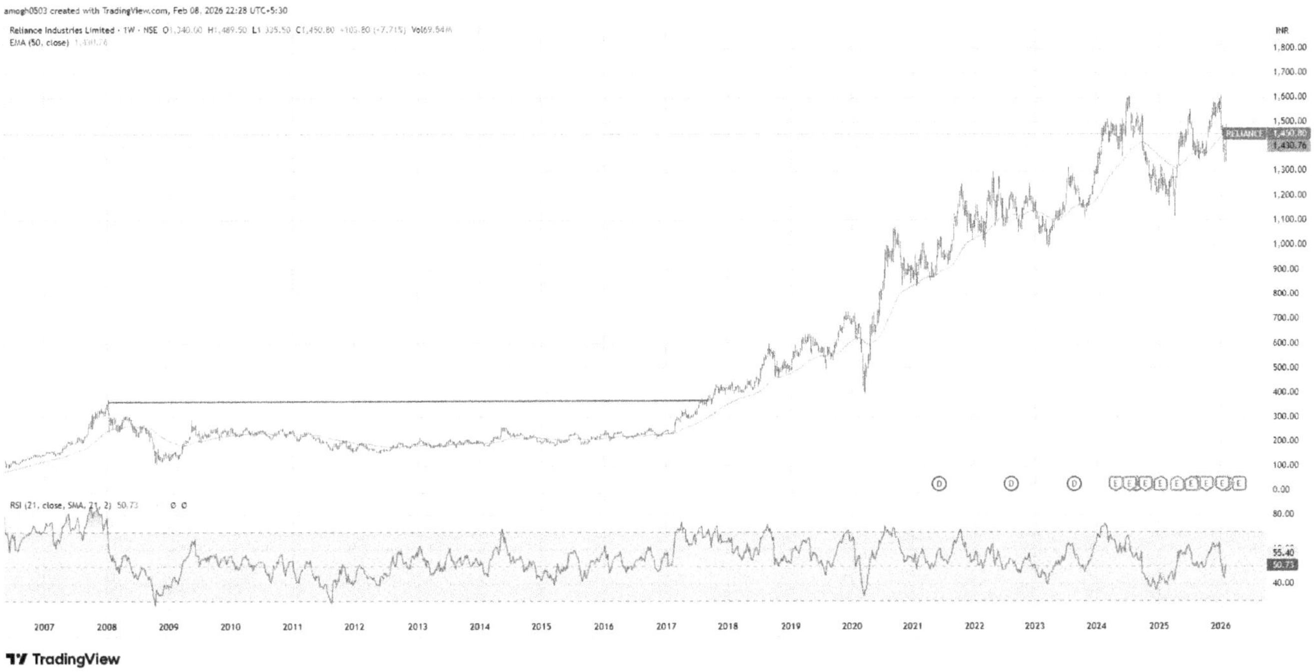
amogh0503 created with TradingView.com, Feb 08, 2026 22:28 UTC+5:30
Reliance Industries Limited · 1W · NSE
EMA (50, close)
RSI (21, close, SMA, 21, 2)
TradingView

amogh0503 created with TradingView.com, Feb 08, 2026 22:29 UTC+5:30
Godrej Industries Limited · 1W · NSE
EMA (50, close)
RSI (21, close, SMA, 21, 2) 43.87
TradingView

amogh0503 created with TradingView.com, Feb 08, 2026 22:32 UTC+5:30
Sun Pharmaceutical Industries Limited · 1W · NSE O1,634.00 H1,729.00 L1,598.20 C1,695.10 +85.00 (+5.28%) Vol19.55M
EMA (50, close) 1,691.96
INR
SUNPHARMA 1,695.10
RSI (21, close, SMA, 21, 2) 49.90
2015 Jul 2016 Jul 2017 Jul 2018 Jul 2019 Jul 2020 Jul 2021 Jul 2022 Jul 2023 Jul 2024 Jul 2025
TradingView

5) **Pattern Matching: The Copy-Cat Effect**

The stock market often moves in herds. Companies operating in the same sector usually face the same headwinds and tailwinds. You can use this to predict moves.

Peer Matching: If **IOC** rallies 20% because of better refining margins, it is very likely that **BPCL and HPCL** will follow suit shortly. If **Bank of Baroda** posts great results and shoots up, **Canara Bank** or **Union Bank** often play catch-up a few days or weeks later.

BPCL crossed all time high

IOCL still has not crossed all time high while both have good results and working in same sector with similar margins

As per pattern matching, IOCL should form similar chart patterns and make an easy returns strategy until charts for both matches.

HPCL has outperformed both previous stock due to its smaller market size while working in same sector and similar business

Similarly, the PSU Bank Index has crossed all time highs and most constituents have followed a similar pattern. Now using this we can find stocks with relative underperformance, but choose only those which have good fundamentals just like top holdings of the index.

Union Bank and Bank of India have underperformed PSU Bank Index while having lesser Price to Book value and better dividend yield

Canara Bank has outperformed PSU Bank Index

New positions can be built in Bank of India and Union Bank of India while the fundamentals support, PSU Bank Index is doing well and until the underperformance continues for these banks using the pattern matching strategy.

Parent-Subsidiary Lag: Many listed companies own other listed companies.

- **Alembic Ltd** owns a stake in **Alembic Pharma**.
- **Zuari Agro** has a stake in **Paradeep Phosphates**.
- **EID Parry** owns a massive chunk of **Coromandel International**.

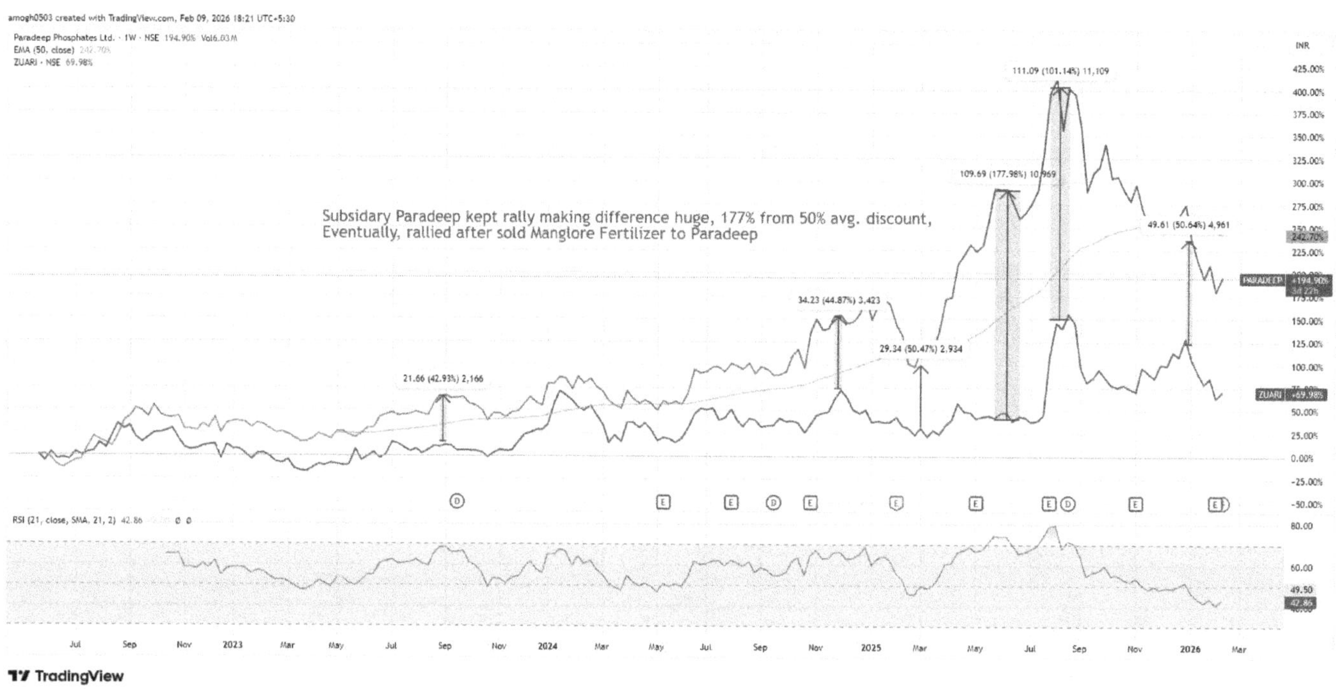

The above chart pattern of subsidiary and parent deviated after July 2025 making buying opportunity in the parent company Zuari Agro

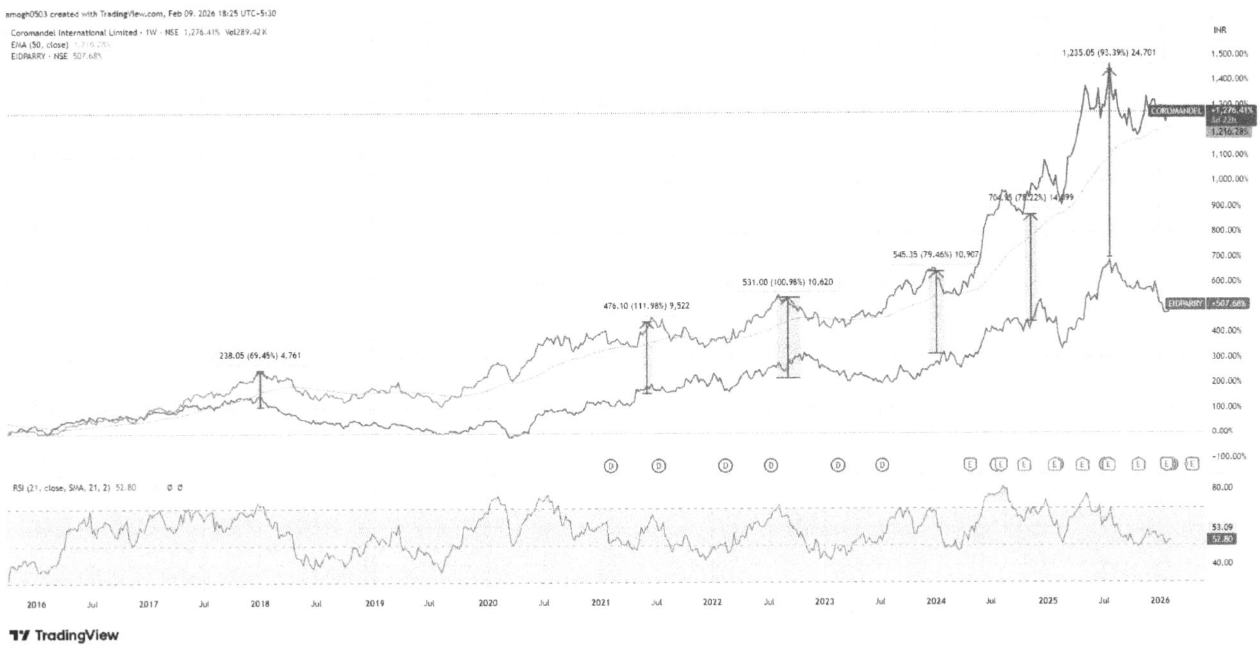

EID Parry and Coromandel International have maintained this pattern and percentage difference well over time, whenever one rallies and pattern seems to be deviated provides a nice buying opportunity in the laggard for long term until pattern matches again

The Pattern: Watch the subsidiary. If the subsidiary (e.g., Paradeep) rallies hard and hits an all-time high, the value of the parent company (Zuari) has mathematically gone up. But the parent stock often reacts with a lag of weeks or months. That delay is your profit window. If the subsidiary is breaking out, the parent is likely next.

The Hidden Treasury List: Parent-Child Arbitrage

Here are the strongest "Holding Company" opportunities in the Indian market.

- **Maharashtra Scooters:** This isn't just a scooter company. It holds a massive treasury of shares in **Bajaj Auto** and **Bajaj Finserv**, often worth more than its own market cap.

- **Pilani Investment:** The ultimate proxy for the Birla Group. It holds significant stakes in **Grasim**, **UltraTech Cement**, and **Hindalco**. When the cement or aluminium cycle booms, this stock eventually re-rates.

- **Kama Holdings:** A backdoor entry in chemicals giant **SRF Ltd**. Kama owns about 50% of SRF. If SRF rallies, Kama's intrinsic value jumps significantly.

- **Bombay Burmah (BBTC):** The Wadia Group's holding company. Buying BBTC is often a cheaper way to enter the **Britannia Industries** growth story.

- **JSW Holdings:** The Jindal Group's investment arm. It offers a direct play on the steel and power cycles through **JSW Steel** and **JSW Energy**.

- **Tata Investment Corp:** One of the best proxies for the entire **Tata Group's** performance, holding stakes in Tata Chemicals, Titan, and Tata Motors.

- **Summit Securities:** The RPG Group's investment arm. It gives you exposure to power transmission via **KEC International** and tyres via **CEAT**.

- **Mahindra & Mahindra Financial Services:** While a business in its own right, its parent **M&M** derives significant value from it. Watch the interplay here.

- **Sundaram Clayton:** Holds a major stake in **TVS Motor Company**. When the auto cycle turns, check the parent stock.

- **Nalwa Sons Investments:** Holds a significant chunk of **Jindal Steel & Power (JSPL)**. A classic value play on the steel cycle.

- **Vardhman Holdings:** The holding company for **Vardhman Textiles**. When cotton prices drop, the subsidiary flies first, and the parent follows.

- **Kirloskar Industries:** A holding company for the group, specifically **Kirloskar Oil Engines**, often trading at a deep discount to its underlying value.

- **Kalyani Investment:** The holding company for the Kalyani Group, offering exposure to **Bharat Forge** and **Hikal**.

Important Note: The "Discount" Trap

These holding companies will always trade at a **"Holding Company Discount"** (usually 40% to 70%) compared to the actual market value of the shares they own. This happens because they cannot easily sell those shares to unlock cash.

Your Strategy: You are not betting on the discount vanishing to zero. You are betting on the **relative move**. If the subsidiary stock moves up 20%, the parent stock should logically move up too, just to maintain that same percentage gap. Do not wait for the prices to match; play the momentum delay.

xv. Growth Stocks and momentum and future driven stocks

Finding a stock is easy; finding a "wealth creator" is hard. The Nifty Index gives us an average growth of about 12%. But to create real wealth, we need companies that run faster than the index—companies growing their sales and profits at 15%, 20%, or even 25% CAGR.

The problem is, everyone knows these companies are good, so they are always expensive. You will rarely find them at a P/E of 10. They trade at high valuations, and when the market falls, they correct sharply.

So, how do we enter without getting burned? We mix **Fundamental Screening** with **Technical Momentum.**

Step 1: The Fundamental Filter

First, we separate the wheat from the chaff. We want companies that have already proven themselves, not penny stocks that operate on hope.

- **Market Cap:** > ₹2,000 Crore (We want established businesses, not micro-caps).

- **Growth:** Sales and Profit growth > 15% consistently for the last 3-5 years.

- **Valuation:** Don’t worry about high P/E yet. If the growth is real, the P/E will sustain.

Step 2: The Momentum Entry (The Moving Averages)

This is where we time our entry. You don't buy a growth stock when it is crashing; you buy it when it is resting or starting to run again.
We use the **Moving Averages (MA)** on the daily or weekly chart to find the sweet spot:

1. **The 200 DMA Support:** This is the "institutional floor." Strong growth stocks often correct during a bear market but stop falling exactly at their 200-Day Moving Average. If a high-quality stock touches the 200 MA (or sometimes the 300 MA in deep corrections) and starts bouncing back, that is your buying zone.

2. **The 50 DMA Trend:** For an aggressive entry, check if the stock is trading above its 50 MA. This shows the short-term trend is positive.

Rule of Thumb: Never catch a falling knife. Wait for the stock to take support at these levels and show a green candle before you buy.

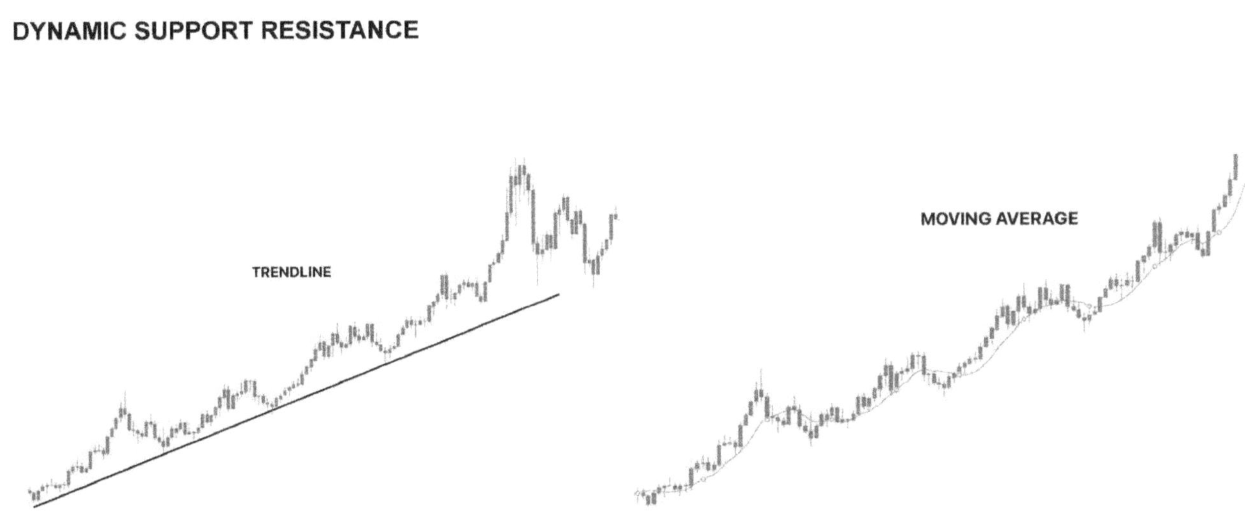

Step 3: Is it Future Driven?

Numbers are past data. We need to look at the future. Before buying, ask yourself one simple question:
"Is this company building something significant or futuristic for India?"
If a company is just selling a commodity, its growth will eventually slow. But if it is enabling a future trend—like Data Centres, Green Hydrogen, Defence Indigenization, or AI—the market will pay a premium for it for years.

Step 4: The "No Listed Peers" Advantage

This is my favourite category. These are companies that are the *only* way to play a specific theme. They have no listed competitors. This creates a "Scarcity Premium." If a mutual fund manager wants to invest in that sector, they *must* buy this specific stock because there is no other option.

Examples of Unique Businesses:

- **BSE / MCX:** If you want to invest in growing trading volumes, these are the only exchange platforms listed.
- **CAMS:** The backbone of the mutual fund industry.
- **IEX:** The monopoly in power trading.
- **Defence Shipyards:** Companies like **Mazagon Dock** or **Garden Reach Shipbuilders**. If the Navy needs a destroyer, they go to them. There is no "Plan B."
- **IRFC:** The specialized financier for Railways.

Summary:
Don't just chase price. Build your list of high-growth, unique business companies. Wait until they cool to their 200 MA or 300 MA. When they find support and the momentum turns positive, that is when you strike for the long term.

xvi. Stocks are backed by Commodities

Every industry relies on commodities in some way. Whether it's chemicals like ethane, metals like iron, aluminum, and copper, or everyday essentials like oil, gas, coal, and sugar—commodities are the building blocks of the market. When analyzing a stock, it is crucial to understand its relationship with underlying commodities. Broadly, companies fall into two categories:

1. The Producers (Direct Impact)

These are the companies that mine, extract, or manufacture commodities. For these businesses, a rise in the commodity price usually means a rise in their stock price, as their profit margins expand.

Examples: Soda ash producers like GHCL and Tata Chemicals; mining giants like Nalco, NMDC, and Coal India; or Hindustan Zinc, which rallies when silver and zinc prices climb. Similarly, sugar stocks tend to surge when global sugar prices rise.

2. The Consumers (Inverse Impact)

These are the companies that use commodities as raw materials to create their final products. For them, a rising commodity price is bad news because it increases their input costs and squeezes their profit margins, often causing the stock to fall.

Examples:

A sharp rise in cotton prices will hurt the margins of clothing brands. The auto industry takes a hit when metal prices soar, and a spike in global coffee bean prices will weigh heavily on the profits of coffee brands. The crude price rise affects refining (IOC, BPCL), tyre companies (Ceat, Appollo) tyres margins whereas the margin of oil producing companies (Oil India, ONGC) increases.

The Strategy:

How to Trade the Trend To stay ahead of the curve, track global commodity prices (preferably in USD). Look for signs of prices "bottoming out" (a potential buy signal for producers) or "topping out" (a potential relief rally for consumers). Always ask yourself: If this commodity price changes, will it expand or shrink this specific company's margins?

xvii. The Liquidity Game: M2, Nifty, and Gold

What is M2?
Think of M2 as the total amount of ready-to-use cash in the economy. It includes physical cash, checking accounts, and easy-to-access savings. Simply put, M2 is "liquidity"—it tells us exactly how much money is floating around in the system.
When central banks (like the RBI or the US Fed) want to boost the economy, they make borrowing cheaper. More money enters the system, so M2 goes up. When they want to fight inflation, they make cash harder to get, and M2 goes down.

M2 vs. Nifty 50: The Stock Market Rally The stock market loves extra cash. When M2 increases, bank interest rates are usually low. People want better returns, so they pour their extra cash into stocks like the Nifty 50.

Expanding M2: More cash chases the same number of stocks, pushing prices up. This usually creates a bull market.

Shrinking M2: Cash gets tight and expensive. Investors pull their money out of the market to pay debts or buy safe government bonds, causing stock prices to fall.

M2 vs. Gold: The Safe Shield Gold is your ultimate backup plan. Governments can print endless amounts of paper money, but they cannot print gold.
When M2 grows too fast, paper money loses its value because of inflation. Since your Rupee or Dollar is worth less, it takes more of them to buy the same amount of gold.
Over the years, gold prices have closely tracked this money printing. While stocks give you growth, gold protects your true buying power.

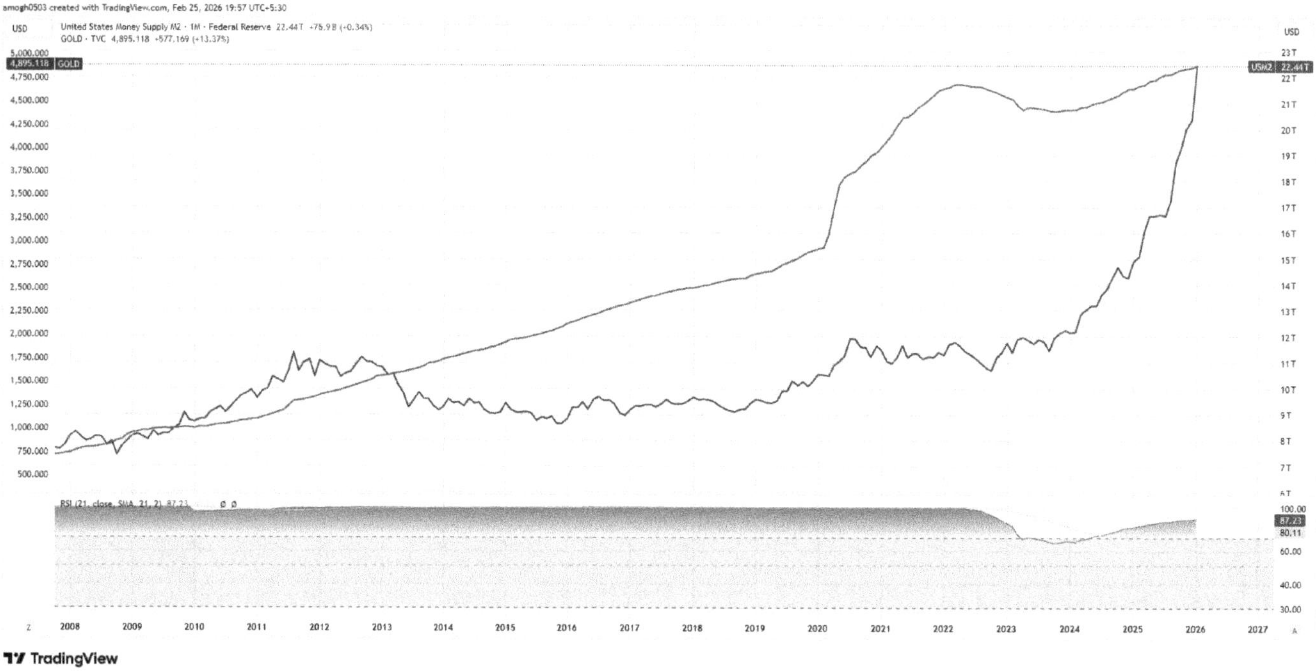

This chart we can see after 2020 m2 money supply of US exploded due to money printing, whereas gold was a long laggard, not even at previous all-time high levels, then after gold had breakout of above 2000$ price it doubled to match the amount of United States Money Supply M2

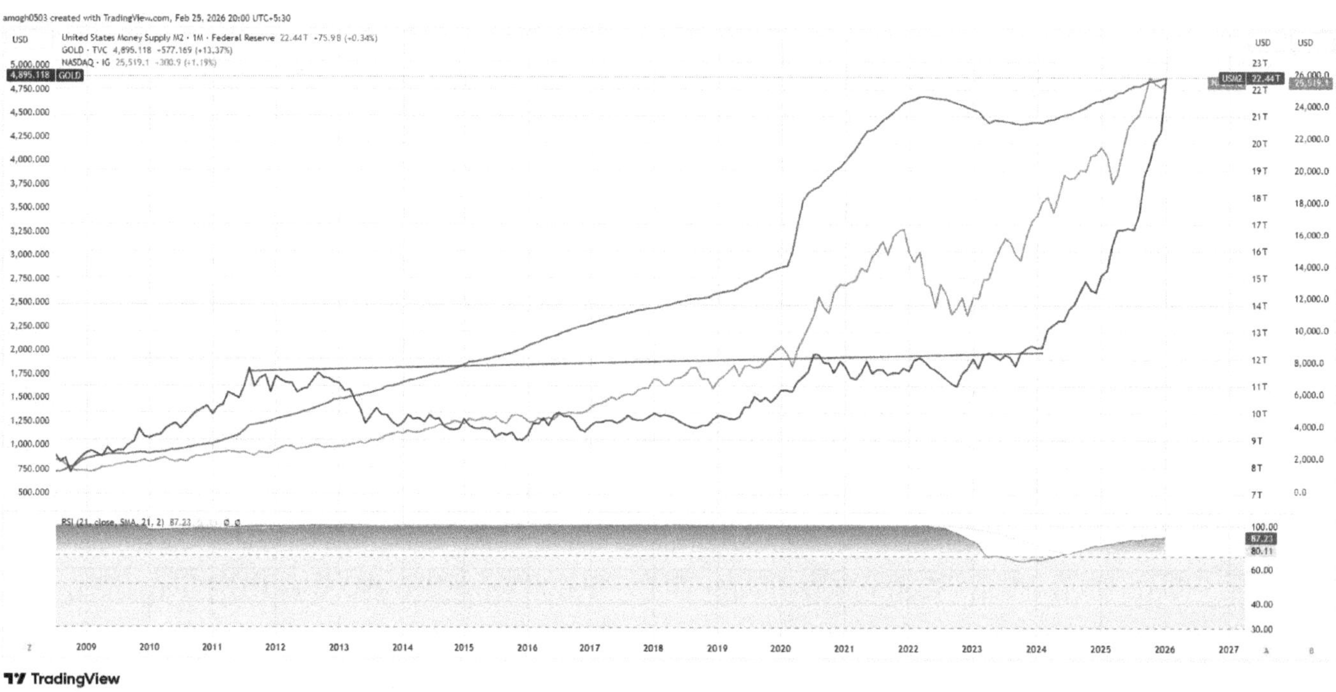

Nasdaq the top index of US was also trading below M2 supply for long time and eventually matched those prices

These types of events are rare when there is large divergence between prices of equity with M2 or gold with M2, they have a long history of being at similar levels, whenever this opportunity occurs, be ready to take a bet on an asset that's below M2.

Let's see in India's context how M2 fared with Nifty and gold prices in ₹, since ₹ is also depreciating against $ and commodities prices are global (in $) this gives a different view for gold prices and other assets.

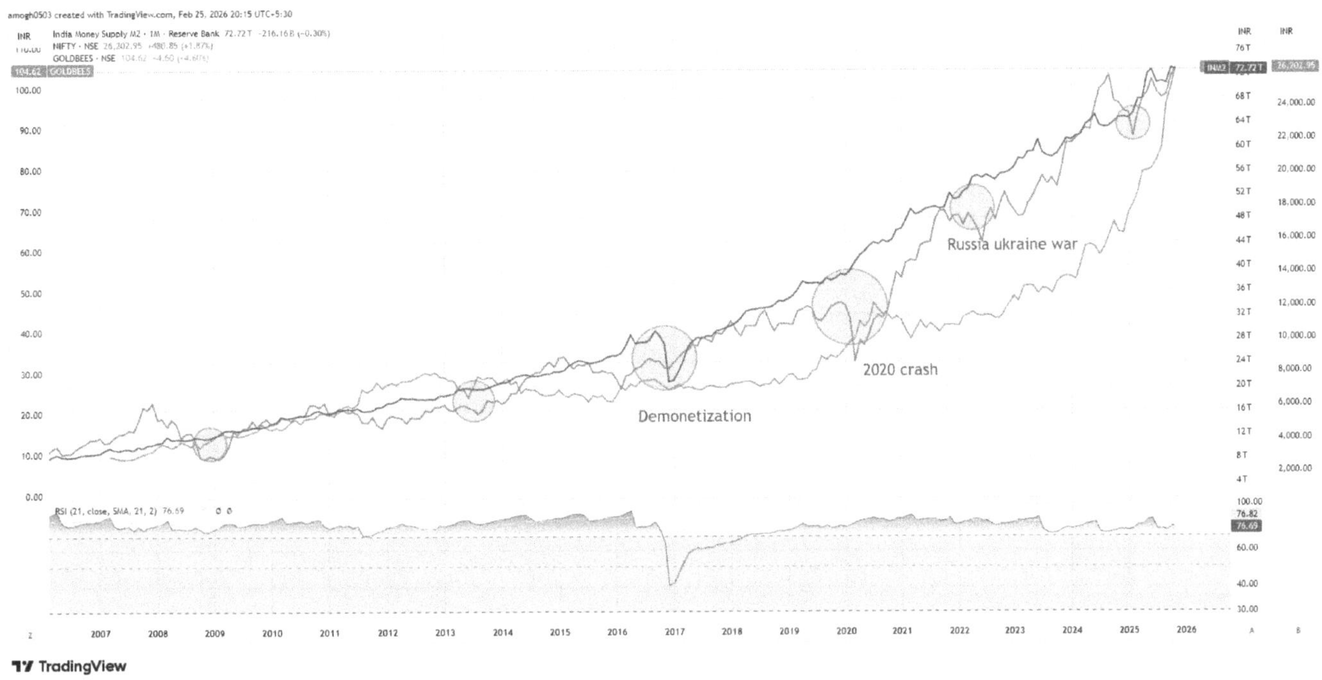

This is the chart of India's **M2** money supply (blue), **Nifty** (green) and **Gold** (golden). I have used Goldbees because it had more price history than gold futures on tradingview.

The yellow circles are the points where assets deviated in large values from M2 supply like 2020 Covid crash equity fell drastically while M2 money supply remained constant and increased after reducing interest rates, during 2022 Russia-Ukraine war M2 was stable while equities fell, only exception is demonetization where M2 fell the recovered eventually. This comparison greatly helps in choosing undervalued assets based on money printing or money supply where sometimes equities are valued lower or gold is valued lower than money supply creating huge buying opportunities, these opportunities are rare sometimes only once a decade to make great money.

Chapter 5

Risk Management

Risk management in the stock market is the structured process of identifying, evaluating, and controlling potential losses arising from investments or trades.

Why is it important?

1. **Preserve Capital**
   If you lose the money, you put in then there's no interest on it that can bring it back. To ensure we stay in the market long enough to benefit from recoveries and growth periods.
2. **Reduce emotional stress and improve decision making**
   Knowing risk management helps reduce emotional pressure and presents panic selling or reckless buying.
3. **Supports long term growth**
   No assets class keeps growing, to make our returns linear and more predictable we should apply risk management.
4. **Learn from market events**
   Historical events like 2008 financial Crisis and 2020 Covid-19 market crash have shown that companies and traders with insufficient risk management suffered more severe losses or even collapsed while others survived.

Techniques:

- **Diversification** – spreading investments across sectors and asset types to reduce the impact of an adverse event in any one area.
- **Stop loss orders** – setting automatic triggers to sell assets mostly for traders. Investors with long term holdings can sell at a 20% drop in stock as stop loss.
- **Regular portfolio rebalancing** – adjusting investments based on changing market conditions to maintain your risk profile.
- **Position Sizing** – limiting the size of any single investment relative to your total portfolio to ensure no single trade can cause excessive harm. Like buying only up to 5% of the portfolio in stock.
- **Continuous Monitoring** – stay updated on market trends, economic changes and global events that may affect assets prices.

Let's learn some practical methods to begin with risk management:

1. Asset Ratio

Holding different assets which are appreciated with time and hedge or generate returns above inflation are good for portfolio and emotional health too.

Mostly ratios should be determined by risk appetite you have like

Equity: Hybrid 60:40, 70:30 or 50:50. But if you are getting started, willing to take risk for higher returns, when investing for 10-20 or more years.

We can reshuffle or rebalance our holdings for high growth based on interest rate environment, inflation or GDP growth.

For 1 lakh folio

10% gold + silver (5000 gold and 5000 silver),

10% in cash/bonds (5000 in liquid and 5000 in gilt)

80% in equity (multi-cap fund or 35% large-cap, 35% mid-cap and 30% small-cap)

Whenever the price of one asset increases and these ratios change, you can sell them and buy another to keep maintaining these ratios.

We can use an indicator like RSI and sell equity for cash when RSI reaches an overbought zone, similarly for gold and silver. Also when they reach overbought zones, we can sell them for cash and then deploy them, later as per need into equity or the asset which has not moved much.

Year	The Event	Max Drawd own (Nifty vs Mix)	Overall CAGR (Nifty vs Mix)	Portfolio Value (Nifty vs Mix)	The Reality Check
2008	Global Financial Crisis	-55% vs -30%	2% vs 6%	3.2 Lakh vs 4.1 Lakh	Nifty tanks. Gold and bonds cushion your fall.
2018	IL&FS Crisis	-15% vs -8%	12% vs 11%	38 Lakh vs 34 Lakh	Equity moves sideways. Bonds pay steady interest.
2020	Covid-19 Pandemic	-38% vs -15%	11% vs 10.5%	45 Lakh vs 48 Lakh	Panic everywhere. Safe assets protect your total value.
2022	War and Rate Hikes	-18% vs -9%	12.5% vs 11%	75 Lakh vs 68 Lakh	The market jumps up and down. You stay calm and rebalanced.
2026	Current Market	-5% vs -2%	13% vs 11.5%	1.3 Crore vs 1.05 Crore	Nifty creates more total wealth, but the mix lets you sleep well for 21 years.

Asset Allocation benefits

2. Is the market liquid?

Indexes like Nifty & Sensex fall about 10-15% every year, but only a fraction of total market value exists (1-2%). FIIs can catalyse volatility but deep domestic liquidity from mutual funds insurance, pensions, and retail SIPs largely offset this swing. Market infrastructure keeps the cash market and derivatives more liquid than hollow.

Period	Typical Nifty Peak-to-Trough (%)	Days to Trough	Days to Prior Peak Recovery	Broad-Market Impact (Mid/Small Caps)
2010-19 cycle	12-14%	45-70	100-180	18-25%
Covid-19 shock (Feb–Apr 2020)	38%	33	250	45-55%
Oct 2024–Mar 2025 tariff scare	14%	80	60	20-25%
2025 full-year correction	23%	~150	6-12 months	30-35%
Jan-Feb 2026 ongoing	9%	Ongoing	TBD	12-15%

Correction Episode	FII Net Equity Flows ($B)	Domestic MF/DII Flows ($B)	Nifty Peak-to-Trough Drawdown (%)
Mar 2020 lockdown	-8.3	+6.9	-38%
CY 2022 global yields	-17.0	+27.8	-14%
CY 2025 record outflows	-19.0 (₹1.58L Cr equiv.)	+82.0 (₹7L Cr)	-23%
Jan 2026 YTD (ongoing)	-5.0 (pace)	SIP +3.7 (Dec-Jan)	-9%

Liquidity Flows During Selloffs (USD Billion)

Even in the worst six month window of 2025, FII sold nearly 15.5 billion $, barely 0.35 % of India's 4.5 trillion $ equity market.

Why only a sliver of money leaves?

1) **Free float vs Total cap**
   Corrections are measured on free float prices, but only the traded free float - usually 45-55% of total shares - change hands.
2) **Rotation, not flight**
   Mid and small caps experience deeper cuts, yet large caps often see defensive inflows. Capital rotates rather than vanishes.
3) **FIIs tug of war**
   FIIs have posted three large outflow years (2008, 2022, 2025) but DIIs absorbed ₹4 lakh crore in 2024 alone, limiting cash leakage.

Therefore, using corrections to rebalance large caps at lower multiples is important. Maintaining tactical buying in cash, but avoiding panic selling, track FIIs flows as sentiment gauge.

Indian equities are prone to volatility, but the data shows a resilient, liquid place rather than a fragile bubble ready to pop.

3. Bull or Bear?

Bull market is technically when the market (index) breaks the previous all-time high by more than 20%.
A bear market is when the market drops more than 20%.

Both bear and bull markets can last long over multiple years, but our strategy must be different in both types of markets.

Risk management is different for both types of markets.
When the index has fallen and reached a state of consolidation, the risk is less when the market is down. You should put in some cash at demand zones or use a formula-based approach: every 5% correction puts 10% of cash into the market. Since the risk is lower at lower prices or bear markets, our allocation should be increased in equity or even gold if it is going through a bear phase.

When the index has risen touching previous all-time highs, or making new all-time highs, then every good rise, we should sell little amounts and increase our cash allocation (liquid funds). Here also we can use a formula like at each 5% rise in index put in the 5% profit in cash (liquid/bond funds).
Since, risk is higher at higher valuations, we should maintain our risk for market fall possibilities by adding other asset classes.
If a folio has a 60:40 Equity: Debt ratio, and the market goes in the bear zone, then risk is less in equities. The 40% debt can be shifted in a phased manner at every drop to achieve a 70:30 ratio.
For bull market 60:40 ratio when market increases, can become 70:30 or 80:20 according to rise of equities so on every overbought signal (cup handle target reached, or long-term RSI nearing all-time highs) or major rise equity can be sold to maintain the 60:40 ratio for portfolio reducing the risk of equity.
Risk management here will reduce large losses and leverage long-term wealth creation.

4. Broad or Narrow

Investors should broaden their portfolio- adding diverse, lower priced stocks when the market is broad during bull markets, and narrow their holdings, focusing on high quality names when breadth contracts in bear phases.

- Understanding Market Breadth

How many stocks participate in a market move. A broad market advance is one which most stocks rise; a narrower advance is driven by just a handful of large caps.

Advance / decline ratio (for nifty and other indices are available on many websites like money control).

Tactical portfolio construction using advance/decline ratio

When breadth indicators confirm broad market strength, for instance **A/D (advance/decline) ratio > 1** and 60% of stocks above their 50-day MA. Broaden the folio in these bull phases by these methods.

Adding mid and small caps that have lagged but stand on strong earnings growth.

Rotation into **cyclical sectors** that typically outperform in expanding markets.

When breadth contracts – **A/D ratio < 1** and 60% stocks below their 50-day moving average then implement these methods for risk management.

Consolidation – trim speculative position, sectors and reduce holdings to core blue chips with strong balance sheets.

Defensive tilt – overweight sectors such as utilities, consumer staples and health care which often show relative strength during contractions.

Hedging – use index options or ETFs to protect against further downside – based decisions.

Conclusion:

Adapting portfolio breadth to market breadth enhances returns and risk management. Increase diversification during broad rallies and concentrate on high quality names when breadth narrows.

5. Do you know about Rolling CAGRs?

Rolling CAGR measures the annualized growth rate for a fixed holding period calculated at equally spaced internal. Each incoming data point 'rolls' the start date forward by one period; the series therefore overlaps but captures every possible period of experience.

The **two-year rolling** compounded annual growth rate CAGR is a powerful way to judge how India's flagship Nifty 50 index has behaved across market cycles. It smooths the daily noise, shows at every monthly observation how ₹1 would have grown each year if bought exactly two years earlier, and reveals whether medium term wealth creation has stalled or compounded.

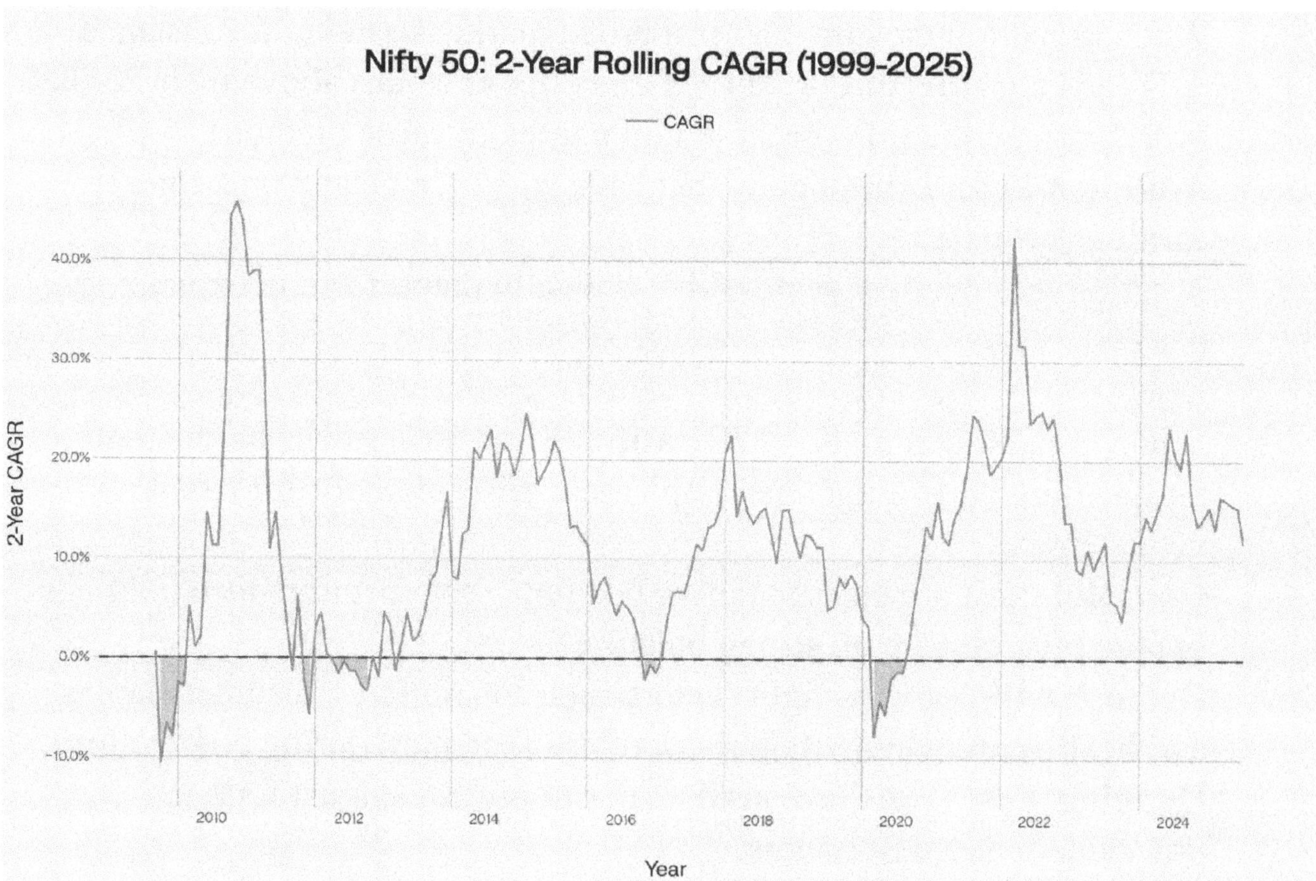

Shaded red bands mark months when the 2-year CAGR dipped below zero per cent.

Cluster (Start - End)	Max Drawdown (Nifty vs Mid/Small)	Months < 0% 2 years Rolling CAGR (Nifty vs Mid/Small)	Macro Context
Oct 2009 – Jan 2010	-12% vs -18%	4 vs 8	GFC aftermath (Nifty crashed 52% from 2008 peak)
Sep 2011 – Nov 2011	-20% vs -30%	3 vs 7	Euro debt crisis and high inflation
Apr 2012 – Oct 2012	-10% vs -15%	7 vs 12	Rupee fell to 56/USD, high trade deficits
Mar 2013	-8% vs -12%	1 vs 3	Taper tantrum and sudden FII outflows
Nov 2016 – Jan 2017	-10% vs -15%	3 vs 5	Demonetization shock and cash crunch
Mar 2020 – Aug 2020	-38% vs -45%	6 vs 11	COVID crash (40% drop and global lockdowns)
Late 2025 – Early 2026	-8% vs -15%	2 vs 6	Massive FII outflows absorbed by strong DII buying

Months 2-year rolling CAGR has been negative

The Dead Zone Ended	1-Year Return After the Drop (Nifty 50)	The Reality Check
Jan 2010	+11%	The market stabilized and steady wealth creation resumed.
Nov 2011	+28%	A massive relief rally as the Euro crisis faded.
Oct 2012	+11%	The economy absorbed currency shocks and climbed.
Mar 2013	+18%	The start of a powerful pre-election bull run.
Jan 2017	+31%	The cash crunch ended, leading to a massive surge.
Aug 2020	+52%	A historic boom that rewarded anyone who bought the fear.
Early 2026	Unfolding Now	The current setup. History suggests spring is reeling again.

What happens after 2 years rolling CAGR goes less than 0%

- **Why does 0% two-year CAGR act as BASE/Support?**

1) Mean reversion of earnings & valuations
   India's nominal GDP historically comprises 10-12% per year. Severe sell offs therefore push price to earnings and price to book to deep discounts.
2) Domestic Liquidity floor
   Post 2003 rise of mutual fund SIPs and provident fund mandates funnels 20000₹ - 25000₹ crore per month into equities as of June 2025.
   The Indian mutual fund industry added nearly 1 crore new investors in the financial year 2025, reaching a total of 5.43 crore PAN-linked investors.
   This might look huge, but India is still under-penetrated; only 3-4% of India's 140 crore population are unique mutual fund investors. Whereas the US has over half of households invest in mutual funds.
   AUM to GDP – This reached an all–time high of 18.2% in fiscal 2024. However, this is significantly lower than the global average of 65%.

Takeaways -

- When the 2-year rolling CAGR falls below 0%, history suggests markets are already in panic territory.
  Deploying incremental lump sums or topping up SIPs in such a window has, so far, produced > 12% CAGR over next 3-5years.
- Negative 2-year CAGR periods usually coincides with Nifty forward P/E < 15x and P/B < 2.5x levels that later delivered outsized gains.
- Seeing your portfolio flat/negative after two years tests conviction. The rolling CAGR chart removes disappointment.
- This also means a negative CAGR for two consecutive years is a rare event that happens only in crisis times.
- Thus, if the market has fallen then the rate of 2 years previous acts as a strong support and signals the market is going to rebound from this level unless it's a crash or will produce good gains from here.

Guide: -

- Track at least 24-month CAGR using free spreadsheets or code, monitor this monthly.
- Deploy 25% of earmarked cash each month while CAGR stays negative.
- Don’t stop existing systematic plans.
- Shift 5-10% from debt to equity while CAGR < 0% and reverse when > 20%.

	Return Statistics (%)					Return distribution (% of times)					
Benchmark Name	Average	Median	Maximum	Minimum	Std. Deviation	Negative	0 - 8%	8 - 12%	12 - 15%	15 - 20%	Greater than 20%
NIFTY 50 TRI	15.49	13.62	47.21	-1.03	8.73	0.08	17.00	16.73	26.13	19.28	20.79

Nifty 50 TRI 5 Years Rolling Return Period

Above chart of 5 years Rolling CAGR of Nifty 50 TRI (Nifty Total Return Index) shows what investor of Indian equities fell over the period of 5 years each while the average return is above 15% but the investing journey has been full of ups and downs where even after investing for 5 years 0.08 % of times returns were negative and for 17% of times only 0-8% market with returns spiking to greater than 20% for more than 20% of the time (5 years) while majority of time returns has been between 12-20. Market returns are lumpy, if you can time your entry and exit well you can make good returns, and shift into less risky assets from time to time.

	Return Statistics (%)					Return distribution (% of times)					
Benchmark Name	Average	Median	Maximum	Minimum	Std. Deviation	Negative	0 - 8%	8 - 12%	12 - 15%	15 - 20%	Greater than 20%
NIFTY 50 TRI	14.09	13.95	22.30	5.13	3.62	0.00	3.69	25.67	32.57	31.87	6.20

Nifty 50 TRI 10 Years Rolling Return Period

The above chart shows Nifty 50 TRI 10 years rolling returns, analyzing how investors felt at each time of the year and when was the best entry and exit times.

6. Stock trends for risk assessment

One of the pivotal principles in stock market analysis is observing trading volumes.

When there's the highest downside volume in many years, it can indicate a potential market bottom (reversal from fall).

General Insurance chart above shows stock bottomed at highest volumes

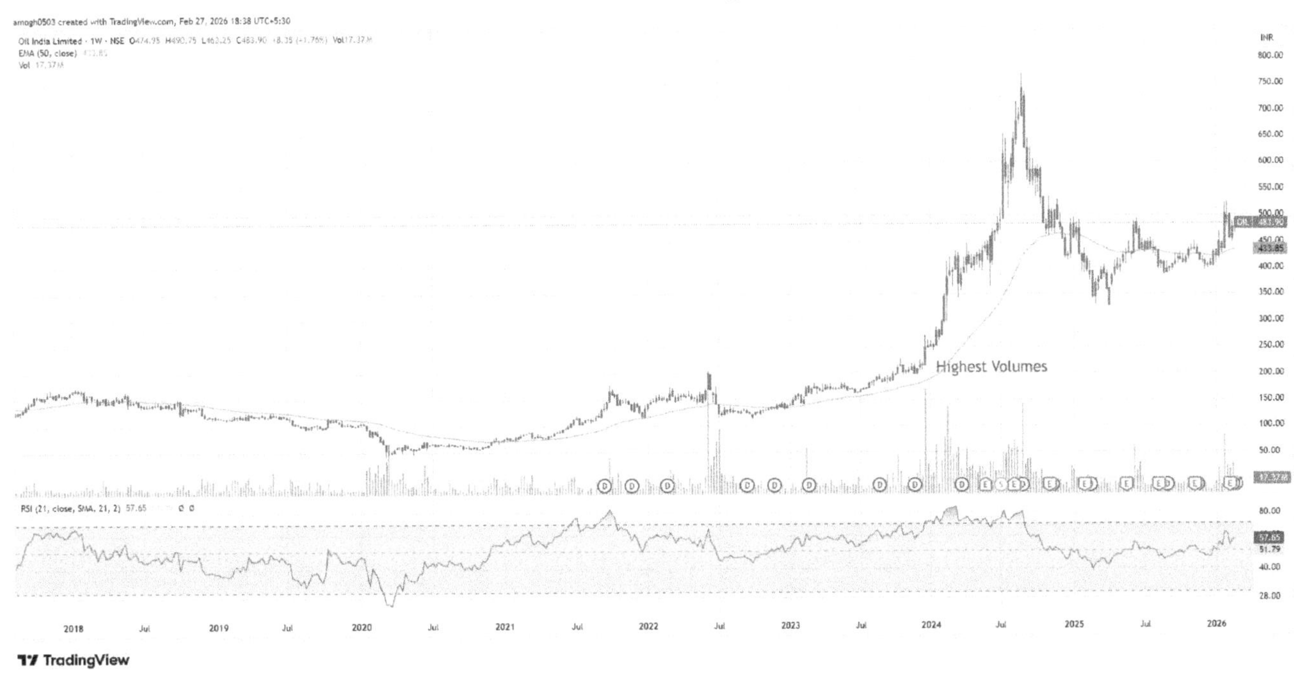

Oil India chart above shows stock bottomed at highest volumes

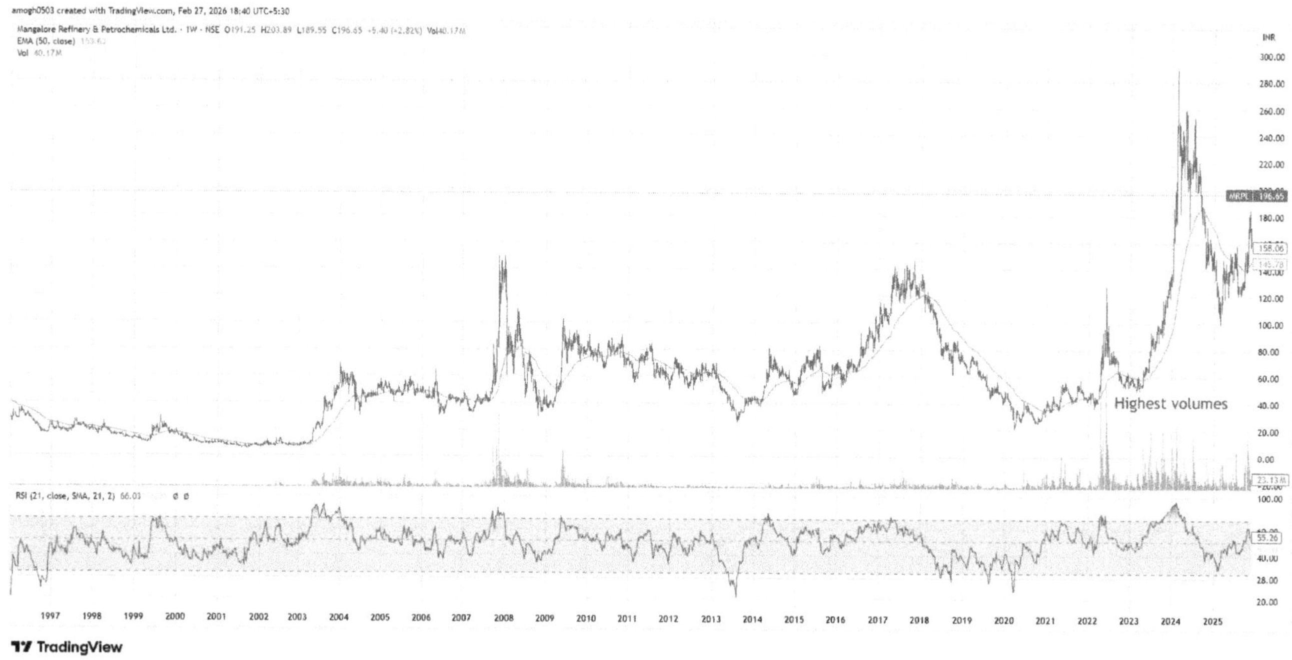

MRPL chart above shows stock bottomed at highest volumes

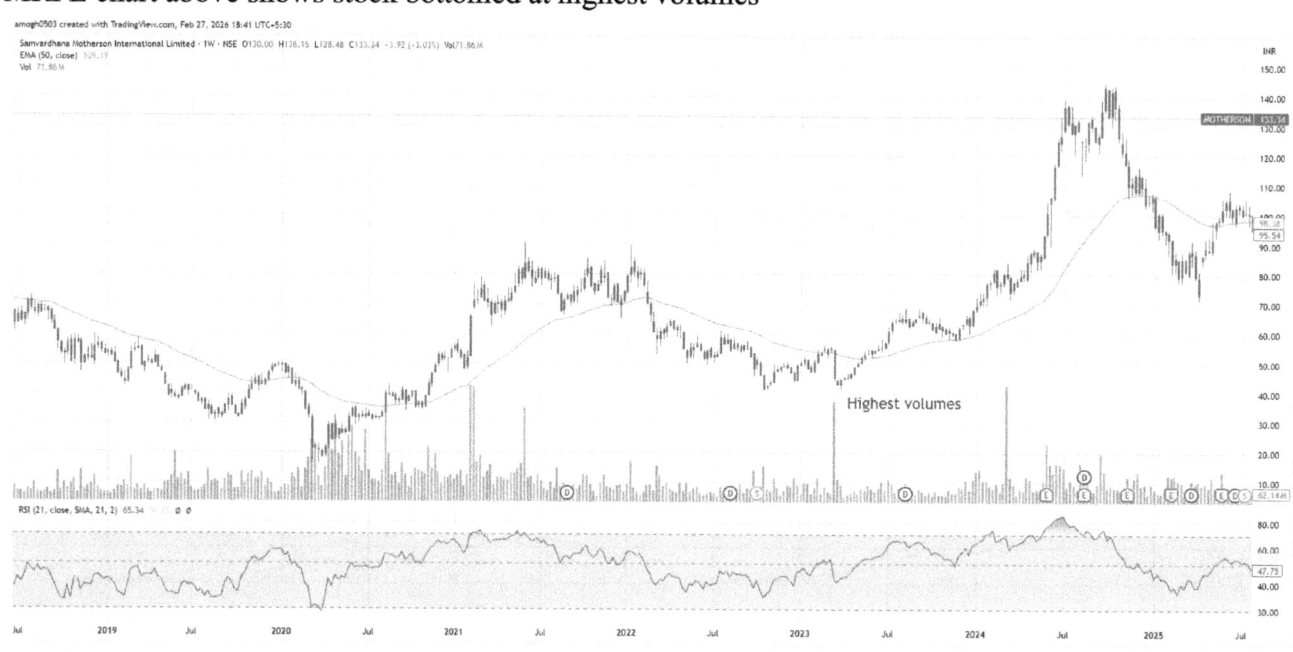

Motherson chart above shows stock bottomed at highest volumes

Conversely, when the upside (buying) volume hits multi-year highs, especially if valuations look stretched or stock has recently given very high returns, suggest a market top or stock top.

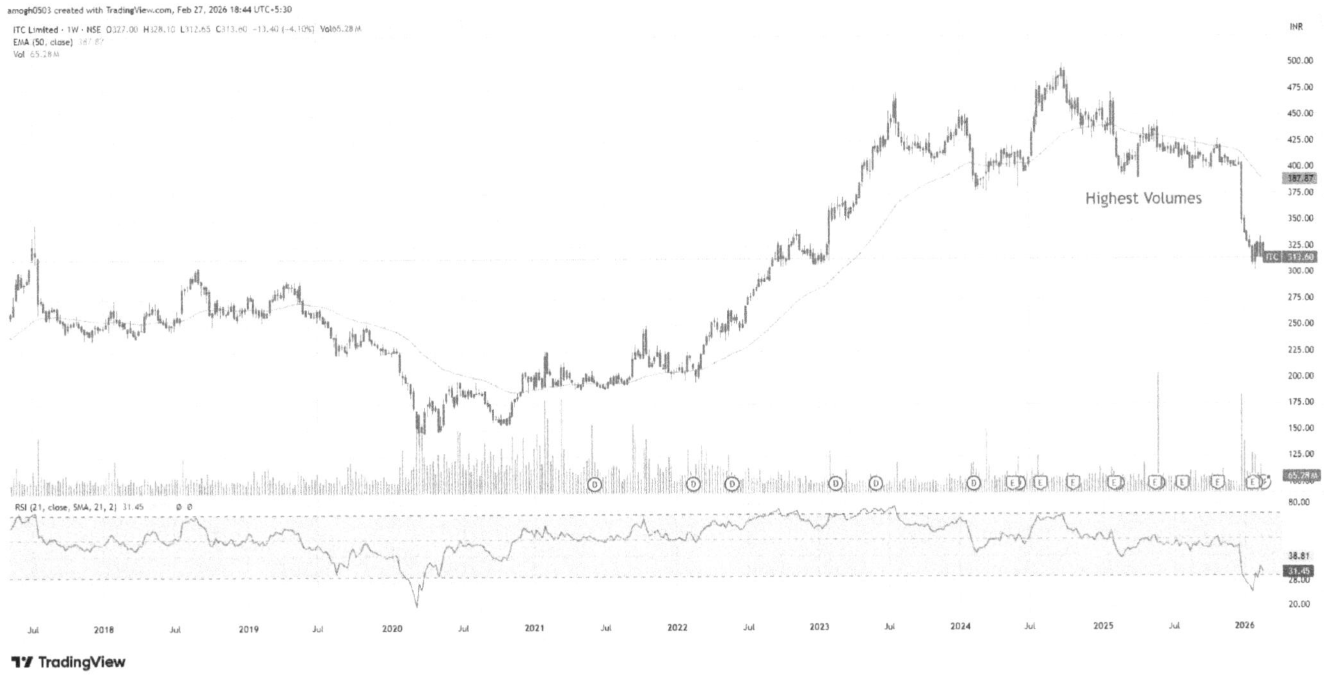

ITC chart above shows rounding top pattern along with highest volumeS

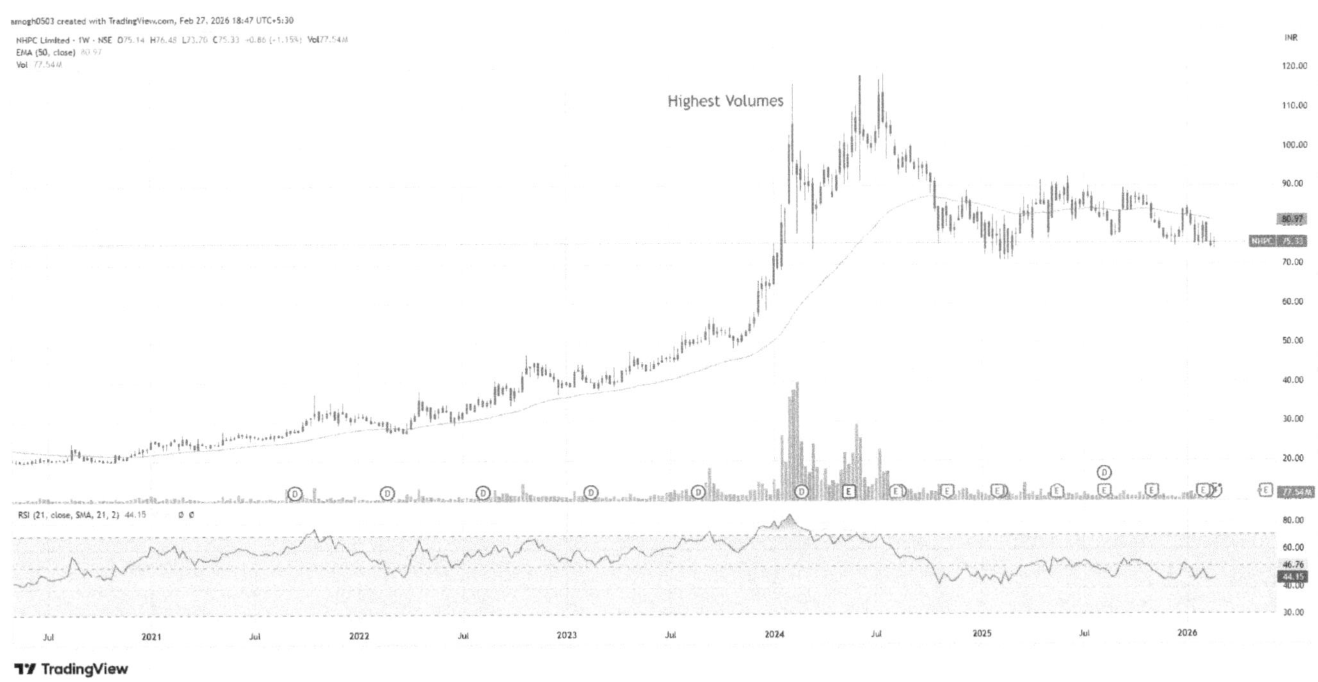

NHPC chart above shows rounding double top pattern along with highest volumes

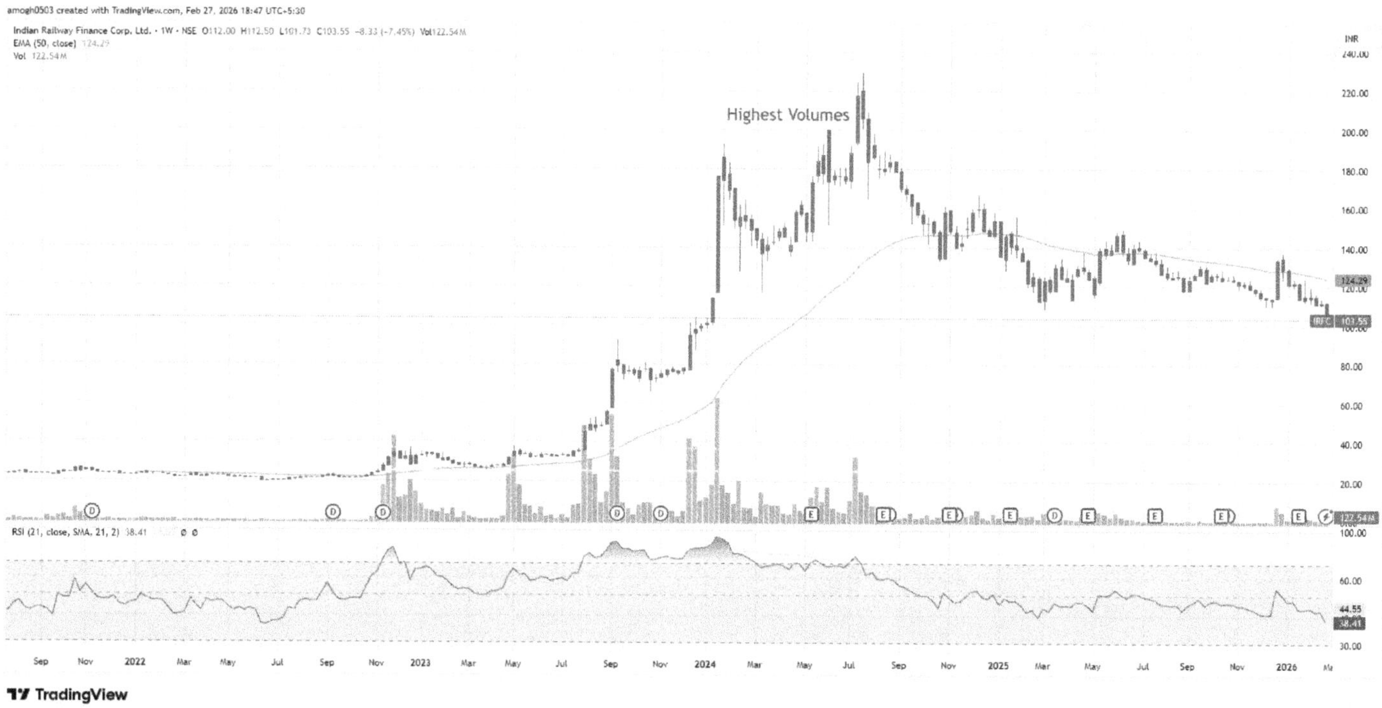

IRFC chart above shows rounding double pattern along with highest volumes and top RSI levels showing over bought

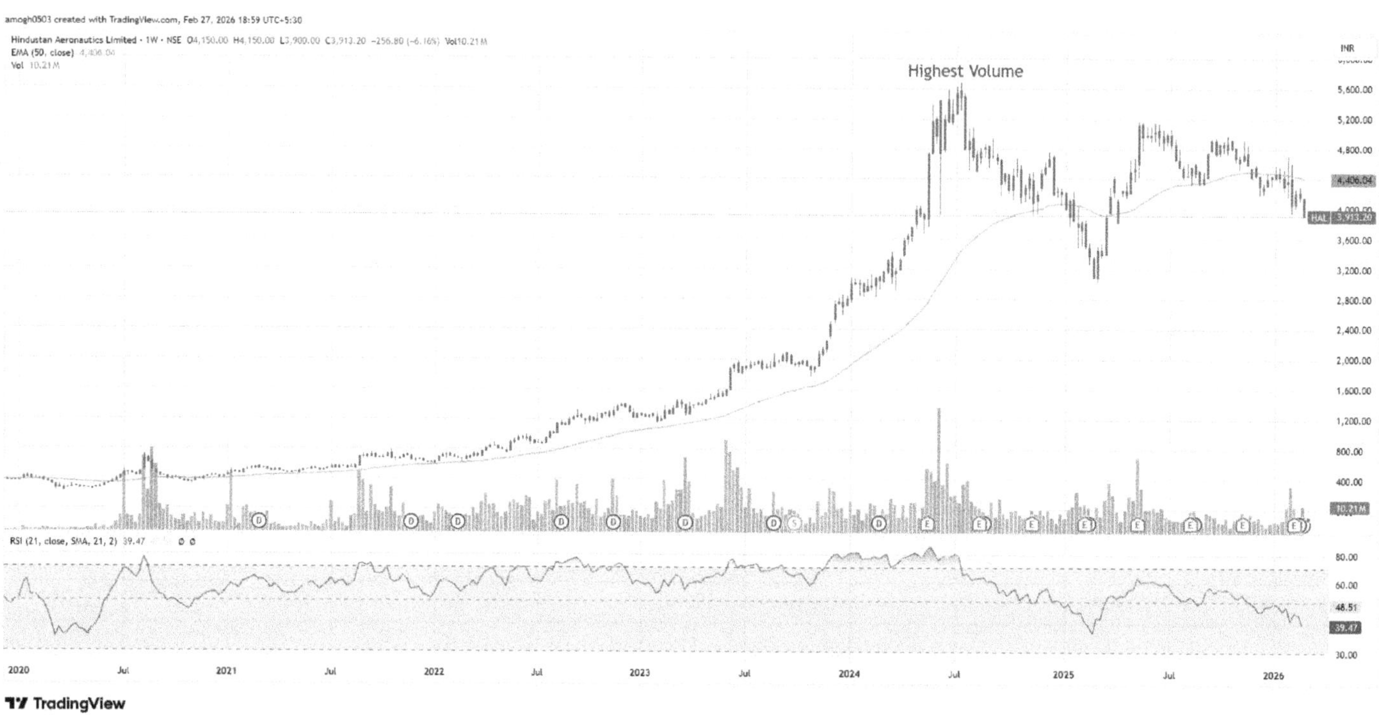

HAL chart above shows rounding top along with highest volumes and highest RSI in multiple years

Just volume analysis tells us so much about the stock stage where if a good stock is falling, buy it only after volumes of multi-year highs come up saving precious money and time. Similarly, when valuations look stretched or stocks have run up multiple times, people are overexcited about a stock, and volumes reaching all-time highs is a good way to book profits.

Balance, your portfolio by looking at these patterns of stocks showing reversal from bottom with volumes can be added and stocks showing reversal at top with volumes can be sold or avoided from buying more, helps in managing risk for losing capital from fall of stock. Also, you can find momentum scores for each stock and make buying or selling decisions based on that.

7. Sona vs Sensex

Indian households mostly have this debate Sona (gold) or Sensex (equity) which is better investment, where there is more return, which is more stable and often Sona is seen as generational wealth but not Sensex since it's a paper-based asset.

But we can rebalance both using mutual funds or stocks and gold, using the low relative correlation to have stability and additional gains. Also, after 2015 prices of Sensex and Gold have been closer in INR each chasing the other every year to make new all-time highs.

Sensex/Goldbees

Finding the ratio of Sensex/(Goldbees*1194) average comes as 1.05 with bottoms at 0.7-0.8, Tops at 1.14 -1.2. Since February 2026, gold reached 1.61 lakh ₹ whereas Sensex was near 81,300 ₹. This is an indication of a temporary bottom, and the ratio should reach the mean of 1, meaning either gold will fall 50% or Sensex will rise to 1.61 lakhs ₹ or gold stays here for multiple years while Sensex reaches these 1.6 lakhs ₹ level.

Making our portfolio 80% equity and 20% gold helps in market falls since gold rises and acts as a hedge on the upper side of equity. Rebalancing the portfolio to match this 80:20 ratio using the above chart is one of the best approaches to keeping your money stable.

- **The Numbers: Why the 80/20 Mix Wins**

Let us look at typical historical returns in the Indian market over a long 15 to 20-year period to see why this specific combination is so powerful:

100% Equity (Sensex): Roughly 13% to 14% CAGR. You get the highest possible return, but you must survive terrifying 40% to 50% market crashes.

100% Gold: Roughly 9% to 10% CAGR. It is safe, steady, and beats inflation, but offers lower overall growth.

The 80/20 Mix (Rebalanced): Roughly 12.5% to 13.5% CAGR.

The Reality Check: By holding 20% in gold and shifting your money when the Sensex-to-Gold ratio hits 0.8 (buying equity) or 1.14 (selling equity), you capture almost all the growth of a pure stock portfolio.

You only sacrifice a tiny fraction of a percent in yearly returns, but you cut down your deep, painful losses in half. You build massive wealth, but you actually get to sleep peacefully while doing it.

Buying equity near or below a 0.8 ratio, selling equity near or above a 1.14 ratio, and adding gold is good risk management.

8. Number of shareholders

If a stock is held across almost all demat accounts in India, how can it rise? There is no room for growth in terms of new demand. Stock will perform just like the index. Major money is made on stocks that are uncovered and later come to public notice.

For high retail participant shares, price appreciation can continue driven not by new retail investors but majorly by deeper existing holders (Institutions, Mutual funds, FIIs).

Identifying a theme or stock early when a smaller number of shareholders are present on it, will be very rewarding when the story reaches every home and every person will try to get only one stock in their demat accounts.

Example:-

Eicher motors in mid 2010 had fewer than 25000 retail folios as motorcycle volume and margins expanded. Its folio count and share price exploded – 8000% appreciation over the decade.

Eicher Motors

Shareholding Pattern

Numbers in percentages

Quarterly Yearly TRADES 2 Recently

	Mar 2017	Mar 2018	Mar 2019	Mar 2020	Mar 2021	Mar 2022	Mar 2023	Mar 2024	Mar 2025	Dec 2025
Promoters +	50.58%	50.49%	49.32%	49.28%	49.23%	49.21%	49.20%	49.14%	49.08%	49.06%
FIIs +	32.45%	30.97%	32.49%	27.71%	29.06%	29.22%	28.63%	28.95%	25.02%	27.01%
DIIs +	4.03%	5.90%	4.55%	11.12%	9.08%	9.95%	11.19%	11.04%	16.55%	14.64%
Government +	0.00%	0.03%	0.11%	0.15%	0.15%	0.10%	0.10%	0.10%	0.10%	0.10%
Public +	12.94%	12.61%	13.53%	11.75%	12.49%	11.52%	10.88%	10.77%	9.26%	9.19%
No. of Shareholders	81,872	93,341	1,17,136	1,09,899	2,52,014	2,63,479	2,66,168	2,63,132	2,49,483	2,60,429

* The classifications might have changed from Sep'2022 onwards.

Eicher Motors Shareholding pattern

Scan NSEs universe for companies with
Number of Shareholders < 50000 AND Sales growth 3Years > 15 AND Average return on equity 3Years > 15 AND Market Capitalization > 2000

At Screener.in you can create screens like this. Create an account > Go to Screens > Create New Screen.

Here, you can create screens to scan stocks from the whole universe of the Indian stock market, experiment there to find stocks that you like to invest in, or filter stocks based on results P/E, P/B, market capitalization and many other factors. Below is a screen I created for stocks with currently less shareholders and sales growth of more than 15% from the last 3 years.

Less Retail Holding Screen

Keep an eye on corporate actions like buybacks: -

When a hidden company announces a share buyback, it purchases its own stock from the market and removes it forever. This shrinks the "free float," meaning there are even fewer shares available for the public to buy. Because you already found a strong, growing company with very few shareholders, this sudden drop in supply acts like a spark. It forces new investors to pay much higher prices to get their hands on the limited stock, rapidly multiplying on your wealth.

9.RSI Signals

Relative Strength Index (RSI) for Nifty over the last decade shows clear cycles of overbought (RSI > 70) and oversold (RSI < 30).

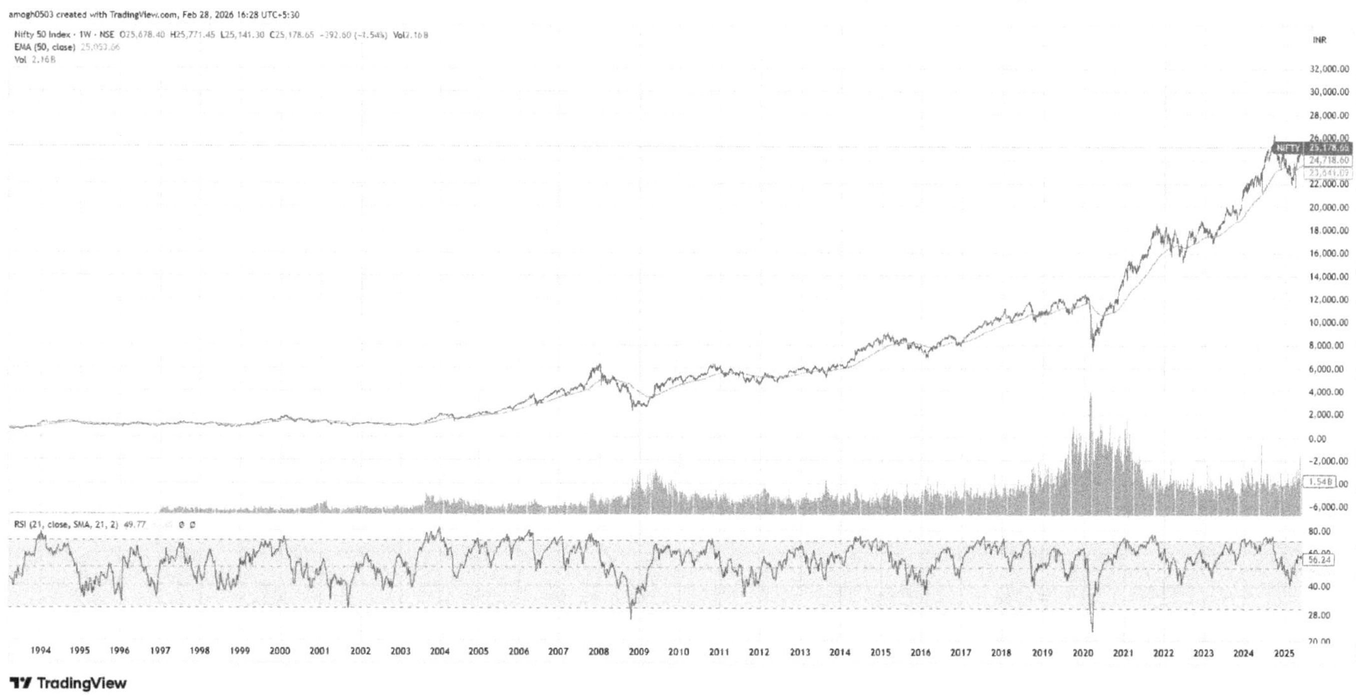

Nifty 50 with RSI 21 days

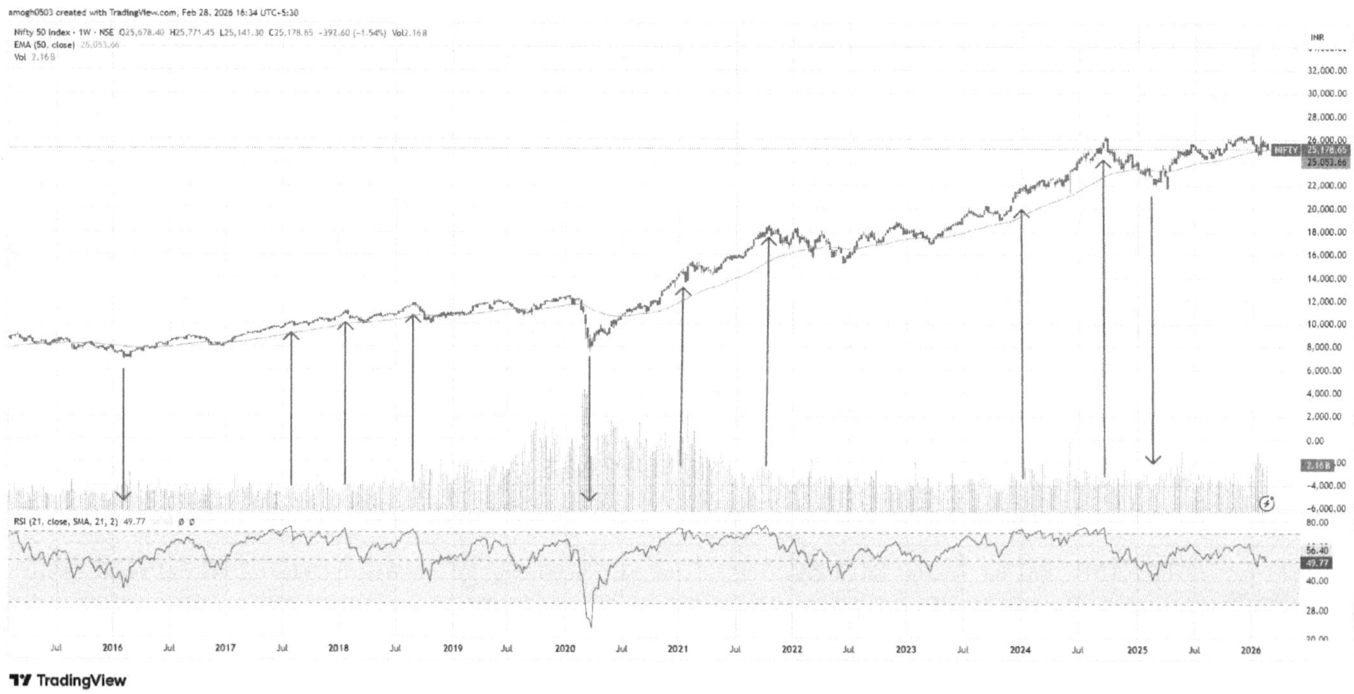

Nifty 50 from 2016 to 2026 RSI trends

Observations: -

Oversold Signals (The Panic Zone)

When the RSI drops near 30, the crowd is selling in fear. But history shows this is exactly when you should be buying:

March 2020: The RSI dipped to around 25, right before a massive, strong recovery.

Oct 2018 & Feb 2016: Both periods saw lows near 30, creating highly attractive buying opportunities.

Feb 2024 & Jan 2026: RSI fell to 40, creating great buying opportunities after which the market bounced back.

Overbought Signals (The Greed Zone)

When the RSI crosses 70, the crowd is too excited. The market is running hot and usually needs to take a break:

Aug 2018: RSI peaked at around 72, followed by long consolidation that gave breakout after 3 years at the end of 2020.

Sept 2021: The RSI peaked around 75, followed by a multi-month consolidation where prices just moved sideways.

July 2024: A brief spike above 70 coincided with the Nifty reaching new highs, followed again by a cooling-off period.

Range of Oscillation:

Over ten years, the Nifty 50's 21-day RSI has oscillated between roughly 25 and 75, illustrating consistent momentum cycles without extreme extremes beyond these bounds.

Investor Takeaways:

- **Tactical Entry Points**: Use RSI < 30 as potential buy signals, especially when accompanied by fundamental or macro dips.
- **Profit Booking**: Consider trimming positions or tightening stops when RSI > 70 signals overbought conditions.
- **Risk Management**: Combine RSI signals with trend analysis (e.g., moving averages) to avoid counter-trend trades, check Heading 6 Emotional machine under chapter 2 for using moving averages to find trends in stock / indices.
- **Long-Term Context**: While RSI provides short-term timing, maintain core allocations to equities for strategic growth.

By integrating the 21-day RSI into a broader investment framework—balancing fundamental analysis and risk controls—investors can enhance timing decisions for the Nifty 50 and potentially improve risk-adjusted returns in their portfolios.

10. Bulls and Bears are blessing in disguise

A bull market occurs when an index rises at least 20 percent from its recent peak. Conversely, a bear market ensues when prices fall more than 20 percent below their recent highs. These thresholds help investors identify market regimes and adjust strategies accordingly.

Bull and Bear markets are far from being mere market extremes, they act as economic reset mechanisms, catalyzing innovations from India's submarine cables to Japan's industrial giants and prompting macroeconomics fine-tuning that underpins more stable growth.

Bull and Bear Markets: Catalysts for Economic Transformation

1. **UK Railway Mania (1845-1856)** Built over 6000 miles of railway, seeding the Industrial Revolution's transport backbone, and spurred engineering innovations. Over-extension of capital into canals and railways led to economic consequences. London and Birmingham railway shares went up 400%, then collapsed by more than 60%. The bulls of the railway, followed by the bear market, ultimately shaped the future transport revolution.

2. **Japan Bubble (1985–1990)** Consolidated giants like Mitsubishi and Sumitomo into global industrial powerhouses and forced deep financial reforms. Crazy land prices and stock overvaluation led to a massive crash. The Nikkei 225 rose 200% to 39,000, then collapsed below 20,000. The painful bear market forced companies to become lean. This quietly created huge multibagger opportunities in tech and auto exports that the panicked crowd missed.

3. **Dot-com Bubble (1995–2002)** Built the heavy undersea internet cables that accidentally sparked India's massive IT and offshore outsourcing boom. Too much hype in unproven internet companies caused the NASDAQ to rise by 410%, only to crash by 80%. The crash wiped out the weak, leaving behind the real multibaggers like global e-commerce leaders and Indian IT giants who used the cheap internet lines to grow globally.

4. **Global Financial Crisis (2005–2009)** Forced central banks to act fast. They learned to cut rates instantly at the first sign of trouble, bringing in a new era of stable global growth. Bad home loans and complex banking products caused the S&P 500 to rise 31%, then drop a terrifying 57%. Panic blinded people to the birth of the smartphone era. The cheap money that followed fueled the next decade's biggest tech multibaggers.

5. **Indian Market Cycle (2005–2008)** Cleaned up the Indian banking system and launched strict rules and circuit breakers to make the stock market much safer for everyday investors. Heavy borrowing to buy stocks and build projects pushed the Nifty up 250%, before it plunged by over 57%. While everyone was busy fearing the crash, it quietly laid out the foundation for massive, unseen multibaggers in private banking and consumer goods over the next ten years.

6. **COVID-19 Crash & Boom (2020–2021)** Led to the explosion of green energy, Indian fintech, and global AI, skyrocketing companies like Nvidia and Tesla to the very top of the world market. As COVID-19 news escalated, markets worldwide began to slide in a sudden, terrifying panic. The crash quietly triggered a massive boom in Indian discount brokers and AMCs, paving the way for a powerful new bull market, richer retail participation, and the rise of new sectoral leaders.

Episode	Bull Peak to Bear Trough (Index)	Economic Consequence	Long-Term Impact
UK Railway Mania (1845–1850)	London & Birmingham Railway shares up ~400 percent; collapsed > 60 percent	Overextension of capital into canals & railways	Built over 6,000 miles of railway, seeding the Industrial Revolution's transport backbone; spurred engineering innovations.
Japan Bubble (1985–1990)	Nikkei 225: ~13,000 → 39,000 (+200 percent); fell below 20,000	Land and equity overvaluation	Consolidated Mitsubishi, Sumitomo, and others into global industrial conglomerates. Deep reforms in financial regulation and Keiretsu governance.
Dot-com Bubble (1995–2002)	NASDAQ Composite: ~1,000 → 5,100 (+410 percent); crashed ~80 percent	Cleared out unviable Internet firms	Enabled India's offshore outsourcing boom via robust undersea cable infrastructure; drove telecom liberalization and submarine-cable expansion.
Global Financial Crisis (2005–2009)	S&P 500: ~1,200 → 1,575 (+31 percent); dropped ~57 percent	Triggered swift, preemptive rate cuts worldwide	Central banks adopted flexible inflation-targeting, cutting rates at first GDP slowdown rather than waiting for recession; stabilized growth cycles.
Indian Market Cycle (2005–2008)	NIFTY 50: ~1,800 → 6,300 (+250 percent); fell to ~2,700 (> 57 percent)	Excess credit and equity leverage	Promoted tightening of bank NPAs frameworks; accelerated reforms in infrastructure financing and launch of SEBI's circuit-breaker mechanisms.
COVID-19 Crash & Boom (2020–2021)	~12,400 fell to ~7,500 (40% drop); rocketed back to ~15,400 (+100% from bottom)	Global pandemic lockdowns and sudden economic standstill	Forced the RBI to pump cash into the system, sparked a massive wave of new retail Demat accounts, and shifted focus to digital businesses.

Historical Bull–Bear Episodes and Their Legacies

Bull and bear markets, rather than mere cycles to endure, are potent engines of innovation, policy reform, and structural renewal. By understanding their timing and recognizing the opportunity in them. Investors cannot only preserve capital but also capture the deep value that follows every market reset. Each time a cycle is over, a new cycle creates new leaders which benefit from the new opportunity arising and change the world forever.

Market Era	The Bull Run (Growth & Duration)	The Bear Phase (Crash & Duration)	The Rebound (New Leaders & Reforms)
1998–2001 (Dot-Com Boom & Bust)	Nifty ~₹800 → ~₹1,800 *(A fast 2-year tech frenzy)*	2000 Crash: Dropped ~50% *(Lasted ~18 painful months)*	**2002 onwards:** Wiped out weak internet hype, giving rise to India's real IT and software giants.
2003–2008 (India)	Nifty ₹900 → ₹6,300 *(A massive 5-year run)*	2008 Crash: Dropped >60% *(Lasted ~9 painful months)*	**2009:** PSU and infrastructure reforms fueled the next rise.
2009–2020 (Global & India)	Nifty ~₹2,700 → ~₹12,400 *(An 11-year steady climb)*	2020 COVID Crash: Sudden panic *(Lasted just 1 rapid month)*	**Apr 2020–2021:** Sparked worldwide digital and remote work adoption.
2020–2026 (Current Supercycle)	Nifty ₹7,600 → Beyond ₹24,000 *(An ongoing 6-year mega-run)*	2022 & 2025 Dips: Speed bumps *(Short corrections, not crashes)*	**2023–present:** Powered by massive green energy, AI, and fintech growth.

Author's Note

ॐ महालक्ष्म्यै नमो नमः

Technical analysis and fundamental analysis are often viewed in isolation. Many believe that technicals are strictly for traders, while fundamentals are the go-to for long-term investing. In reality, what works most consistently is pure rationality. It requires looking ahead to see where the world is moving, understanding government plans and incentives, and forming a clear vision of how global conditions benefit specific businesses. It is about recognizing the blessing coming in disguise

Once you have formed that vision, you can apply the technical and analytical skills you have learned over time to capitalize on those opportunities.

Investing is a serious business. Whoever manages risk effectively is the ultimate winner. The market operates as a loser's game—the one who loses the least, wins.

May the learnings in these pages stay with you and bring you a happy, prosperous life.

Congratulations on reaching the end of this book!

Happy market journey.

www.ingramcontent.com/pod-product-compliance
Lightning Source LLC
LaVergne TN
LVHW070910210926
848482LV00017B/1036

* 9 7 9 8 9 0 5 8 4 8 9 6 4 *